Traveling the South Pacific

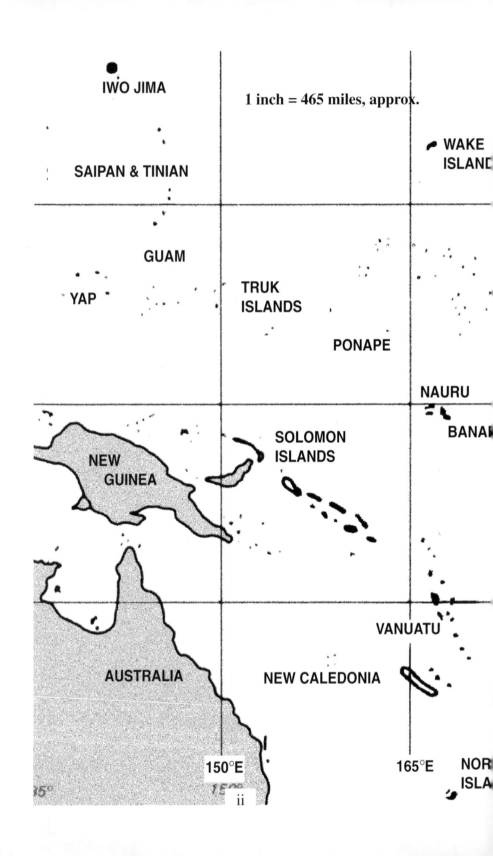

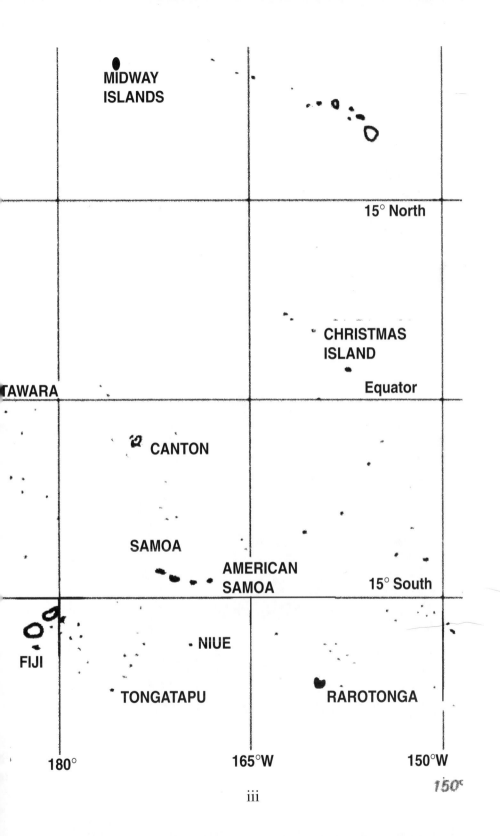

MIDWAY
ISLANDS

15° North

CHRISTMAS
ISLAND

Equator

TAWARA

CANTON

SAMOA

AMERICAN
SAMOA

15° South

FIJI

NIUE

TONGATAPU

RAROTONGA

180°   165°W   150°W

iii

Traveling the South Pacific
Without Reservations

By
Evangeline Brunes

Edited by Robert E. Bell
Penrith Publications
Mechanicsville, Virginia

Published by Penrith Publications
                      Mechanicsville, Virginia
Printed and bound in the United States of America.

Library of Congress Control Number 2001132261

The Library of Congress cataloging in Publication Data:
Brunes, Evangeline
    Traveling the South Pacific, without reservations /
Evangeline Brunes, -- 1st ed.
    p. cm.
    Includes index.
    ISBN: 0-9710519-6-8

    1. Polynesia -- Guidebooks. 2. Rarotonga (Cook
Islands) -- Guidebooks. 3. Fiji -- Guidebooks. 4. Samoan
Islands -- Guidebooks.   I. Title

DU510.B78 2001   919.604
                                              QBI01-200675

Table of Contents

All photos are by the author unless otherwise indicated.
Cover photo shows the fales (cottages) at Va'vau.
The dancers in the photo on the back cover are E. Matike
a popular music and dance ministry from St. Mary's
Catholic Church in Arorangi

DEDICATION

We often pray for guidance, but when it comes in some astonishing, unlabeled way we call it coincidence.

While preparing this manuscript, each time I got to the section in which I spoke of Martha, who was instrumental in my coming into faith, I wondered where she was and what had become of her and her family.

Rewind the scene to the 1960's where two young Mid-Western suburban homemakers enjoyed survival coffee breaks while their ten children played and their husbands climbed their separate corporate ladders.

Our husbands' transfers sent us in different directions and we lost contact.

"Sending this note to a thirty year old address seems as futile as putting a message in a bottle and throwing it off a cliff" prefaced my earnest hope that it would somehow reach her.

Four days later Martha called. They say that timing is everything. In retirement, her husband had already written a book and established Penrith Publications, LLC to publish it and others. He would be happy to be my editor and publisher.

To them goes my unbounded gratitude (coupled with a bit of guilt for turning their placid retirement upside down), gratitude for the heroic effort that has gone into bringing this book to fruition; for their love, friendship, and encourgement through it all.

Editors Note

The episode described on page 273 of this book and the comment in the dedication on the opposite page are illustrations of seemingly minor events in our lives which have a profound effect on the lives of ourselves and others. We are often unaware of the influence which our words and actions have on other people.

A typical cottage on Rarotonga

Chapter One

Compass Point

There was nothing impressive about his appearance. He was of average height, but thin, with a shock of unruly blonde hair that fell over his forehead above wire-rimmed glasses. From his appearance, I would have guessed that his was a very ordinary occupation.

It was a warm day and the congregation seemed restless until he began to speak.

"We were assigned to a village which was 120 miles down river from the last outpost. My wife and our two children were with two native rowers in the lead canoe and I followed in a second dugout with all our supplies."

As linguists with New Tribes Mission they had spent a year and a half in the bush of New Guinea developing a written language for a remote group of tribesmen before their work of Bible translation began.

It seemed an open door...an invitation that would give direction and purpose to my life that had been shattered by divorce. My children were grown and all the props of my comfortable life were gone.

The letter I received from New Tribes Mission indicated that I could apply in person at their linguistic school in Camdenton, Missouri. Our home in Ohio had just gone into contract for sale and I would be driving to California to live in our intended retirement home in Santa Barbara until that house sold. I could stop in Camdenton on the way.

A farewell luncheon with my friend was a welcome break from packing. On the way home, we stopped at a travel agency where she was booking a cruise. While waiting, I idly picked up an old copy of *Ford Freighter Guide*. It included a small segment about Silk & Boyd, Limited, an interisland shipping service linking the Pacific Territories. Although their schedule was determined by cargo, they did accept passengers. Stops were made at outer islands in the southern Cook Group on irregular schedules six to eight weeks apart; in the northern islands every six months or so. Perhaps, I thought, that would be a good test for me to determine whether I could live in a nonmonetary society far from the neighborhood restaurant and Walgreen's.

The letter from Bob Boyd of Silk and Boyd, Limited, in response to my query, was a classic which introduced me to an obscure island group of which I knew nothing; islands located in the South Pacific as far south of the equator as Hawaii is north.

"Deck passage," it indicated, "is only for indigenous Polynesians who have traveled that way since childhood. Staterooms are available for Europeans. While sleeping on a cargo hatch under the stars may sound romantic, with more than seventy passengers facilities can be strained and an assortment of livestock leaves a fragrance which is least desired." Their letter concluded with, "All in all, an Outer Island visit is a must for every visitor to the Cook Islands, the As Always Isles, your unspoiled, unforgettable paradise."

When I arrived in Camdenton, two hundred missionaries, who were home on leave, were in conference at the New Tribes Mission headquarters. As I waited in the lobby, the atmosphere was electric. Snatches of conversations I heard from small groups around me covered every remote corner of the globe. I felt that I had come home.

My lengthy interview with the director of linguistics at the school went very well. Although I had no training in linguistics, they could provide that. My dozen years working as a volunteer with international students at Ohio State University had given me a wealth of cross-cultural experience, which would be invaluable.

"How long has your husband been dead?" the interviewer asked.

I hesitated before telling her that I was divorced and that my former husband had remarried.

Her apology was sincere.

"I am so sorry," she said. "On a couple of occasions we have accepted someone who was divorced, but it didn't work out, so it is now against mission policy."

I was stunned by the finality of her response. It had seemed like such a comfortable situation, as though it was meant to be.

During the following decade, I moved from Santa Barbara back to Ohio, to Florida, then to Arizona. Each time the reason for my move involved property or one of our six children. Eight new grandchildren were born in those scattered places. Each time I stood alone at the nursery window, the same devastating feeling of loneliness overwhelmed me. There must be more than this, I thought.

My financial situation became seriously eroded in spite of my efforts in a series of minimum wage sales jobs. There were only two things I knew for sure. I could accept a life that was severely diminished or I could choose to create a future so different there would be no point of reference to the past.

Travel had been one constant during marriage. As my husband developed a national corporation, business travel took us from coast to coast. About every other year we would get someone to watch the children and go on a special trip. Our last trip together was to India and Sri Lanka where we spent a month with students who had returned home and with families of students with whom I worked. They had shown us very affordable ways to travel. We discovered splendid palaces and dak bungalows, government rest houses and small inns far from tourist's tracks.

I began doodling on placemats and napkins as the concept for *The Solo Traveler* slowly emerged. I could go back to India to research budget lodgings and self-publish a newsletter "for the traveler with more time than money".

Sri Lanka was convulsed by continuing insurrections of the minority Tamils. By the time I was ready to leave, there were also State Department advisories against travel to all the places familiar to me in India. The Punjab and Kashmir were both off limits to American travelers. Again, an unexpected change of circumstances had altered my direction and turned my compass point toward a new destination.

I reread the worn, yellowed letter from Silk & Boyd, Limited. The terror of venturing out alone to an unfamiliar place made me hesitate, but it was an impasse I knew I would have to overcome to bring *The Solo Traveler* to life.

Finally, with a renewed passport in hand, I began calling airlines to find one which flies to those enchanted Cook Islands. It was the fifth airline that suggested Air New Zealand. I took the last of my savings and bought two *Lonely Planet* guides, $1,200 in travelers' checks and an "open" ticket that would be good for six months. It would take me from Los Angeles to Rarotonga, Nadi in Fiji and return to LAX.

I didn't know then that the last of Silk & Boyd's two freighters, the *Manuvai*, had run aground on a reef at Nassau, just southeast of Puka Puka, two years before, on the 27th of December, 1988. The only constant thing in travel information is change, often before the ink is dry. A newsletter with up-to-date information would surely be useful.

Hallway at Are Renga with resident cat

Chapter Two

Rarotonga

Rarotonga is a small island about three thousand miles east of Australia, about as far as London is from New York.

Because I would be arriving three days before Christmas, my son insisted that I call ahead for at least the first night's lodging. Together we read and reread the "bottom end" listings in a Lonely Planet guide.

In moments, by direct dialing 011 682 20 050, I was speaking to Tangi at Are Renga. This was a new kind of travel for me; alone, open-ended and without reservations beyond the first stop, a Maori operated budget-friendly plantation geared for backpackers.

Adrift in the somnolent drone of night flight, I walked down the aisle between rows of sleeping passengers. We were flying at thirty seven thousand feet somewhere over the Equator. Just before dawn the screen flashed our location. Tahiti was behind us...Aitutaki and Rarotonga just ahead. I let the past go and began a new life, the center of which is the Southern Tropics of the Pacific.

A light drizzle fell as I stepped onto the tarmac. The arrivals lounge was filled with people, both men and women, wearing wreaths of flowers as crowns and garlands around their necks. Ladies were dressed in flowered cotton pareus and flip-flops, men in shorts and knit or flowered shirts.

When I left Los Angeles it was during an unusually cold spell, so I wore slacks, a heavy sweater and light jacket. Quickly, it became apparent that I was overdressed for the tropical climate. I had brought much more luggage than I needed. A few changes of light- weight cotton clothes and a couple pairs of sandals would have been enough.

As I waited at the Immigration Desk, half distracted, I scanned the faces of those who had come to meet arriving passengers.

"Why have you come to the Cook Islands?" the official asked.

"I will be writing a magazine article," I responded innocently.

"You cannot work here. You cannot write," he said firmly, sternly adding, "Come to the Immigration Office first thing Monday morning."

I am the kind of person who will stand on a city street corner at midnight with no car in sight, waiting until the red light turns green. I flushed. I was in trouble even before I had arrived!

Once through baggage check, I looked among the parked vans for one marked Are Renga. Two girls approached me.

"Are you Eona?" they asked.

Although my name is Evangeline, family and friends have always called me Iona, and Eona was as close as people in the islands got to it.

I told them about my problem with Immigration. Monday would be Christmas Eve and I wanted to know exactly where I had to go.

"It is in the brown building just down from the airport. We'll pass it on the way."

At the time, I couldn't have guessed that I would be drawn into this family and, for a decade, watch them grow into young women and then parents, as the family at Are Renga grew and prospered; as the island which was their home went through subtle changes.

Their father, Bob Estall, brought a half dozen young backpackers and loaded their packs, along with my several small pieces of luggage, into the back of the van as we crowded into three rows of seats. It was my introduction into the incomparable experience of "budget" travel. They were the ages of my children. If they were surprised to find an older American woman among them, I never knew.

We followed the coastal road, the Ara Tapu, along the lagoon. You cannot describe Rarotonga without using superlatives. All the clichés from travel brochures unfold in one gorgeous view after another.

We passed through a little village made up of small farmlets, raked, swept, neat and tidy. From the airport it is just three miles to Are Renga.

I followed the girls down a trail toward the back of the ten-acre plantation. We entered the lodge through a broad verandah on the backside of the building, which overlooks the plantation and mountain peaks beyond. Doors lined the bright, wide hallway opening into nine self-contained one room apartments, each complete with a small kitchenette and rustic bath.

James Estall and his wife began constructing the three buildings near the road in 1976 shortly after the airport was extended to accommodate international flights. They were pioneers in Cook Island tourism. Altogether they have twenty three units.

When James' wife died, his son, Bob, and Bob's wife, Tangi, who is a nurse, came to manage the property. Four generations of the large extended family live on the far side of the plantation where dozens of young coconut palms and groups of colorful bougainvillea and frangipani and fragrant gardenias are set in a neatly clipped emerald green lawn.

Rarotonga, pronounced with a soft "g" as in song, is the largest of fifteen islands in the scattered Cook Group. From the southernmost island, Mangaia, to the far reaches of the northern atolls it is about nine hundred miles.

Because of the long, close association with New Zealand, English is as commonly spoken as Maori. The mantle of democratic government and culture, New Zealand style, rests easily over ancient traditions. But underneath, ta'unga are still there somewhere in the villages and hills for this is the heart of Polynesia. Just eighteen thousand Maoris remained in the Cooks; half of them on Rarotonga where the people are a charming blend of simplicity and sophistication.

I had neglected to exchange money at the L.A. airport and found the banks closed on Saturday morning when I arrived. Shopkeepers near Are Renga looked at my American money and shook their heads. It might as well have been confederate or poorly counterfeited bills. Useless. But they gave me anything I wanted, saying, "You can pay me anytime."

An Australian newscaster on a shop's TV announced that Cyclone Joy - upgraded to 4 out of 5 - is packing 200 km. winds and is about to hit the coast at Cairns, Australia. They fear a tidal surge there. I realized how far I am from home.

Minutes before it began raining, I got back to Are Renga, lay down and slept heavily. It was dusk when I awoke to the sound of a young Swedish couple taking turns reading to each other. A girl with a British accent showed me how to light my gas stove and gave me matches. She assured me that the tap water is safe.

With a cup of instant coffee, I went to the verandah where a young German man was eating a fragrant rice dish out of a frying pan at one of the patio tables.

"When you are not lucky in love you have to learn to cook," he joked.

My bed is adequate, a home-built pressed board frame with a clean cotton-covered foam mattress about six inches deep. I have a table and chairs in my kitchen. All the basic things I need are furnished. There are glasses, dishes, cooking and eating utensils, shiny kettles and a fry pan.

When I told Tangi at the time I made my reservation that I am traveling budget she suggested their shared single rate of $15 in Cook Island or New Zealand money, which were used interchangeably. The favorable exchange rate of $1.65 to the U.S. dollar allowed me to extend my stay on Rarotonga.

When the heavy night rain eased to a drizzle, I took my umbrella and walked to church, which is about a half mile into the village of Arorangi. The church was built in 1849 of huge coral blocks brought from the sea. In great pits, driftwood and trees were set afire with broken coral heaped on top. The fire was tended for a week or more. Coral and ash became powder that formed mortar when mixed with water and sand. Whitewashed walls are two feet thick. Jalousie windows, surrounded by stained glass, are open on both sides. The high altar is decorated with hand crocheted pieces and fresh flowers. Bouquets of orchids, white lilies and gardenias decorate the front of the church. Polished hand-hewn pews are made of Kauri wood.

I had read about the outstanding a capella singing in the Cook Island churches, but nothing could have prepared me for the burst of sound as one woman's lusty voice began the himene, joined by others in perfect harmony. Deep bass voices answered. Intermittent guttural chants from the men are a vestige of pre-mission worship of their ancestral god, Tangaroa. To Western ears it is shockingly discordant at first, but lovely as it becomes familiar.

At my door, Tangi has left fresh eggs, two mangoes, a watermelon and three sweet potatoes from their garden. I had forgotten how good farm fresh eggs are where chickens range free!

On Monday, Christmas Eve, I was still without Cook Island or New Zealand money so I walked about six miles into Avarua. My stop at the Immigration office was brief. I showed a young, somewhat indifferent, customs agent my letter from the magazine and my business card explaining my intent. Without even glancing at the letter, he said that I would be allowed to stay up to six months by monthly extensions with a $30 application fee for each renewal.

"But you cannot work. You cannot write."

Sweeping with a kikau broom at Are Renga

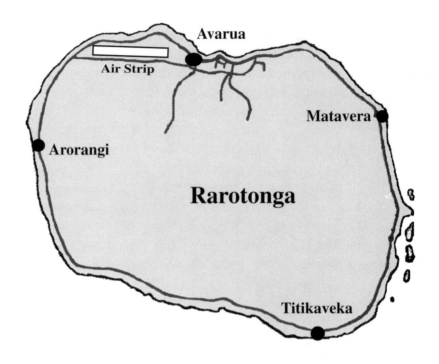

Rarotonga is a small island, just 32 kilometers, about 20 miles, around the Coastal Road, Ara Tapu, in circumference. It is about 3000 miles east of Australia and about as far south of the Equator as Hawaii is north, roughly 20°of latitude.

Chapter 3

A Tropical Christmas

The colors were right. Canopies of flaming red blossoms of flamboyant trees stood against deeply green tropical foliage, but everything else about Christmas in the Cook Islands was like a delightful child's game of opposites.

The Christmas Eve pageant in the CICC (Cook Islands Christian Church) Sunday school hall was scheduled to begin about seven in the evening. All day decoration of the hall was in progress. I estimated that four hundred fifty balloons had been inflated and were hung in a fish net secured to the ceiling along the center ridgepole from the door to the stage. Palm fronds, slit at the tips, were braided to cover the posts. Plaited palm branches, garnished with flowers, covered the front of the stage. Pressure lanterns were set across the stage as footlights.

At half past eight the pageant began. It was filled with surprises. Two young men sang *White Christmas* in a false nostalgia on an island where snow can only be imagined.

A young couple played Mary and Joseph, but our traditional manger scene was not the focus. "Joseph" scolded and shamed his "Mary" for being pregnant, striding back and forth on the stage. Suddenly, on one of the highest rungs of a ladder at the edge of the stage, illuminated by the beam of a flashlight, the angel appeared to inform Joseph of the Divine Conception. Mary and Joseph left the stage happy about the angel's message.

At the end of the pageant small children, arranged and encouraged by a lovely teenager, danced a graceful hula. Then a scramble for the balloons as the net was released.

I remembered a pageant long ago. It was in a snowbound village Up North in the heart of the Minnesota lakes region. Each Saturday morning for a month we gathered in the frigid church wearing our snow suits and rubber boots with scarves tied around our heads and mittened hands. Because I was too young to go to school or to memorize a piece to recite, I was put with the group of children carrying placards with a single letter on each. We would assemble in the correct order with the help of loving parent volunteers until our time came to march nervously onto the stage. Somehow, my little group of four, which should have formed STAR came out backwards. The congregation roared with laughter as we announced the next event in the program, RATS OF BETHLEHEM. It was a polar opposite setting, but the heart of Christmas is the same everywhere.

As I walked home to Are Renga, laughing groups of children and their parents moved through the dark streets, their flashlights making pin pricks of light like a hundred fireflies.

The couple from England left at two thirty this morning. Bob came down on a motor scooter to tell them the plane was flying early. Departure and arrival times in Auckland and Los Angeles made our mid-ocean schedules less convenient.

The three remaining backpackers are Pieter, a Swede who is a forty two year old school teacher; Friedeman, a bearded German from the Black Forest area who has a marvelous voice and Anita, a pretty, petite blonde girl from Denmark. She is leaving on Sunday for an eight or nine-day cruise on the freighter, *Nga Maru*. It was in port so she approached the captain, Jens Jensen, and negotiated a price...$200 with cabin and meals. They will probably visit five islands, although a freighter's itinerary is always subject to change.

After a morning promising blue skies, a gray mist covered the island and for an hour it rained torrentially. Pieter and I brought the laundry inside to the lines on the verandah, but soon the sun was out with birds twittering, so we put it back on the outdoor clotheslines. He told me that he teaches History to fifteen and sixteen year old students. He is currently on the way to visit his daughter who is a student in New Zealand.

The lane that runs behind my bedroom window leads from the coastal road to the Ara Metua, the ancient road that was built a thousand years ago, according to legend, by a chief named Toi. Along the lane, papaya and arrowroot fields prosper in the rich volcanic soil. At the end of the lane, not much more than a half-mile behind Are Renga, is the Cultural Village. It was built by Cookie Sadaraka, a man from Aitutaki, and his Kiwi wife, Lois. Although on a smaller scale, it was patterned after the Polynesian Center in Hawaii, which is associated with the Brigham Young University.

In the first nine "are" or huts, a girl spoke of Cook Island pre-mission history showing artifacts. Cannibalism was mentioned lightly, but the emphasis was on the successful cultural adaptation of the early Polynesians living on an isolated island with few resources.

The coconut palm was, and still is, used in countless ways. Coconut husking was demonstrated. The stem end of the husk was struck on a sharpened stick set firmly in the ground, which allowed the husk to be peeled away. A blow from a bush knife opened the nut cleanly in half. The refreshing milk of the nut was drunk, the meat of the nut was grated and squeezed through a fiber which grows between new fronds at the crown of a young palm tree. The resulting coconut cream is the basis for much of Polynesian cooking. The empty half shells are used for cups or to make ukuleles. Coconut fronds are plaited into baskets and lengths of material used for roofing thatch.

In the fishing hut, Danny Mataroa explained how kiko ro, a natural "net" made from palm fronds, is used to scare the fish into an ever narrowing circle where they can be speared and put into palm-woven baskets. He showed us how to kill the fish by biting the back of its neck. In olden times, he said, "utsu" was used to stun the fish. It grows on the Barringtonia tree. Fibrous on the outside, the white utsu nut was crushed and sprinkled on the water. When fish eat it they are stunned, but they must be cleaned and eaten immediately before the deadly poison gets into the meat of the fish. Reef-walking shoes were made of bark of giant hibiscus, woven and tied with sennit, a rope made from coconut fibers.

Candlenut, which is oily inside, is strung on the spine or midrib of the coconut frond and burned as a torch. So it went, from one hut to another as life in pre-mission days was explained. There was a hut for Maori medicine, one to demonstrate umu cooking in the ground ovens, one for costume making, another for carving of split log drums and statues of the gods.

In time for an island lunch, we arrived at the Are Kariei, the house of entertainment. The young people who were our guides served lunch followed by a finely choreographed show of Polynesian drum dances. The rapid, graceful movement of the girls dancing the tamure is mind-boggling. The young men dance close to the girls, never touching, a teasing, knee-knocking dance impelled by the rapid rhythm of drums. Young warriors, long removed from the need to protect their shores, dance the huka shouting fiercely and threatening the audience with spears; then they invite the audience to come onto the floor to join the dance. It is all in fun and the pale papa'a leave the floor with even greater respect for the grace and skill of the Rarotongan dancers wondering, how do they do that?

There are traditionally five drums. Three of them, pate, are made of hollowed slit logs.

To get the proper tone, the three drums must be carved at the same time by the same person. The other two drums are made of the hollowed lower part of a coconut palm trunk, covered by goat skin that is stretched taut and tied with sennit. Ukuleles are made from a coconut half-shell with a hibiscus limb for the neck.

On the afternoon of New Years Eve Friedeman returned from Aitutaki. Pieter came home from the lagoon with a dozen small fish, which a fisherman had given to him, strung on a thin limb. He cooked them whole while I peeled cucumbers and tomatoes from Bob's garden. Friedeman joined us for dinner on the verandah. A wide-ranging, compelling conversation continued until the full moon hung above the mountains in billowy clouds that suggested a moon in motion. The New Year had begun...1991.

Mynah birds, saucy raucous brown/black mynahs, have been imported to destroy an insect, which was threatening coconut plantations. They have displaced indigenous birds, which are now found only in the mountainous interior. Shore birds are also absent on Rarotonga, perhaps because it is so isolated in a great expanse of ocean or perhaps because their eggs were consumed to extinction.

This morning, after an early high tide, I went shell collecting. I found some perfect shells, like miniature conchs. Then I saw one unlike any I had ever seen, a luminous silky opaque white with colorful rings around. When I picked it up, I saw that it was occupied...but not by the original owner. There were three legs sticking out which belonged to a nervous, enterprising little hermit crab. I tried to shake him out, but he crawled completely inside. I cannot take a living shell, however desirable, but there were many shells on the beach, any of which could give him shelter. I took this shell to the water's edge and tried to let the little fellow escape and swim away, to no avail. By then his tenacity had stung my conscience and I set the shell on the beach still cool and wet from the receding tide. Cautiously the little fellow began dragging the shell toward the place that I had found him, higher on the beach. He was not a pretty thing, red spotted with spiny legs protruding in all directions.

I watched him, curiosity mingling with respect, which turned to wonder as he dragged, then pushed, then pulled the burden of his lovely shell higher on the beach. He was undaunted by obstacles such as footprints in the sand that were to him deep ravines. He conquered each obstacle, pulling the shell along.

When my shadow fell over him, he momentarily retreated into the shell. I thought, How much I am like this spiny, homely creature, clinging to my lovely burdens which are becoming far to heavy for me to carry...houses, cars and furniture, all beautiful shells in which we hide and in which we find pseudo-security and a false identity.

When I returned from shell collecting, one of Tangi's daughters was busy with a large basket of frangipani weaving flower eis (in Hawaii, called leis) for a group of Tahitians who were scheduled to come on the next flight. Tangi said they may be going to Ariana Bungalows instead, but Bob and the girls will still go to the airport with welcoming eis to greet them. There seemed to be fierce competition for business among middle and bottom end establishments. Top-end hotels were usually booked by travel agencies as part of packages or by tour groups.

Several new people came in on the plane last night. I asked if anyone would like to join me to walk to Edgewater Hotel to attend Island Night. Without dinner, I told them the cover charge is NZ$5.

We were all on tight budgets, so Kim brought a pitcher of ice water and seven glasses from the bar. Our group included a Canadian couple, a Japanese couple, and Ian and Mark, from England. Mark had been traveling for seven months from Bangkok east. He said that Sumatra was nice and he liked Taveuni in Fiji. He had stayed at Susie's Plantation on Taveuni's rugged south coast, where he dove right from the beach.

I watched the girls dance and studied their incredible movements. They danced barefoot, feet flat, knees slightly bent, bodies lowered just a bit.

All the dancers wore costumes that were hand made from the inner bark of the wild hibiscus or paper mulberry tree. They were decorated with shells and flowers. The women's were ankle length; the men's "grass skirts" came just to their knees.

After an excellent show, we walked the mile and half home in a light drizzle.

In the night when the nearer sounds are still I could hear the distant surf pounding on the reef, which reminded me again how small this island is in so great and powerful an ocean.

Children learning to dance at Avorangi Elementary School, Rarotonga

Chapter Four

Backpackers

Lethargy, commonly called "Polynesian Paralysis", had begun to define my schedule. I had decided to go on Monday to the Immigration Office to renew my visitor's permit for another month. This had to be done two weeks before expiration of my current permit.

Are Renga had been described as the best backpackers place in the Pacific by several young travelers who have been out for several months. The only complaints about Rarotonga have been that, at low tide, the lagoon is often too shallow to really swim and that in some places the reef seems dead. But this comparison was from divers who had seen Australia's Great Barrier Reef and the White Wall of Somosomo Strait in the Fijian Archipelago. The water here was clear, the beach and lagoon bottom were white sand, transportation around the island was easy and the people were sincerely welcoming, with an innate warmth that seemed genuine.

Each time planes came in they brought new guests; each time they left they carried our new friends away. Though the dynamics of the group on the verandah was always changing, without exception there was a generosity of spirit, a universal acceptance, that I had never experienced when traveling upscale as half of a couple.

The market by the harbor in Avarua was set up casually among trees across from the main street of the city, where everything one needs was available. With a population of about four thousand, Avarua was the only trading center in a thirteen hundred seventy-mile stretch of ocean between Papeete in Tahiti and Apia in Samoa. Off the back of trucks you could purchase a variety of produce: watermelons, mangoes, papayas, ripe coconuts and green drinking nuts. There were arrowroot cakes, palusami and unfamiliar foods that were cooked and wrapped in banana leaves. And, of course, there were T-shirts hanging on lines stretched between trees. But it was the fish that caught my eye. A stringer of silver fish hung from a tree limb where a Maori woman, selling fish, sat on a cooler filled with fillets.

"The parrotfish is good today," she suggested.

I bought $5 worth with little idea what I would do with them.

Bob and Victoria, Canadians, were on the verandah when I returned. When I mentioned the fish, Bob offered to cook them for me. He had lived in the islands. This journey, which began in Vanuatu and continued through Fiji, was one of pure nostalgia for him.

He hurried off into the plantation and returned with two coconuts, which he brought to James Estall, Jr., who was in the wash shed grating nuts for their family dinner. The electric grater quickly produced a big bowlful of juicy coconut, which Bob squeezed through a cloth. After sautéing half an onion, diced, and a clove of garlic in butter he added the coconut cream, fish fillets and two taro leaves, which he had chopped. When the poached fillets were done, he removed them and cooked the sauce down a bit, pouring it over the fish. There was plenty to share, so we served it on the verandah. That was the beginning of frequent multinational potluck dinners that became feasts.

The next day Wayne, an Alaskan fisherman from Petersburg, bought a yellowfin tuna.

While Wayne filleted the tuna, Bob began gathering coconuts. Andreas made a tropical fruit salad and the girls cooked rice, kumara and taro. Clark made his specialty for dessert, fried bananas with orange caramel sauce. Both the oranges and bananas were from the plantation. Clearly the men were the superior chefs.

Joe Smith would sit back after eating and, sucking on his pipe, he would relate adventures that spanned more than a dozen years of traveling the warmer latitudes around the globe. Shanghai, Jamaica, Bali, Perth...ordinary places to this extraordinary, rootless man whose main goal was avoiding the English winter. Well read, he was pompous and a little arrogant with more than a touch of cynicism, but his travel tales held us all spellbound, all the more interesting because of his Scottish humor and accent.

He mentioned losing his wallet, obviously to a pickpocket, at the Nadi airport. He had exchanged $900 just before getting on the plane. Philosophically, he said, "Well, it's just that much less to leave the grandchildren," then added pensively, "If that's ALL you lose at sea..." as his voice trailed off to unspoken memories.

His sailboat, his only home, was docked at a marina in Aberdeen.

"There is a place in Scotland," he said, "where palm trees grow; an area warmed by the Gulf Stream." But, in confidence, he said, "Living on a cruising yacht sounds romantic, but when a chill wind blows and you are standing at the gate to the showers by the dock with your towel in your hand and realize that you forgot your key, reality quickly erases romance."

The next week he planned to return to Scotland to settle his affairs and sell the boat. Reacquainted with a childhood sweetheart whose mate had also died, he intended to return to Perth to marry.

I gave him a breadfruit and suggested that he boil half of it and slice the other half to fry as "chips". I reminded him to peel it under water to avoid the rubbery sap oozing all over his knife and hands.

That evening, an agonizing cry came from Joe's room. Cindy and I arrived at the same time. While moving the pot of breadfruit from the stove he had bumped the table, spilling boiling water down his leg. Cindy shouted for everyone to bring ice cubes and clean towels, which she put on the raw, deep burn.

I remembered that, in the Maori medicine hut at the Cultural Village, they spoke of a cactus which helps heal burns without a scar. I ran to the house and asked if they had the cactus for burns. Theressa, with a flashlight, took me to the garden where she cut aloe and put it in my hand.

By the time I got back to the lodge, Vicki and Bob had returned from dinner. She was a trauma nurse; he was part of a British Columbia search and rescue team. When she saw the aloe, she said, "Oh, that's great!" as she squeezed juice from the aloe onto his leg, which was deep pink from knee to ankle. She loosely bandaged it, giving him pills for pain. Then she and Bob went to the hospital for saline solution, gauze and other supplies. Bandages were expensive and in short supply. Because they had to be changed frequently, we washed and boiled them and hung them to dry. Care had to be taken to avoid infection because in the tropics wounds can become seriously septic.

Bob and Vicki extended their stay in the Cook Islands, giving up an opportunity to visit Tahiti, so they could take care of Joe at home until he was able to travel back to New Zealand for treatment. The accident seriously compromised his plans.

An article in the Cook Island News said that the *Nga Maru*, the freighter Anita is on, has been delayed at Atiu because of unsettled weather.

Possessions are few among travelers. Gift exchanges are a frequent part of solemn and emotional leave-taking at flight time, especially from long-term travelers who are going east, those returning to North America or Europe where everything is easily available. A towel, a length of clothes line, a plastic water jug, half a bag of sugar, a couple onions or a bit of cooking oil are small gifts given in a sincere and caring way. There are exchanges of addresses, promises, hugs. There is a difference between travelers and tourists!

Nels was soft-spoken. His ponytail reminded me of the 60's. The worn leather pouch he carried easily over one shoulder marked him as an experienced traveler, but even so, I wouldn't have guessed that he and Carin had been traveling Asia for two years. Carin's speech had a hard, coarse edge. With flashing dark eyes she seemed more gypsy than Swede, a pretty woman about forty, older I guessed, than Nels.

Within an hour after their arrival their room had been transformed! They pushed the two beds together and covered them with an Indian cotton spread printed with an elephant motif. A mosquito net was hung. The table was covered with a batik cloth, a candle was added and a vase of fresh flowers from the garden.

At first they kept to themselves, but on their last morning they came to me on the verandah. They knew that I was just beginning my trip.

The conversation went to India. Not the exotic and beautiful place I remembered from my visit in 1970. They knew the streets. She had lain in a mud hut for seven months recovering from what they thought was tuberculosis while Nels tended her, afraid to see a doctor. If her illness was documented it might make their return to Sweden difficult.

There was a dichotomy in her personality, which I found hard to reconcile. Gentle with children, she had a soft center that she rarely allowed to show. I watched her explain how to use their fishing gear, two small hooks and lines, as she gave them to the Maori boys, Tero and Aster. Nels commented that, because of those fishing lines, they were able to travel and live on $100 a week between them.

Carin gave me a small, empty rusted tin, which was obviously important to her. "This," she said, "will keep your punk from crushing." She explained that I will encounter mosquitoes, which can carry deadly diseases and I must keep coils of punk for burning.

Nels told me of their favorite places in India and Malaysia and Indonesia, places away from the drug trade. Carin confided to me that they had bought jewelry and had shipped it home wrapped in old clothes to avoid customs. All fourteen boxes got through. They will sell the jewelry "on the black" at flea markets.

On the way to Avarua, one passes the Meteorological Observatory. The young man attending it said they pass hourly reports to Nadi and Kelburn, Wellington, the main station. In the summer their weather comes mainly from the northerly sector closer to the Equator (December to April) and in winter (June to September) from the south.

"Coming from the Antarctic, it can get quite chilly...down to eighteen degrees Centigrade [64.4° F]," he said.

Cyclone Sally surprised them at night one New Year's Eve. Great boulders came ashore. They have designated Terora College as the "hurricane safety house".

When I passed Avatiu Harbour, I saw the *Nga Maru* in port. I got off the bus to inquire about Anita.

"She went into town about forty five minutes ago."

The advantage of a city with just one major street allowed me to find Anita quickly. She looked fit and tan!

"I haven't eaten so well since I left home!"

She related one adventure after another, including a bush beer party on one of the islands.

"On two of the islands we couldn't go ashore because the sea was so rough."

Even at best, they are wet landings where freight and passengers are taken over the reef in a small boat. I understood Anita's concern when she said, "Don't try it, Iona. You need to be really fit to go up and down the rope ladder into the reef boat."

Although the account of such a landing was written more than a century ago in *Amerika Samoa*, some things never change. On taking a canoe across the reef:

Turning toward the channel, he kept his eye on the following seas and waited for a wave of proper size to project the boat through the reef with enough momentum to hold her inside the lagoon against the furious backwash which would follow. At the precise moment he cried, "Alu! Alu! (Go! Go!)," and the men took to their oars an pulled the boat through the passage, mastered the backrush of water and moved onto the beach where they jumped over the sides...the boat must be narrow, swift and maneuverable and the steersman and rowers must be masters of their art, for failure in passage results at best in a swamped boat and wet passengers...and at worst in a smashed boat and death for its occupants on the jagged coral rocks.

Paul Theroux, who kayaked around many of the 41 islands he visited, described such landings in the Marquesas when going ashore from the freighter Aranui:

And the whaleboats came and the older passengers were carried in the arms of Marquesans. It was accomplished quickly, but I was struck by these arrivals and departures through the surf...like rescues, just as wet and urgent and precarious.

(from *The Happy Isles of Oceania*)

Clark, just nineteen years old, a Canadian with deep-set dimples, red hair and freckles, was my favorite. He was on his way home after five months in Australia and New Zealand. Hawaii would be his last stop so, with little money left, he welcomed just hanging around. One day I mentioned that a professor of economics from Hawaii would be speaking the next evening at the University of South Pacific campus downtown.

"But the bus stops running at four o'clock," I mused, then dismissed the idea of going.

First thing in the morning I heard the "RmmmRmmm" of a motorcycle outside my window. Clark had spent $15 to rent a blue Suzuki motorcycle for twenty four hours. All day he practiced riding it.

"I'll pick you up at six," he insisted.

I rode behind him, one hundred sixty pounds of scared-stiff dead weight.

The first person I met while waiting outside for Clark to park the motorcycle was the Curator of the Museum, which was housed in the library building across the street from the University.

Learning that I am an American, he said that he had attended Ohio State University in 1982. He knew both Dorothy Brickman and Kevin Harty, the Director of the International Students' Office and her assistant. I had worked with them for ten years until 1982.

When I mentioned that the University of Pennsylvania Museum in Philadelphia has an excellent collection of Polynesian artifacts he said that is probably good because it is very difficult to maintain the museum displays on Rarotonga because of deterioration from the heat and humidity.

Professor Kelly spoke passionately about the way Hawaii had been sold and developed to the point that there is no longer any place there for indigenous Hawaiians. She said that they have been totally dispossessed of their lands. She was particularly critical of the Japanese role in Hawaii's over development. A lively open discussion followed.

Rarotonga seemed aware of the dangers. Until then, there was a law that forbade anything to be built higher than a coconut palm, which eliminated the high-rise nightmare of some other island nations. Land was controlled by the Ariki, the high chiefs, and could be leased, but could never be bought or sold. It was held in trust in perpetuity for future generations. In later years, a problem arose from young people borrowing money from banks to build houses, then, unable to make the payments, losing the family property.

Throughout the islands there were twenty four Ariki. In addition, there were mataiopo and rangatira (sub-chiefs) and unga (commoners). In *Tin Roofs and Palm Trees* (1977) Robert Trumbull explained that under the Cook Island system of communal possession of land, a single acre may have dozens of owners and land disputes are frequent. But despite the complexities, Rarotongans had retained control of their land!

Clark and Eric, a Californian he had met in New Zealand, went to the beach looking for a photo opportunity, hoping for a colorful sunset. We sat on the beach taking turns listening to the news on Clark's Walkman. Julie and Carol, Canadians, were also there. Looking for a stick to throw for the dog that was the adopted pet of guests at Are Renga, Eric stepped on the grass, barefoot, into a nest of ants. He walked back and forth in agony, stepping into the lagoon to try to get relief from the itch and pain of multiple ant bites. Then he left with Julie and Carol.

By the time Clark and I got back from the beach, Julie had driven Eric to the hospital on a motor scooter she had rented for the day. Clark had their room key in his pocket at the beach, so Eric had not been able to get his wallet and I.D.

Bob and Tangi were taking Akihiro and Akiko, who had just returned from a few days on Aitutaki, to the Airport Lodge, which absorbed overflow when all the rooms at Are Renga were booked. On the way, they dropped us at the hospital where Eric had been given two injections, but his eyes and ears were still swollen, his face and body covered with rash. By the time he and Julie had reached the hospital, his windpipe was severely restricted.

Clark rode home on the back of Julie's bike. I waited until Eric's condition stabilized and took him home in a taxi as he was too drowsy from shock and medication to ride on the bike.

At ten that evening fourteen of us crowded into James Estall's little living room to watch the news. We were at war. Hundreds of planes were flying on bombing raids to Baghdad and Kuwait. It was the last telecast I would see until the announcement was made that hostilities had ceased. Desert Storm seemed unreal, a world apart, to us there in the islands.

Chapter Five
Expatriates

While waiting for the bus at Cooks Corner, I asked a young man the time.

"Ten thirty," he said.

From my relieved response, he seemed aware that my concern about the time was because it was Saturday and the buses would soon stop running.

"Which way are you going?" he asked.

"To Are Renga."

"If you don't mind riding around the island first, I'll take you there."

I asked his name.

"Euan Smith."

During the drive he told me that he had come to Rarotonga in 1973. As one of four partners, he had started Air Rarotonga. At the time of our conversation, they had five planes and flew twenty five thousand passengers a year; 45% of their passengers were local people; 55% tourists, split about equally among New Zealanders, Aussies, Americans and Europeans. Although U.S. tourists were fewer in number, a greater percentage of Americans tended to fly on to the Outer Islands...either on two or three day packages or day-trippers.

His wife had a baby boy the day before...6 lbs. 10 oz., their third child. He said that, although there are more accommodations and conveniences, life on Rarotonga hasn't changed much since 1973, nearly twenty years.

"When I return from other places, I see what I often take for granted. I believe this is the last best place to raise our children."

On one side of Are Renga rap music blared from a boombox; from the other side came the unearthly harmony of himenes being sung at the Cook Island Christian Church.

Tourism is not the only cause of change. Returnees from New Zealand bring new mores and new expectations. Although church was in progress a young Maori wearing a muscle shirt raced past on his motorbike wearing an ei katu, a crown of flowers.

Massive coral and limestone walls surround the cemetery in front of the church in Arorangi. There, the tombs of Papeiha and early Western missionaries rest beside this street of change. Ropes of cowrie shells...shell eis mean good-bye...decorate pictures mounted on tombs of more recently deceased deacons who were honored by burial in the crowded church cemetery.

More than ever before I felt the Spirit of God in the church this morning. The theme of the sermon was, "How can you be saved and all your family?" Much of the sermon was in Maori, but the service began with "Holy, Holy, Holy" sung in English. Mid-service, "The Lord's Prayer" was sung in Maori. In the end, "He is Lord" was sung in slow, reverent, heavily accented English.

The Pastor stressed that by becoming children of God we are drawn into a life of privilege, obedience and service. That we can serve only through obedience. An ordinary thing, having been possessed by a great person, becomes a thing of value...a book, a walking stick, a pen...having been the possession of some great person, though ordinary, becomes a prized object worthy of being in a museum. And so it is, when an ordinary person becomes possessed by God, he becomes vested with dignity, value, greatness.

Is this the Source of the exceptional grace and dignity, the total lack of self-consciousness, that I see in the Maoris of Rarotonga?

I had forgotten the admonition of the Immigration officials and began to get serious about my deadline for Travel Age West. I determined that the following day I would begin my walk around the island to research upscale lodgings.

Because my ear was bothering me, I stopped again at the hospital on my way downtown. I waited in the lobby from nine forty five until eleven forty five, but the time went by quickly. The Maori woman who was the lead singer at the church in Arorangi was there with her teen- age son. He had conjunctivitis, which was rampant. They called it "sexy eye". When people learned that I was staying at Are Renga they opened up to me. She invited me to her home where she tie-dyes fabrics.

I was called into the emergency care room, the only place on the island to find treatment, as there were no private practice doctors. There, I met a very professional female doctor from the Philippines. She noted a white gelatin-like coating in my ear. She asked an assistant for the ear syringe. They seemed to have misplaced it. While they continued to look for the syringe, an emergency patient was pushed in from an ambulance on a gurney, groaning with pain, surrounded by anguished family and friends.

"Could you come back Monday?" she asked as she turned her attention to the emergency at hand.

The Perfume Factory was not easy to find, but was worth the effort. At Cooks Corner, you walk inland toward the mountains and turn left at Cable & Wireless.

John Abbott, an Australian who married a Rarotongan stewardess, ran a very casual business. A sign above the inner door said "FACTORY PLEASE ENTER." The showroom was filled with the fragrance of exotic soaps and perfumes. In the factory, women in pareus were laughing and gossiping while they wrapped soap. Ingredients for the soap were mixed in a machine resembling a small cement mixer. The mixture was poured into a homemade wooden frame where it set overnight before being hand cut.

John sold about fifteen hundred bars a week. He used thirty five hundred twenty gallons of coconut oil a year, shipped to him in forty four-gallon drums. Some was produced locally, but most of it was shipped from Fiji and Samoa. To process copra, it is put into an extractor; high protein flakes come out one side, oil from the other. The oil is then filtered and the flakes are pressed.

His line of perfume was called Mi'i, which means unforgettable. Local frangipani, jasmine and gardenia were blended with oils from North Africa and essential oils from Grasse, France.

He was working on a new product for export...Tangaroa Rum Coffee Liqueur, which was being made from coffee produced on the island of Atiu. He said that a new freighter line, Ute, was establishing a route to North America, so exporting to that market would be easier. Wholesale price for the soap was NZ$1.50 FOB Rarotonga.

As we spoke, John tipped his head, patting his left ear as though it was bothering him.

"I went to the hospital," he said, "but they couldn't find their syringe."

He seemed to be a totally happy man except for sadness over the recent death of his wife.

I found a wealth of books in the South Pacific collection at the library. *The Lagoon is Lonely Now*, written by a resident of Arorangi, smelled musty as I turned the pages. This is a climate where maintenance of anything is problematical. Perhaps this accounts for the lack of acquisitive nature of these people, long accustomed to communal living. But as they enter the cash economy things seem to be changing.

There were cautions in guidebooks about clothes line theft, although they tempered the warnings by blaming losses on floppy eared dogs that were observed bothering items dangling from the clothes lines. I had lost nothing in two months, so I had relaxed my guard, sometimes leaving things on the verandah lines overnight if they were slow to dry.

It was just ten o'clock, but I had fallen asleep early. I awakened to a commotion in the hall.

"They got my bike tools, too!" one man shouted with expletives.

That certainly exonerated the playful puppies.

When I got to the verandah, I saw that two of my favorite white shirts were gone, irreplaceable there on the island. The thief, in haste, had dropped my bras and panties on the floor and left two other shirts on the line. Don had lost his black silk shirt with a colorful dragon embroidered on the back.

We were frustrated and angry to have had our possessions violated, upset that we hadn't heeded warnings that the communal theory of ownership was sometimes extended to tourist's possessions.

I was still steaming mad when I went back to bed and was slow to fall asleep. When I felt a drop of water on my leg I thought, it isn't raining anymore. I turned the light on. A large gecko froze where he was on the ceiling just above my bed.

He lived in the attic above my room, going in and out through a hole in the ceiling of my kitchen just above the stove. He was a welcome pet because he was an expert at eradication of mosquitoes. After showering I forgave him and fell asleep, smiling.

Dancer at the Cultural Village, Rarotonga

Dressing Richard in Rarotonga style

Chapter Six

A Walk Around the Island

It will be interesting to see if the controversial Sheraton Hotel will be finished. The land is cleared and steel girders are up. I have been told that the road will be changed to go behind the hotel to give it beach frontage. At present time, bags of cement, purchased long ago, are being sold off because in this humid climate they have begun to harden. If it is finished it will force existing hotels to a competitive higher standard.

The Rarotongan Hotel was the first stop on my walk around the island. The premier hotel on the island, it was government owned but a bit down at the heels.

After settling into my hotel room, which was in the wing that had recently been refurbished, I made an appointment to interview the sales manager. J. J. Browne was a nephew of the Prime Minister, but I did not know that at the time.

He apologized for the condition of the hotel. It was built in 1977 and was in need of general renovation. He said that the government was building the Sheraton, similar to the one at Cairns in Australia. He showed me the architect's drawing of the proposed new Sheraton, which would consist of several low buildings built around landscaped lakes because the land on which it was to be built was low and marshy.

When I mentioned that I was staying at Are Renga, he responded explosively, "Riff-raff...nothing but riffraff stays there."

I felt defensive and personally insulted. I tried to explain to him the difference between travelers and the typical guest that stays at the Rarotongan on a short holiday or package trip. According to statistics Dorice Reid, who was then working at the Visitor's Bureau, gave me the average visitor stays ten days and spends $822.33. The greatest constraint in the growth of tourism, she told me, was the limited number of incoming seats. The typical visitor to Are Renga tended to stay longer. Money was spent in the village to buy groceries, to rent motorbikes, take scuba diving lessons, visit restaurants and the Cultural Village and for trips to Outer Islands. So, even though his rent was less, the economic benefit to the community was there.

"Most of the young people who stay at Are Renga are professionals on leave from successful jobs," I continued, but my defense left him unimpressed.

He explained that government policy is to go after the high-end tourist who is on Rarotonga for a short visit. Mr. Browne was young...handsome, polished, educated, privileged.

At five o'clock I went to the Management Cocktail Party for new guests. Stiff. Formal. Mr. Browne was there along with another man from the staff. I asked him how he felt about the Sheraton.

"I am Sheraton," he said.

He explained that he had managed the Bangkok Sheraton for fourteen years. He had been brought in to upgrade the Rarotongan through its period of renovation and anticipated sale; then to manage the new Sheraton through the construction phase and opening.

"My wife is Thai," he continued.

"Do you know of Somsak Lohachala or his father Chumbphol Lohachala?" I asked.

"Somsak's father was a General in the Royal Thai Police, in charge of security for the King. But that was several years ago."

I hastily wrote Somsak's name and his father's on a piece of paper hoping that his wife would know of them. I was aware that his father had attained an eminent political position during the intervening years. But just as I handed him the paper new guests arrived, so I had no opportunity to explain that Somsak was one of the international students who had become part of our large adopted family during the years I worked with the Office of International Students and Scholars at the University.

I had innocently blundered into an arena where the seeds of doubt and suspicion flourished. As I walked past the Sheraton construction site the next day I was oblivious to the intrigue that would follow.

At the construction site a bronze plaque affixed to a stone monument declared:

This plaque was placed here by the Honourable Geoffrey A. Henry, MP Prime Minister of the Cook Islands on 25 May 1990 in appreciation of this historic site being made available by Pa Tepaeru Ariki for and to mark commencement of the construction of the Sheraton Cook Island Resort.

Walking around the perimeter of Rarotonga is not such an adventurous undertaking as it sounds. It is just twenty miles around. The six villages are almost evenly spaced around the Ara Tapu, as are the twenty three small resorts and hotels. In addition, the bus passes every half hour in one direction or the other and the drivers frequently stopped and asked, "Are you okay?" So I never felt isolated. At any time, in less than an hour, I could have been back at Are Renga.

I stopped to visit a woman who was sitting in a house with an open doorway both front and back. I could see the lagoon from her front step through the back door. She was weaving a large pandanus mat. I walked on the beach. I took pictures of a man grating coconut sitting astride a bench that resembled a sawhorse, with a sharpened shell that functioned as grater on the end. With quick, experienced movements, he grated a bowl of coconut as quickly as James had with the electric grater. I admired the catch of fishermen who pulled their outrigger up onto the beach. I fell in love with an island too beautiful to attempt to describe.

At Avaavaroa Passage, The Channel of Plaintive Calling, I paused to watch fishermen waiting for the incoming tide to carry fish into their nets. The channel was named for the young lovers whose canoe had been swept from the lagoon and lost in the rush of tidal backwash.

Near Titikaveka I saw a sign, Apartment for Rent. Behind the hedge I found the oldest European-built plantation house on the island, dating back to the early 1920's, which was built by Boss McKegg who was, according to custom, buried in the garden. The large, airy house had interior walls of tongue-in-groove, hurricane shutters, exquisite Samoan mats on the floor. The man who met me, an American, extended his hand with a smile that swept me in.

"I am Anthony McBride."

He showed me the apartment, charmingly old fashioned, clean and neat, then he showed me the garden. I could easily see that his heart was there.

"I am a planter," he explained, using the colonial island term proudly. "I began in Hawaii when I was nineteen. When it got too crowded, I moved on to Samoa. I married a beautiful girl there and we settled in Fiji. We had a forty-acre plantation, mostly kava, which is the biggest money crop. When we had an opportunity to buy the lease on this place, we sold the plantation. Kept just one acre on which the house is located. We live there half of each year and come here for half the year. We rent the house in Fiji by the half year for F$800 to $1,200 a month, depending on how long they stay."

Tony was a polished man, lean, hard, utterly charming, with the deep leathery tan typical of planters who spend hours in the tropical sun year after year.

I didn't meet his wife, Nima, until my next visit.

I had walked less than two hours from Are Renga to the Rarotongan on my first day, so I wanted to cover a greater distance on my second day out.

Just before I got to Rick Welland's studio a boy about four feet tall, not yet ten years old, I would guess, tried to mug me. He was walking toward me carrying a woman's purse, wearing a flower behind each ear...a picture of perfect innocence. As we met, he said, "Come let me show you my...."

I couldn't understand him and didn't want to hurt the child's feelings. He was insistent and took me firmly by the elbow to lead me down a lane. Whenever I hesitated, he repeated what he had said. Still not understanding, I asked, tentatively, "Your crab?"

He repeated it again, slightly irritated.

"Your camp?" I continued.

Suddenly a flag of caution went up and I stopped, seeing what appeared to be nothing but a half constructed house at the end of the isolated lane. He tried to grab my purse and I jerked it back, saying, "No!" firmly. Then he tried to open the flap to reach in as he grabbed it again. I jerked it and as I whirled around shouted, "No!" again. He grabbed for my duffle. Failing to get it, he hit me...not as an assailant who meant to harm me, but like a frustrated child who hadn't gotten his way.

I hurried as fast as I could back to the Ara Tapu and felt safe again when I got out of sight of the child. I hoped to meet no more like him along the way. That was the only time I felt threatened at all in eight and a half months traveling alone through a dozen islands of the South Pacific!

Beyond the motus at Muri Beach, where all the places I stopped to research had no vacancies, there were fewer places to stay. It was already late afternoon when I stopped at Sunrise Beach Motel, where I found a nice, affordable bungalow with a panoramic view of the rocky beach.

Wild waves were breaking on the reef, which was near the shore. Because I was not accustomed to the sound of surf so near, I kept waking. There were no screens on the windows. Without my resident gecko, it was the first time I was aware of mosquitoes. Too late, I remembered Carin's advice about always carrying punk to burn against their dangerous aggravation. In the semidarkness, I was aware of a shadow moving slowly across the kitchen wall. When I turned the light on, I saw a huge brown thing, like a crusty spider as big as a dinner plate crawling down the wall. He crawled slowly sideways, not quite as sure-footed as a spider, and much, much larger. With a brisk swoosh of a towel I brushed him out the open door.

I was up at first light and reached KiiKii for breakfast; Avarua in time to take the last Saturday bus home to Are Renga. I had walked the road from Avarua to Are Renga many times and had been around the island by bus and auto, but it was not the same as walking it, which made me feel that I had come to know the island better.

Well into my second month, I had finished my rough draft for *Travel Age West*, lacking only some statistics, names and rates.

Because the lodge was full, Tangi put me in one of the units by the road when I returned from my walk. It was spacious, but had low ceilings and a metal roof, with windows on the east, south and west sides with little shade. When compared to the cool and breezy, open-sided, thatched roof Right On the Beach Restaurant at Manuia Beach Resort, one wonders why the islanders adopted western-style homes!

On my way to mail a letter at Depot #2, I decided to follow the Scuba Diving sign down one of the lanes that led toward the mountains, to the Ara Metua. Well-maintained plantations bordered both sides of the road. Cautiously, I approached the house. A dive boat on a trailer stood in the yard. A large open shed in back was filled with air tanks and other dive equipment.

At the open window, I called, "I'm looking for Greg Wilson."

A big grin appeared on the face that popped up at the window.

"You're looking at him."

A stocky man, robust, though not tall, he gave the impression of being a very big man, not one you'd want to mess with. I had the feeling that he was a capable man who could handle anything; that you could put your life in his hands and feel good about it. He was as tanned as a reddish-blonde could be.

He said that he would be leaving town in two days for an Air New Zealand promotion of Cook Island Diving in Las Vegas. He was as excited as a kid over his first visit to the States.

"I'm going to Disneyland!" he said, asking if I could come back in a couple weeks.

Our interview then began informally. Just returned from a dive, he said, "I need a tub," as he stepped, singing, behind the curtained shower in the corner of the dive shack. I busied myself studying a collection of seashells on the table, shyly taking in the large room that seemed to double as "home".

Scraps of varied colored linoleum covered the concrete floor. Radio equipment and a computer dominated the living room. There was a kitchen in back and, beyond that, a workshop.

Still glistening wet from his shower, he offered me a drink, then popped a beer and sat across the table.

With no apology, he said, "You have to get the salt off."

When I asked him about the dive, he became the wonder-filled kid that is left somewhere in the heart of all of us. They had seen a shark and octopus and thousands of brightly colored fish. Visibility was about two hundred feet so it had been an exceptional dive.

I asked how he had gotten involved with diving.

"My Dad ran an oyster farm in Mahwrangi Harbour. At fifteen I started working with him, diving. I still have an interest in it. When I went from Australia to New Zealand for my mate's wedding, I saw an ad in the New Zealand paper and came out to work on airport construction in '71."

Alarm bells rang so he dashed off to the next room to turn some valves on air tanks.

"It's a wonderful life," he continued. "I lucked into doing what I'm doing and getting paid for it. Seventeen years with no accidents."

"What's diving all about?" I asked, trying to tap into his feelings about this job he loves.

"Coral and fish. It's like Alice in Wonderland. Compared to what's above the water...well, there are canyons and tunnels and caves. Creatures you can't describe in a colorful garden of coral. And the feeling! It's an indescribable feeling of weightlessness.

Freedom. A step away from reality it is. It's a sort of escapism that's addictive. My favorite dive is the Pinnacles. There are lots of ocean fish, barracuda, tuna, trevally. But I take only certified divers there. Inside the lagoon, water is four to ten feet. Depths outside the reef easily reach one hundred feet and there's a drop off which starts at eighty feet and descends to more than twelve hundred feet."

He said he takes two boats out with about fourteen people. In four days, for NZ$395 he teaches dive lessons for PADI certification.

"Most people have a lot more ability than they think they do."

When I asked about dropouts, he said, "We don't call it failure. At least they had a go at it!"

Two girls at Are Renga were taking his classes. They felt perfect confidence in Greg's hands. When they fell back into the water they just knew Greg was right there and every time they got into trouble he was always right beside them.

Cam said the bodily freedom was the thing that amazed her most. "I did a ballet on a pipe and somersaults. I felt that I could fly!"

In the classroom he was very demanding. He told them about the dangers...how the body and oxygen and pressure functioned in that environment, about weights and air balance during ascent and descent. And, especially, he cautioned them never to swim near a passage in the reef. Tides come in and go out through the passes and strong currents can quickly carry the unwary swimmer out to sea.

Paddy Walker, retired icon of the New Zealand fashion industry, now lives on Rarotonga and is active internationally in Pacific Women's issues. She also works tirelessly to promote Polynesian culture among Rarotonga's youth

Chapter Seven

Intrigue

January 29. It was the first day of school after summer vacation. Yesterday, the children had to go in the morning to clean up the schoolhouse, which is located in the center of Arorangi village right on the beach.

I had lunch at Trader Jack's with Dorice Reid and her friend from New Zealand, Paddy Walker.

On my way home I stopped at Immigration to pick up my passport and renewed visitor's permit.

"You must speak to Tutai Toru, the Principal Immigration Officer," he said as he ushered me curtly down a hall into a private office.

Without rising, Mr. Toru pointed to a chair across from his desk, indicating that I should sit down.

He said, emphatically, "You may not work here. You may not write!" He hesitated, then added, "Those who are trying to sneak into employment here will be found out."

Then, considering his words carefully, he said, even more firmly, "Those who are pretending to be independent, but are working for an international organization, will be found out."

His voice seemed to take on a seriously threatening note, but I couldn't even fathom the shape of his concern or what reason he might have had for such a wild, implied accusation.

It was enough that I felt guilty over the notes I had taken to fulfill my obligation to the magazine. I tried to soften the brittle edge of our conversation by praising the beauty of Rarotonga. I asked if he had a copy of Immigration laws that I could borrow.

His answer was evasive.

"You can buy a copy from Parliament. Policies keep changing. When Parliament convenes in February, one of the first orders of business will be rewriting Immigration laws."

Only professionals are allowed to immigrate, he explained. The Monetary Board controls all professional recruitments under the Recruitment Scheme. Overseas investment can be a firm 2/3 locally owned; 1/3 expatriate.

Clearly, this was not intended as a social call. I decided that this time, I must take the admonition not to write more seriously.

Mike, a young Californian, said again, "You must go to Taveuni. It is extraordinary."

He was scheduled to fly out that night. I told him about my interview at Immigration...about Mr. Toru's mistaken presumption about my identity and nebulous "connections" I didn't have. I told him that I am, for some reason, being watched.

"If I put my notes in a package addressed to my home, when you get to California, will you drop it in the mail? I don't understand what is going on. There could be some risk."

"No problem!" he grinned.

I packed away my copy of *Cook Island Politics...the Inside Story* and took out my *Fiji, Lonely Planet Guide*, vowing to be simply a well-behaved tourist until I traveled on.

The full moon had, once again, risen in the saddle of the two sentinels, Te Reinga and Maungaroa, which had become the backdrop for my days as the verandah again became the center of my life.

There was an unusually high tide, so I went to the beach early in the morning to look for shells.

Father Fred was gathering a kind of sea moss, which had washed ashore during the night. With a pitchfork, he was putting the moss into a wheelbarrow, taking load after load to use as fertilizer on his small garden just behind the row of casuarina trees, which lined the beach. Though frail, this small, spry man exuded enthusiasm.

The church to which he was attached was St. Mary's, which was across the street from Are Renga. We all used the churchyard as a shortcut to the beach.

I made an appointment to see him in the afternoon.

Gerard de Leeuw (which means lion, he explained) was born December 1, 1910, one of fifteen children. Thirteen are still living: four older brothers, four younger brothers and four sisters.

"We were a Catholic family of the Father of Sacred Hearts Parish in Ginneken, now part of Breda, in Holland. In my youth, I read a book written by Father Damien, the Leper Priest, which changed the direction of my life."

He joined an order of priests dedicated to sending missionaries to the most isolated islands in the world.

"We wore white sauternes in those days. In Seminary, I learned five languages, Latin, Greek, French, German and English, in addition to my native Dutch. I apologize for my English. I have spoken Maori for so long."

However, I found him fluent in English.

He left Holland in 1940. At that time you could see Hitler's soldiers at the border. Holland was still neutral, but filled with German spies. Letters that he sent home were censored, en route, by the Germans. Until 1945, he was out of touch with Holland.

"I arrived in Rarotonga before the end of March. Friars in Avarua at that time were part of the Apostolic Church under Rome. Until 1946 I covered Matavera, Titikaveka and Arorangi by bicycle. It was a sandy road then. I knew everyone on Rarotonga."

"At the time," he said, "Avarua had only two stores...Donald's and CITC (Cook Island Trading Center). During the war everyone was very poor and lived only off the land because no boats came."

Service on Rakahanga followed his assignment on Rarotonga.

"Life was very simple. The people made copra and fished. Houses were kikau (palm thatch) then. The people seemed happier. They were more connected."

To make copra they collected the nuts after they fell, husked them and cut them in half. They waited until the meat was a bit loose and used a metal piece to get the nuts out. Meat was put on corrugated iron to dry. Drying was important because the oil can cause spontaneous combustion. Once, a ship was two days out to sea and had to return because of a smoldering fire in the hold."

After Rakahanga, Manihiki for seven months followed. In 1948 he went to Penrhyn. Freighter was the only way to travel. The *Tiare Taporo* would call in the northern islands about twice a year. The northern islands were too sandy to garden.

"Rice and flour would come on the boat, but after a few months it would be full of weevils." He paused, as if remembering. "A man doesn't need much to live on," he said gently. "I'm always satisfied with whatever I eat."

He was in Aitutaki for three years, back on Rarotonga three years; then he was returned to Aitutaki for two years.

"There was a power plant at the airport so once a week I went by bike five miles to use a room the engineer had fixed to develop and enlarge photos. One day, because there were bees in the wall, the engineer put a light bulb between the walls to drive them out. It burned the building down. I lost many of my photos of the old days in the fire."

After Aitutaki, he went to Mitiaro; then he retired on Raro.

"It doesn't seem like the same place now...too civilized. All the people I knew are gone."

He was a dedicated and interesting man whose memories spanned the greatest period of change in the Cook Islands.

When I sat by lamplight on the verandah later rewriting my notes, I felt that it was somehow a clandestine activity, until I looked up and saw three other travelers writing in their journals.

Paddy Walker was the speaker at the Professional and Business Women's Luncheon at Paulina's, a second floor restaurant overlooking the harbor. Dorice Reid, who invited me, was also at the speaker's table, so I took a table alone, which I shared with Piri Puruto's wife. A divorcee from Sydney, with three children, she had met him on a cruise from Tahiti and they had married three years ago. Although he was no longer young, he does an amazing tourist show climbing palm trees.

The buffet luncheon looked sumptuous. I reached for the spoon in a bowl of salad bright with onions and tomatoes and cucumbers. The woman behind me exclaimed, "Oh, good, raw fish!"

When I hesitated she explained that ika mata is delicious...raw fish marinated in lime juice until it loses its translucent appearance and becomes white as though it has been cooked.

Paddy was an excellent speaker. She shared two memorable illustrations: "A small boy watched day after day as a sculptor chipped away at the rock. In the end the child looked at the finished art and said, 'I didn't know there was a lion in there!'"

Her closing was, "We are all like angels with one wing. We can fly better if we cling together."

The substance of her talk was a review of the South Pacific Women's Conference she had recently attended in Bangkok. Both Queen Sikrit, who hosted the meeting, and the Queen of Tonga gave papers, so it was apparently a high level meeting concerning Pacific women's issues.

I looked around the room at the prominent women on the island...either socially, like the table with the women from the Henry family...or by virtue of their business or profession. At least half of them were dressed in pareus...beautiful women. When I returned four years later, I seldom saw a woman in island dress.

A recent article in the Cook Island news told of the penalty given a young person who had accepted a stolen bottle of rum ($33 value) and bottle of coke ($3 value). He had not stolen them, but he had accepted them, knowing they were stolen. He was given a year in prison.

In retrospect, I am so happy that I didn't make a police report about my stolen shirts. I thought of the humiliation and anguish it would have caused the family of the thief. On a small island with nowhere to go, reputation is everything.

I have heard that there is no word in the Maori language that means to steal.

A group of about forty people from Aitutaki conducted the service at CICC today. The ladies were dressed in white, wearing delicately woven white rito hats; men in navy blue pants, white shirts and navy blue ties. They were excellent singers that filled the massive church from wall to wall with flawless harmonies.

They announced that on Monday night at 8:30 there would be a performance at the Sunday school building.

All afternoon the electricity had been off. The officials called it "power shedding" and it somehow involved the construction project to expand service. I was not sure the performance would go on as scheduled.

With flashlight in hand, I walked through the darkened village to find that all the doors of the Sunday school building were open. The usual happy chaos of children and dogs mingled with the concerted efforts of the performers to gather and light as many pressure lamps as they could locate.

When the curtain opened, instead of the smartly dressed choir I expected, the dance troupe was dressed in traditional costumes for drum dances.

The Pastor's son, Raymond, who was just two years old, was on stage through most of the performance. Among a forest of moving legs, he would look up at the vigorous male dancers. Then he mimicked their knee-knocking. Indulgent, as always, the performers just smiled and tried not to step on him until one of the ladies in the audience would take him off stage again. Girls who were four or five years old left the audience and were dancing impromptu in the aisles and below the stage, doing all the steps and hand movements the big girls did.

Some of the numbers in the long show seemed a bit risqué judging from the audience reaction. It was mostly in Maori, so the precise humor was lost to me.

Their performance was the dress rehearsal before going on to Fiji where they would perform for a month, traveling around to various islands.

I marveled that so much talent came from an island with a population of only twenty three hundred ninety one persons.

I chose a perfect day to take the bus to Paddy Walker's house. It is a few doors beyond the Little Polynesian Resort, which is owned by Dorice Reid and her sister.

Paddy's house is small, white with a broad verandah that overlooks the lagoon. Her rattan furniture, which she had sent from New Zealand, was painted white. Her couch and chair upholstery was tie-dyed cotton with a pattern of huge breadfruit leaves. Two tones of green were colorful against crisp white and were contrasted by bright yellow dining room cushions and pillows. Spreads and curtains of pareu material, starched, brightened her bedroom... hot pink and white. Simple elegance.

On the coffee table were the latest issues of *Vogue* and a New Zealand glossy magazine, *Fashion Quarterly*. The February/March 1991 issue had an article about Paddy with a full-page picture, telling of her recent retirement to the Cook Islands. A multidimensional woman! For twenty years she had dominated the fashion industry in New Zealand, later working with the Australian Wool Board and the Indian government promoting their cotton and silk fabrics.

We had a delicious lunch of chicken salad sandwiches on whole wheat bread from the church operated bakery at Titikaveka. She spoke about her music. She composes delicate music for the piano. One, called *The Reef* almost echoes the sound of surf in the distance.

After lunch we followed a stone-defined path through the low hedge to the beach where Paddy went for a swim while I walked to Muri. Three quarters buried in the sand, I found a giant clamshell, still hinged.

She had an appointment with the Minister of Education who is also the Minister of Prisons. She was planning a cultural program for the children of Rarotonga involving storyboards, which the prisoners would carve. The program would help prisoners develop skills and pride and make the children more aware of their history and culture.

Her appointment required her to leave at twenty past two, so I walked down to Anthony McBride's house about a mile and half, just beyond the Agricultural station. Tim, a handsome young half Samoan was just getting home from school, carrying a surfboard. Tony was on the roof, so I put my finger up to silence Tim and told him not to bother his Dad; that I would wait in the garden. Every kind of tropical plant that fruits or flowers was there. An orchard of huge mangoes was in the back and, on the other side, a jungle path found the stream, which ran under a bridge to the beach at Muri Lagoon.

While I was walking his wife, Nima, came out to take in the laundry. I had just a little while before the last bus, so as Nima and I visited, Tony gathered fruit for me to take home. From the refrigerator he took some short fat bananas with darkened skin.

"You eat these with a spoon," he said, "like pudding."

As we got to the road, Nima said, "I will go and get something for us to sit on."

She came back with a scrap of towel and a large breadfruit leaf. We crossed the road and sat in a very cool, breezy spot under huge ironwood trees. She wore a pareu. When she sat cross-legged, I noticed that she was tattooed above her knees. She is from a large village on 'Upolu Island in Western Samoa, far from Apia. Their four sons all have U.S. citizenship.

Later, I learned that it is not culturally acceptable for Samoans to carry on conversation while standing, which explained her getting something for us to sit on.

I also learned that high born girls of chiefly families are sometimes tattooed.

Cook Islands Christian Church at Avorangi

Chapter Eight

Sir Albert Henry

At four a.m. I was awakened by heavy rain beating a staccato on the metal roof, like the sky was a water tap, which had been opened up. I could not see the gecko in the darkness, but I could hear his squeaky, hissing purr.

After the fifth or sixth day of rain, I had lost track of time. The other residents of Are Renga were getting restless. Four of them moved to a place across the island with a bar and dining room, which had discounted its rates. Three hopeful sun-seekers tried to get on an outbound plane last night, caring little in which direction it was going. They just wanted to leave the rain. The flight was overbooked, so they reluctantly returned.

The sound of wind worrying the palms breeds restlessness. During this monsoon downpour, which had been heavy and nearly continuous, I had grown to understand the madness, which inspired Maugham's classic story *Rain*. Though the road behind us was still open, the area between the lodge and the road, which is a flood plain, had become a mini-sea into which the delighted children had launched fragile canoes and rafts.

But you must understand that these are not cold, miserable rains like we have Up North. With umbrella and rubber sandals life went on. When the rain let up a little, I went back to the library for more books. There I found regional books that tapped into the life and culture...books that would never be available at home.

I have seen the bust of Albert Henry in the cemetery of the Cook Island Christian Church in Avarua where he is buried. He was wearing wire-rimmed eyeglasses with shell eis around his neck. Although carved in stone, his presence seemed very real. While Prime Minister, Albert Henry was knighted by the Queen of England, after which he fell from grace, accused of electoral fraud. I found a book written in 1979, the year after he had lost his office accused of misappropriation of funds.

Sir Albert Henry, His Life and Times by Kathleen Hancock told of the beginnings of the ruling dynasty of the Cook Islands. She helped balance a harsher view expressed in *Cook Island Politics, the Inside Story.* In the beginning Kathleen Hancock wrote: *Collecting information in the Cook Islands is a wild mixture of fascination and frustration, and you begin to understand why a whole generation of New Zealand government auditors has retired in confusion from these islands fighting to free themselves from the cobweb of rumor and innuendo in which they find themselves entangled. No wonder their reports are marked 'confidential' and never see the light of day. Those poor men know better than anyone that in the Cooks no two tales tally.*

I began to have a glimmering of understanding of the suspicions I had aroused as I moved around the island probing, interviewing people and asking totally innocent questions that were somehow touching raw nerves. Determined to avoid getting tangled more deeply in that web, I began focusing on the tourist view of life in those beautiful islands.

Kathleen Hancock's biography showed the deeply personal side of the Henry family's beginnings.

When Papeiha, the native missionary, and John Williams of the London Missionary Society came from Tahiti in 1821, the Paramount Chief was Tamatoa, an ancestor of Albert Henry, on the island of Aitutaki. After establishing a mission on Aitutaki, John Williams took two women with him who had been kidnapped and left there. He was hoping they could help him find their home island, Rarotonga. In 1823 the mission on Rarotonga was begun when he left Papeiha there.

Eighteen years passed before another missionary reached Aitutaki. Henry Royle found the mission in social disarray. The island was filled with escaped convicts, beachcombers, drunkenness and violence. His life was difficult, but he persisted. By the end of his first year an Aitutakian of chiefly descent befriended him, Teraopu Tataura. Tetaura adopted Royle's Christian name of Henry.

Twice the mission's enemies burned the churches Royle's small congregation had built. They lived in constant fear and under threat, but holding services in open air, he continued.

A devastating hurricane hit Aitutaki. At the same time, an earthquake raised the floor of the seabed. Aitutakians believed this was the wrath of Royle's Jehovah and the mission flourished.

In 1843 Mrs. Royle became ill and took passage on a whaler to Australia.

Henry Teraopu Tetaura married a daughter of Geoffrey Strickland from Mauke, an adventurer who had families on Mauke, Samoa and Tahiti. Henry Tetaura's oldest son, Geoffrey added his father's Christian name to his in the Cook Island custom.

Geoffrey Henry was the first to establish Henry as the family surname. He married Metua Kamiri, a girl from Mauke. She was pregnant when she accompanied Mary Royle, who was ill, to seek medical help in Rarotonga. Metua was advanced in pregnancy and while gathering eggs one morning in the Avarua mission hen yard her baby, Albert Royle Henry was born (1906).

When Mary Royle died, her sister, Harriet Royle was lonely on Aitutaki. She decided to return to Sydney and took Geoffrey and Metua with her. Albert was only a few months old when they left him with his paternal grandparents, Henry and Minora Tetaura.

Geoffrey and Metua returned after a couple years of training in Sydney. He became head teacher when Albert entered school.

When Albert was initiated into manhood, in the Maori tradition, his hair was cut. He was seven years of age. Left unattended for several nights under a mango tree to prove courage, he shook in terror, tears rolling down his cheeks. At thirteen he went to St. Stephen's College in New Zealand.

Her book gave a fascinating glimpse into the early life of the man honored by the bust in the cemetery.

The gardens at Are Renga, the small budget priced hotel on Rarotonga. The peak in the background is Maunga Roa.

Chapter Nine

Rain

During breaks in the rain, the merciless sun turned the soaked earth into a steam bath, making the island a giant greenhouse. Each afternoon fluffy whipped-cream clouds rose to form towering white caps around the mountain peaks.

On such days I would leave my door open to catch any stray bit of breeze as the overhead fan slowly rotated, moving the heavy air in my room. Sweat trickled down my spine. My arm smudged ink on the limp paper as I wrote.

I was sitting at my table over morning coffee reading when I looked up and saw a man wearing a business suit fumbling with the key to the door next to mine. He was carrying a briefcase. He wouldn't have been noticed in Chicago or Indianapolis, but a man in a business suit was something I had not seen since I had left North America. He was my own age, or perhaps just a couple years older. I caught his Kiwi accent when he said, "Good Day." But he was a man in a hurry who rushed off without further conversation.

It was about four o'clock when he came home.

"Would you like a cup of coffee?" I offered. And so, we began a conversation that lasted until afternoon turned to evening.

His business card read, "We sell anything, anytime, anywhere" and his territory covered the Pacific from Chile to Asia...and through Asia to Arabia.

Once, in the early '70's on the way to Arabia, he was crossing Iran with a "blanket train", a caravan of trucks loaded with blankets to sell. They would drive across the desert to a rendezvous point...totally unmarked, which looked like every other sandy stretch of undulating dunes...and wait. In an hour or two a camel caravan would arrive and the trading would begin. But this time, entering Iran, the convoy was being held up by Immigration. They were looking at a possible delay of one hundred ninety five days. Desperate over the delay, he devised a plan and took the head driver into his confidence. Outside the border station he lit up a cigarette, blowing smoke generously toward the open window of the guard shack. He demonstrated how he had spent a couple hours practicing tapping the bottom of the pack to flick out a couple cigarettes with a casual flourish. As the driver approached, just in front of the window, he asked, "Do you like American cigarettes?"

"Oh, yes, thank you," the driver responded, as rehearsed, and lit up, creating a cloud of Lucky Strike smoke. The charade went on until one of the guards asked if he could have one. The trucks were waved through for the price of a carton of cigarettes.

I mentioned to him a letter I had received from my daughter in the afternoon. She had asked, "If we have another baby, would you be able to come home and spend six months with us helping with the children?"

I was flattered by her request! With a demanding career, even the first child's care had been difficult and expensive. In her letter she gave no indication whether it was just an idea or if, indeed, she was already pregnant. I had pondered this all afternoon with that sort of glow peculiar to grandmothers.

He continued to regale me with one story after another, each funnier than the one before. Tales from forty years of travel covering half of the southern latitudes.

When I got up to light the lantern, he asked, "Would you like to go out for a bite to eat?"

I had nothing to offer him from my refrigerator, so I thought, Why not?

He had rented a car to conduct his business with clients scattered around the island. The rain had stopped, but rivulets from the mountains joined the sky's deluge deepening the flood plain beside our lodge, so we took the back road out.

Now, I have always had a problem with disconnected conversation. Hours may pass and I will pick up an aborted conversation as if there was no break in it and continue.

On the way to P.J.'s Carryout, I mentioned the letter from my daughter again and told him that I had been speculating all day on whether or not she was already pregnant. I was already feeling the excitement and joy of having another new grandbaby.

He went in to pick up some chicken and fries. We drove to a spot he knew at Muri Beach where we walked through the dripping palms and wet sea grass to a fallen coconut log which made a perfect place to sit by the beach. A hazy moon was momentarily obscured by passing clouds; then came out to make a silver path across the ripples of the lagoon. A gentle lapping of waves completed a picture of perfect serenity. As he opened the bag and handed me some fries and a chicken leg, I continued our previous conversation.

"It does seem like we're going to have a baby," I mused.

His immediate response, "I've had a vasectomy," nearly made me choke on the fry. I was blushingly aware that we were suffering a momentary communication gap.

Pretending I hadn't heard, to avoid further embarrassment, I drifted back to small talk.

I think the angels must have been smiling while watching two old people sitting on a damp coconut log having a picnic in the moonlight.

Seven new passengers arrived during the night and as the days went by we once more became a comfortable family of strangers.

Mathias, a large, sensitive German man in his mid twenties, came home excited about the shells he had collected in the lagoon at Aitutaki. He laid them out on my table, showing me his treasures, one by one. His favorites were the trochus...large conical ones, aside from black pearl oyster shell, the only shells islanders seem to prize. Several people came in to see them; then they drifted off to Therese's room where he showed them how he had learned to dance the huka from Aitutakians.

The group settled on the verandah for a game of cards and I went back to my room to read.

In the morning Mathias was looking desperately for his bag of shells. He was afraid they had been stolen. We searched everywhere. I walked the lane toward the Ara Metua where the borrowed bicycle had been found. Then Therese noticed a strange bag in the corner of her room. He had forgotten that he had put them there when he demonstrated the dance.

Because I shared his agony over the lost shells, Mathias insisted that I take one of his prized trochus. As he gave me the shell he said, "You are what we call in Germany," and he searched his mind for the English equivalent, "a great soul."

It was a surprising place to find an explanation for my muted personality. In the library Wayne carried in his backpack, there was a copy of Joseph Conrad's sea stories. In *The Shadow Line* the author described the cook who was ...*the best seaman aboard who had taken cook's position because of a heart condition. And he was the only one the climate had not touched...perhaps because, carrying a deadly enemy in his breast, he had schooled himself into a systematic control of feelings and movements.*

I had been born with a heart valve that hadn't closed at birth as it was supposed to, so my activity had always been seriously curtailed. It is a simple problem to correct now, but in those days heart surgery had not even been imagined. I was seventeen and had survived beyond the normal limits for one with my condition when I first read of the surgery. The risk was far too great to ask my parents to give the consent required for a minor. By the time I had the surgery at the age of twenty one, I had trained myself to live by measured responses, to hoard my energy. I developed a love of books and quiet conversation that persists.

The Shadow Line was set in the tropics and my experience on Rarotonga has made me a more understanding reader.

Yesterday the electricity was off again from 11:00 a.m. to 11:00 p.m. Tony organized a party, which grew to be about twenty seven people because he included guests from the bungalows by the road.

Everyone brought a pressure lantern as well as a dish for the potluck. The tables on the verandah were all decorated with bouquets from the garden.

As we finished dinner...an extraordinary feast...a double rainbow arched the sky with one foot on Te Reinga, the other on Maungaroa. I think we all felt that we already had found the pot of gold in this place through the remarkable companionship we enjoyed among so disparate a group of travelers.

Greg, an Australian musician, had come to Rarotonga to learn to play Maori drums. Night after night Greg went to the mountains, where he was being taught the rhythms by a family of Maoris who lived there. For us, he played the instrument the aborigines use to make the twang, twang, twang...the kobing.

Tony, a young Englishman, read a romantic poem he had written to his former girlfriend. Had his journey begun, as many journeys do, more a running from than going to?

Ian Gregory, from England, also was leaving on the night flight. He spent his last day on Rarotonga gathering plumeria blossoms from which made eis for everyone as a surprise departure gift.

A friend of Greg's, who writes song lyrics, said, "I'll write a poem...anybody got a piece of paper?"

Within half an hour he had written:

> *Gathered here on Island Night*
> *Preparing for Tony's outbound flight*
> *Far from home and stress and cares*
> *Far from people splitting hairs*
> *Losing track of time of day,*
> *Living life the only way.*
> *Forget your flag and patriotism*
> *Try to see a different vision.*
> *It's good that people turn to travel*
> *And different problems to unravel.*
> *I only hope away from home*
> *We all remember, "When in Rome."*
> Written by Dave Powell

Printed with appreciation, but without permission because I don't have a clue where he is.

Since I was the only one in the South Pacific who had brought an apron instead of a bathing suit, I offered to wash the dishes. The next day the kids from all the units (the ones that hadn't flown out) came to claim their pots and pans and dishes from the verandah.

Rarotongans on their way to church

Chapter Ten

Cannibals and Converts

Books filled my rainy days.

Cannibals and Converts, Radical Change in the Cook Islands, is a collection of writings of Maretu who was born in the Ngatangiia district of Rarotonga about 1802. He was a child in 1814 when the first Europeans came ashore. They were a wild group that stayed for three months causing warfare and all sorts of trouble. Tahitian missionaries came in 1823; traders much later. The colonial era had not yet begun when Maretu wrote this story in 1871 in the Rarotongan language.

It is a story of wars and intrigue, destruction of their heathen gods and building and rebuilding Christian churches. He wrote of painful changes such as the forced introduction of cotton cloth, the tragic break up of polygamous families of chiefs who sought baptism, of hurricanes and epidemics.

As presented, it is a scholarly work with an extensive index, bibliography and annotations. It is a penetrating look at life in pre-mission days and the church from the native point of view. (copyright 1983 Marjorie Tuainekore Crocombe)

Mission Life in the Islands of the Pacific was written by Rev. A. Buzacott in 1866.

He spent his life in the Rarotongan Mission and is buried in the cemetery of the CICC in Avarua. His writings tend to be formal. They were probably intended as a church chronicle for instruction to missionaries who would follow him. His description of their early impressions of the island and efforts to establish Christianity among a people with pagan gods in a beautiful but strange and isolated place seems sincere and without exaggeration. His resourcefulness as both engineer and medical practitioner is surprising.

A chapter is included on missionary journeys to visit teachers who had been established by John Williams on islands as scattered as Tahiti, Samoa, Tanna and New Caledonia. Attempts to land were made on Niue and New Hebrides, but were given up. They intended to establish a mission on Niue, called Savage Island, but learned of a plot to kill the teachers as soon as they landed. They later learned that two Niueans they had returned to Niue had been killed immediately. Because they feared disease and epidemics that came from the outside no one was allowed to land. John Williams had recently been killed at Erromongo in the New Hebrides, so landing there was also reconsidered. It was compelling reading about men who gave their lives to the Christian mission in the Pacific Islands.

Pioneers of the Pacific is an absorbing series of stories covering a broad sweep of Pacific history. On Captain Cook's second trip, he sailed all the way around Antarctica. He crisscrossed the great expanse of ocean between New Zealand and South America disproving the theory of a landmass in that area. Winter storms drove him into gentler latitudes where he mapped islands from Easter Island to the New Hebrides, from the Marquesas, Societies, Tonga and Fiji to New Caledonia. The voyage lasted over three years and covered about seventy thousand miles. During that extended period of time he lost no man to scurvy. He gave his crew near-beer brewed from malt instead of rum, forced them to eat sauerkraut, flavored their pudding with anything that looked like a green vegetable. He insisted on the use of lime juice.

His third and last voyage began on July 12, 1776, searching the American coast for the North West Passage. During that troubled time, Benjamin Franklin ordered all American ships to treat his vessels, *Resolution* and *Discovery*, as friends. The French government issued an order, "That famous navigator, Captain Cook, shall be treated as a commander of a neutral and allied power."

On this journey, he came upon the Hawaiian Islands (called the Sandwich Islands), which he had previously missed. He observed that the Polynesian nation was "the most extensive nation on earth."

On his first visit to the Hawaiian Islands he was welcomed as the returning god, Lono. On his second visit he was killed by a mob of warriors on the Kona Coast in conflict over his whaleboat, which was necessary to his mission and had been taken by the natives.

Sandalwood, whaling, the China trade...each wrote a chapter in Pacific islands history. The 19th Century brought the London Missionary Society. Pacific pioneers, both altruistic and mercenary, wrought massive cultural change in the islands.

Pacific Island Portraits brings to life the great navigators of the Pacific beginning in the 16th and 17th centuries when explorers were searching for the fabled landmass, Terra Australis Incognita; then it told of the clippers that ran before the strong and steady westerlies that blew in the Roaring Forties, those dangerous lower latitudes.

There is a well-researched section on the work of the missionaries. (From the *Patterson Papers* held in the archives of the Society for the Propagation of the Gospel, Westminister and the Southern Cross Log, Auckland)

John Coleridge Patterson was the first settled missionary in the Banks Group island of Mota (1857). He was a genius in linguistics. He had begun seriously questioning the mission boards attitudes toward the native agency. He was aware that John William's remarkable success was attributed to his use of new converts as teachers, which he left on islands not yet contacted to pave the way for the European missionaries that followed. In this controversy he upheld the view that "we must consider the qualifications of ones native clergy in relation to the work they have to do. They have not to teach theology to educated Christians, but to make known the elements of the Gospel Truth to ignorant heathen people. If they can state clearly and forcibly the very primary leading fundamental truths of the Gospel and live as simpleminded humble Christians, that is enough indeed." He believed strongly in the natural equality between the races. He felt that literacy was an unnecessary burden for adult Melanesians.

At the time, mission work was severely strained by the conduct of whalers and traders and the kidnapping of young men to be sent to the mines in Peru or for labor on plantations. Labour recruiting, the infamous blackbirding, set mission work back as missionaries had to approach islands with caution.

On September 20, 1871, Patterson was clubbed to death on Nukapu, Santa Cruz, where he had landed from the *Southern Cross* three times before (1856, 1857, 1870). His body was found in a floating canoe wrapped in a native mat, covered by a palm branch knotted in five places. Five young men had been abducted from Nukapu by "recruiter" Emma Bell only a few days before Patterson's visit. Arrow attack on the ship also killed an English and a native missionary.

There were lighter books, too. *Island to Island* by Alistair Te Ariki Campbell (1984) is a search for Jock and Teu Campbell who died young on the remote atoll of Penrhyn leaving four orphaned children. Their grieving Penrhyn family sent the children to relatives in New Zealand. Forty years later, Teu's family greeted the adult children as "the children who were lost overseas". It is a journey filled with nostalgia as they met their mother's family.

The schooner *Tiare Taporo* was mentioned in a letter from Jock Campbell to his mother, dated February, 1921. It was the same freighter the priest, Father Fred, had said was the outer islanders' only link to commerce with the outside.

Jock's job was working as a trader with A.B.Donald, Ltd., whose headquarters was on Rarotonga. Rarotonga was then on the main shipping line between New Zealand and San Francisco. Mail ships called regularly. Tiare Toporo ran from Papeete to Raro and to the outer islands.

Jock described the weather in his letter. "We had heavy northerly swells and huge breakers came right over onto the edge of the village. The lagoon consequently became very full for two days after the sea subsided. A very strong current ran out of the passages at both ebb and low tides. We have this time of year, changeable weather.

Bright skies and dead calm at times. Then a sudden overcast. Dark clouds race up followed by a wind that whips up the lagoon with whitecaps. Then heavy rain which stops suddenly as it starts. Then clear skies and calm again." It was a pattern that had become familiar to me during the monsoon.

He accepted a job with Boss McKegg of the Cook Island Trading Company and took a position in the trading store in the remote northern atoll of Penrhyn in 1923. There he established his family who later came home in search of their lost relatives.

The Frisbies of the South Seas is a sentimental recollection of growing up as one of five children of author Robert Dean Frisbie and Ngatokorua a Mataa, a Puka Pukan who died in 1939 while the children were still small. The author, a girl named Johnny, was the eldest of the four who lived with their father. For a while they lived in Arorangi on Rarotonga, but mostly they lived with him on the remote northern atolls near the island from which their mother came.

Tin Roofs & Palm Trees by Robert Trumbull (1977) described the islands during a major period of change after the airport was extended to allow international flights.

The Lagoon is Lonely Now by Ronald Syme also spoke of that period of change on the island. The author is a long time resident, who at the time of my visit, still lived in Ngatangiia. Tangi said everyone called him The Professor. He was married to a Rarotongan who ran a small village store there.

I loved the rainy days!

I began taking pictures of the family at Are Renga who had made me feel so much at home. James Estall, the grandfather, had returned from visiting some of his children in Australia and New Zealand. He was a kind, vigorous man in his seventies who still oversaw the family operation and often helped with the laundry. Bob, his son, tall, handsome, quiet, was always busy on the plantation. Tangi, Bob's beautiful wife, friendly, fun, was sometimes outrageously outspoken. Marion, her daughter, and her husband, Kura, also worked on the plantation. Maire, their newborn infant when I arrived, was a bright-eyed four month old by the time I left. Theressa, Robert, Aster and baby Agnes completed the family.

Two of their other daughters were away. Tero and Eikura, who were not related, lived and worked with the family. James, Jr., a nephew, and his wife, Pauline, who danced at the Cultural Village, and their little Marianna also lived and worked as part of the extended family whose life I had been privileged to share for a little while.

The family worked casually and harmoniously together. Sensibly, rooms were serviced only before guests arrived. Thereafter sheets and towels were exchanged weekly or as needed by bringing them to the office. Even the toddlers sometimes picked up a kikau broom and played at sweeping the hallway while their mothers worked. I sometimes joined Tangi as she sat on a mat on the hillside polishing pots and pans between groups of guests while Agnes napped or played around her.

I watched the young travelers come and go. There were many single travelers, most in their thirties. Many of them were on extended trips. Sometimes alliances were made; attachments formed for companionship or economy, which occasionally dissolved in tears or handshakes; regrets or relief at flight time. Some were married couples whose trip was the result of saving and sacrifice.

By March the monsoon was ending and the days were comfortably cool as it was early autumn.

John and Sarah and their children, Julie and Euan often came to visit me on Saturday after church. They brought a picnic lunch and we walked across the street where we put a blanket in the shade of the casuarina trees along the beach. The children swam and played while we visited. I had met them soon after they moved from New Zealand during my first weeks on the island.

Their things, en route from New Zealand, were coming on the *Nga Maru*. John, who had lived in the islands as a young man, saw the move to Rarotonga as a solution for unemployment in New Zealand. It had been a year since he had lost his job and there weren't many opportunities for a man nearing fifty. When a job came up on Rarotonga, Sarah agreed to make the move. They had made the commitment and sold their home. All their bridges back had been burned.

After lunch John said, as if it was a new sort of game, "Let's tell Iona how we really feel about moving to Rarotonga."

Sarah burst into tears. "I feel like I m going to die here from the heat and there will be no place to be buried!"

As soon as she said it, her fears seemed more like foolishness. But she went on about the difficulty she was having feeding her family with all the unfamiliar tropical foods. "Meat and other imported things are too expensive!" she said.

Julie, who was thirteen, began sobbing.

"The kids at school all speak Maori and when I ask them what they are saying, instead of speaking English, they say 'Oh, nothing.'"

I could see her anguish over being left out and missing her friends at home.

Euan was just as passionate in his response.

"If you try to go back, I'll go to the other side of the island and hide! I'm not going back to New Zealand!"

A twelve-year old boy had found freedom he never had in the city...a lagoon for fishing, jungles for exploring, canoes and islands just off shore. The reef was filled with strange and beautiful creatures. In addition, the school system was not all that demanding for a child accustomed to the more structured New Zealand schools.

John was happy that the festering silence among them was broken. He said, "Sometimes I feel so guilty that I brought you here."

We began to talk about the bothersome things...which were permanent problems and which were temporary inconveniences. After that things began to turn around.

Year after year, Christmas letters tell of kaikais and concerts, cultural events and church programs, honors and countless community involvements as they were assimilated into a life-style they don't regret and would never choose to trade for the life they left behind in New Zealand.

About six p.m. I went for a walk through Arorangi. Just before I reached Tom's Dairy I heard drums. I stopped outside a hedge to listen. A little girl said, "It's my father. You can go and see them."

So I went around the tall hibiscus hedge, the kind that typically screens a village home from the street. Singers and drummers were on the verandah; eight girls were dancing on the lawn. They were practicing a new routine so their dancing was a little ragged, but it showed promise. The father, a large man with a heavily bandaged hand brought me a chair. Jokingly, indicating his hand, he said, "Sometimes the bush knife miss."

He told me they are rehearsing a show for which they have a four-month contract to perform in Japan.

On the way home, I met Garth Young who is an accomplished musician with a music store at Cooks Corner downtown. I had suggested that tourists would like to purchase tapes of the himenes sung in the Arorangi church. He told me that the tapes he had printed in New Zealand had been off-loaded on an island to make room for other freight, so they will be delayed.

In one of the shops on the way home I found an apple, snappy and crisp, a texture in complete contrast to our island fruits. Imported from New Zealand, it was eighty cents, but everything an apple should be.

Au Maru Palace in Arorangi, Rarotonga

Chapter Eleven

Death of a Queen

Therese was a blonde girl from the States. She was beautiful in the California casual sort of way...a valley girl. I couldn't decide if she was naive or reckless, but it gave the impression of an irresistible sort of innocence.

When I went with her to the Cultural Village, I introduced her to some of the dancers. She charmed the young Maori men. She expressed a sincere interest in their island-made musical instruments.

Ina came to teach Therese how to play the ukulele, tuning it first to the universal my dog has fleas. When she left, he stayed on the verandah to talk to us. Ina is a kind, gentle young man, innocent and unguarded in his conversation. He is an excellent drummer and dancer. I cannot guess his age, perhaps somewhere between twenty and thirty.

When I asked Ina if he thinks life in the islands was better before or after the missionaries came, he paused for a while before answering.

"After. Remember huka? Fierce, angry people then. They would be there," and he waved his arm toward the mountains, "and they would come here and want to kill me."

He patted the sturdy low coral block wall of the verandah.

"They taught us how to build better houses." Indicating the coconut tree, "Every year we had to make new roofs. Now we have tin roofs. Better."

"Did you ever live in a kikau house?" I asked.

He seemed pained.

"I was born on the floor of a kikau house. I asked my Mom, 'Why not a bed?' She said, 'we didn't have a bed. Only floor.'"

Later, in Fiji and Samoa, I understood.

A soft, warm rain was falling as I stood beneath the canopy of a tree a respectful distance away watching the burial of the queen.

The coastal road was closed - the Ara Tapu - the only road that circles the island. Mourners had been coming to the palace since dawn bearing gifts of food, as the doors of Au-Maru Palace stood open welcoming them.

The palace was across the street from Napa's Store where I frequently bought eggs and fresh vegetables for my dinner. Ngapoko Napa was the wife of Arorangi's paramount chief, Tinomana Napa Ariki. Mama Ngapoko had passed away the previous morning after falling ill, but in the tropic heat of the South Seas, where there are no mortuaries, burial is swift.

The village of Arorangi is one of six pie-shaped divisions of the island of Rarotonga extending from the mountains to the reef. Each village had its own paramount chief or Ariki. In these islands land cannot be bought or sold. It is owned in perpetuity by the clan, claimed by hereditary rights and its use is controlled by Ariki who remain respected and powerful. The clan of Tinomana had a special place in the island's history.

In pre-mission days, Tinomana was harassed by Ariki of stronger tribes and he had been driven into the hills. It was a time of famine. This was especially terrible because cannibalism was common.

When Papeiha, a Tahitian Christian convert from Raiatea, was brought to Arorangi he came into a complicated society of chiefs and sub-chiefs with priests called ta'unga. Tangaroa and Maui were among the dozens of gods they honored. Tinomana's mana or power was so diminished that Papeiha's teachings had a strong influence on him. Soon, with his help, there was a thriving Christian congregation among his people.

I chose to stay in Arorangi so I could walk to the massive white Cook Island Christian Church in the village. It was within the walls of the cemetery in front of the church, near Papeiha's grave that the Queen's burial was taking place.

Listening to the sweet/sour chords of the himenes being sung in the church, I was at first unaware of the man who had come to stand beside me, his footfalls cushioned by the layer of wet blossoms beneath our feet. Although a Maori, he was from the distant island of Penrhyn, a lonely atoll with less than five hundred people. He and his wife had just arrived after spending nine days on the deck of an interisland freighter. They were hoping that the city, Avarua, with a bustling population of four thousand would present opportunity for employment, perhaps in government. Although in the larger context of world affairs, the island of Rarotonga seems insignificant, to the man from Penrhyn it seemed a magnet of opportunity.

A handsome, articulate man in his thirties, he was also an "outsider", a member of no clan on Rarotonga. We stood side by side watching the burial of a queen.

Last night I rode the back of Danny's motorcycle to Manuia Beach where Ina was playing ukulele with a combo. He had invited Therese to come and watch him. She had not wanted to go alone, so we were about to walk over when Danny and Phillip came, each to invite Therese out...Danny to Bible Study; Phillip to dinner, but she told them of her commitment to Ina. They drove us to Manuia Beach, dropped us off, and said they would be coming later.

The group Ina played with was Tina's. She was a Samoan singer who played the guitar. She was one of three sisters who were a famous performing trio in New Zealand. Her husband also played guitar along with her thirteen-year-old brother on the drums.

Danny and Phillip joined us. Danny, who was the principal dancer at the Cultural Village, picked up a guitar and soon Phillip also joined them onstage for a long, entertaining Polynesian jam session. Tina, to introduce the newcomers to the audience, asked their names, and the night went on. Ron Mead, the manager of Manuia Beach, was cooking the barbecue. A couple on their honeymoon danced barefoot by kerosene lantern on the beach sand floor. Ginger, the golden cat, jumped up and sat beside me purring. Polynesia perfect.

Therese wanted to buy a ukulele, so David, one of the newcomers at Are Renga, Therese and I walked with Ina to the prison on the Ara Metua. Ukuleles are made there by the prisoners, in the traditional way, from a half coconut shell. With Ina's help she chose a pretty one with a good tone. She and Ina played together on the walk home.

One of my last days on Rarotonga, the *Cook Island News* printed an article revealing some of the mysterious problems surrounding the construction of the Sheraton Hotel.

Seventy two million dollars that had been borrowed from an Italian bank had disappeared! I had, unknowingly, been dancing around the periphery of the stage on which a high-stakes game of international intrigue was being played.

Was it my reference to Somsak whose father was a general in the Royal Thai Police that had been misunderstood? I began to understand the paranoia over my identity; the suspicions that hung heavy around me. I somehow had projected a false identity, a mystique that had put me in serious jeopardy.

Rarotonga had become so familiar to me. I had grown to love my family at Are Renga. I recalled the night my son and I had gone through the "bottom end" listings of budget accommodations. It had been a blind choice, but a very fortunate one.

Each time I thought of going on to Fiji the dark and shapeless fears of venturing on alone assailed me again. I knew that the only way to erase those fears was to face them.

My plane to Fiji was late leaving. It had lost an engine, so we waited while a different plane was brought in, delaying our departure time until after midnight.

On the plane to Nadi, I removed the shell eis and let events of the past three months run through my mind.

I realized that the core of the greatest travel adventure of my life revolved around the verandah at Are Renga. It was on the verandah that Tangi taught us to tie a pareu; that Phillip showed us how to plait a length of palm frond into thatch for a kikau roof. I tasted ika mata there and octopus and kava, which had been brought by a traveler coming from Fiji. It was there that I learned to make coconut cream and weave flower eis of frangipani. There were memorable Island Nights and travelers tales. It was on the verandah that Joe Smith healed under our watchful communal eye. That is where I read the books from the South Pacific collection of the library that had given me insight into island life and history. On the verandah I heard the drumming of monsoon rain on the galvanized iron roof. I had watched the full moon rise three times behind the mountains.

On the verandah I had given a hug to friends that had quickly grown so dear. And from the verandah I went through my own tearful ritual of departure on that last night.

I glanced at my watch. We should arrive in Fiji in an hour.

Chapter Twelve

Fiji

I never intended Nadi as a destination, but as an air hub; a place to rest, to transit on my way to Samoa, which was referred to as the Polynesian Bible Belt. It seemed a safer sort of place for a woman alone.

I had called *Book Passage*, my favorite travel bookstore, the month before I left for the South Pacific and asked if they had any books about Fiji. They sent me *Changes in Latitude* by Joana McIntyre *Varawa* and the *Lonely Planet* guide. Joana McIntyre, an American, gave an intimate view of tribal life on Vanua Levu. Living in a bure with neither electricity nor running water, she wrote of all night yaqona drinking, trevoros and nightmares, wild pigs and feasts, hurricanes mingled with guitars and moonlight fishing trips. It did little to make me feel comfortable about going alone to Fiji. The *Lonely Planet* guide reviewed Fiji's dark history, a people so feared they were avoided by even their neighbors, the Tongans and Samoans... "...an unknown area inhabited by unpredictable cannibals and strewn with dangerous reefs."

Of course, that was a long time ago, but it didn't sound like an easy place to travel.

Yet, *Lonely Planet* reported, "On a recent press trip, several big league travel writers with well over a million and a half kilometers under their belts were informally polled as to their all-time favorite destinations. Without consulting one another, each of the journalists answered 'Fiji'." Okay. They were on FAM trips being wined and dined by the tourism promoters. They probably stayed at the Regent of Fiji. I've seen the slick ads in glossy travel magazines. But what would it be like for the independent budget traveler?

The more I read about Fiji the less confident I was that a woman traveling alone could navigate those strange cultural waters.

Nima, my Samoan Cook Island friend, who had lived in Fiji and still spends half of each year there with her family, cautioned me, "Don't walk in Fiji like you do on Rarotonga."

I neglected to ask her why.

Before leaving Rarotonga I had selected a hotel from among those listed under "places to stay...bottom end" in my *Lonely Planet* guide. It was the fifth listing that caught my eye, "It is an antiseptically clean, modern hotel..."

When I wrote for a reservation I indicated the flight and time of arrival, but because of the delay, I did not expect to be met.

Nadi International Airport was larger than I expected and more modern. In the terminal, arriving passengers were approached by drivers who held up signs indicating which hotel they represent. In the center, a staffed desk offered brochures of lodging establishments, resorts and tours...a branch of the Fiji Visitor's Bureau.

As I approached the desk for information, I noticed a tall young Indian man scanning arrivals. When I asked if the driver of Nadi Bay Motel was there, they directed me to him. He put a hand out in greeting, took my luggage and asked if I had stopped to exchange money. I had not even thought of it. He directed me back to the bank, a branch of the Bank of New Zealand (BNZ), the only bank in Fiji, which was open twenty four hours a day, seven days a week.

As I was standing in line waiting to exchange money a rush of panic swept me as I remembered the dozens of warnings. Joe Smith had been standing in this line and had been pick-pocketed in this terminal. I was in Fiji and had left my luggage with an absolute stranger at two in the morning. All the precautions that I had promised myself I would take had evaporated!

My turn in line came and I accepted a handful of strange money. The face of Queen Elizabeth looked reassuringly at me from the coins, reminding me how far the British Empire had reached.

I changed US$25 for $34.08 Fijian money and was charged a $1 fee. During my stay in March/April 1991 the exchange rate hovered around $144 Fijian to US$100. (When prices are mentioned, they are in Fijian dollars). Currency denominations were in dollars, coins in cents.

Rushing back into the arrivals lounge I found the hotel driver waiting patiently beside my luggage. I followed him to the van. The psychological impact of careening down a narrow, darkened highway on the "wrong" side of the road in the middle of the night cannot be overstated. And looking at the speedometer on which speeds are indicated in kilometers did nothing to lessen my anxiety. Later, I learned that we were on Queens Road, which runs from Nadi Airport through Nadi Town along the rugged mountain road and Coral Coast one hundred twenty two miles [197 km.] to Suva.

The driver introduced himself as Felix. He told me, as he drove, that he had been orphaned at the age of eight. With no one able to care for him, he lived in the marketplace in Suva eating whatever he could find, sleeping in doorways, until someone took him to the Methodist Children's Home. "There," he said, "they not only fed me, but they loved me and taught me that God is my father and that Jesus Christ gave his life for me." The story of his difficult childhood and the Grace he had found in the loving care of Christians continued as we drove through the night.

A security guard opened the gated doorway. We passed a small souvenir shop on the left. A bulletin board in the hallway on the right advertised dozens of inviting opportunities for tours to nearby island resorts, attractions and beaches.

The receptionist/desk clerk, a beautiful young Fijian, Mrs. Salote Moceica, immediately knew who I was and with an engaging, dimpled smile, apologized that they had a full house and were assigning me to a temporary room.

The lobby, a combined lounge, dining room and bar overlooked a spacious, sparkling pool. Felix took me down a short hall beyond the pool, up a stairway, which ran along the wall and overlooked a large open area, balconied over a lawn and clothesline. At the head of the stairs we turned down a short hall. He stopped at the first door. Felix fumbled with the lock saying that perhaps it was the wrong key. I asked if I could try it and the door opened into a small room with a bed on one side and kitchen cupboards on the other. He put my luggage in the corner and I lay on the bed, falling quickly into a deep and dreamless sleep.

Laughter, mingled with the unfamiliar sounds of Fijian wakened me. Mbula! After the soft, vowel-rich Maori it would take time to become accustomed to the harsher sounds of Fijian.

The sun was high and intense. I fumbled through my duffle to find my clock. It was nearly eleven, but that was on Rarotonga. How many hours different?

The communal bath, which accommodated only four rooms on this hall, consisted of a sink at the end of the hall and two doors opposite the guest rooms which opened to a modern tiled toilet and huge tiled shower, both spotless. The jalousie window beside the basin's mirror revealed a garden filled with bird song. A line of coconut palms defined the neighbor's large residential yard. From this second floor window the coconuts were just beyond reach. Palm fronds, shining in the sunlight, rustled in a light breeze.

After showering, I went downstairs to get my bearings. When I asked a young Indian waiter where I could get breakfast, he showed me to a small, claustrophobic dining room off the bar, the only weak spot in an unexpectedly nice, inexpensive hotel. Everything I saw confirmed the accolades in the *Lonely Planet* guide, which had brought me there. It was perfect for the solo traveler. The option for privacy existed or an easy mingling with other guests and the friendly staff.

After breakfast, Sanjay carried my coffee to a poolside table. Felix returned from meeting a plane and joined me. Our conversation of the previous night resumed.

"Though I am a Christian, my sister is still Hindu. Would you like to go to pujah with me tonight?" He promised to pick me up in the lounge at seven.

It was noon before I went back upstairs. A pretty, shy Melanesian housekeeper approached me.

"Your room is ready now."

She brought me to one of the two doors off the wide, airy bath/ hall, numbered 21A. It opened to a comfortable room with two broad windows overlooking the pool and beyond, vast cane fields. In the far distance, beyond the palms that lined Wailoaloa Beach, waves danced in the brilliant sunlight.

My room had drawers, a closet, a comfortable king size bed. Unaccustomed luxuries. It seemed a splurge, but at $20 a day with the long-stay 10 % discount, it worked out to $19.32 a day including tax. As with everything else in the last decade, budget motel rates also have risen a bit so an updated guidebook should be consulted for current rates.

The open area beside the stair, which had been empty at night when I arrived, was abuzz with activity. The girl who had shown me to my new room was sitting at an ironing board. She wore a long pale blue flowered sulu with a short tunic, called a jaba. I learned that her name was Olimaipa Yalikanacea. A girl, busy hanging towels on the outdoor lines, smiled and boomed the traditional greeting, "Mbula", insisting that I repeat it after her. She wore a black skirt, red and white striped top and a huge pink hibiscus behind her ear. She told me that she is from Lautoka. Her name is Kasanita Raikoti and she insisted that she would teach me Fijian.

Fijian language is part of the broad Austronesian family of languages that spans the area from Madagascar through Polynesia. During three thousand years of use, the language has fragmented into nine hundred distinct languages, but there are many similar words throughout that area proving the language connection. David Cargill, one of the early missionaries, developed the Fijian alphabet. Consonants are filled with pronunciation surprises: b is pronounced "mb" as in remember; c is pronounced "th" as in other; d is pronounced "nd" as in sandy; g is pronounced with a soft "ng" as in ring; q is pronounced as "ng" plus a hard "g" as in finger.

Half, of the population of the Fijian islands, are descendants of Indians who were brought as indentured laborers for the cane fields. They speak Hindi, though it has evolved from several Indian dialects including Hindustani and Urdu. Conveniently for the traveler, English is taught in all Fijian schools and is spoken by almost everyone.

When I asked Kasanita where Nadi is, she corrected my errant pronunciation.

"Nandee," she said. "Wait for the bus under the mango tree on the other side of Queens Road."

The hotel sets on the road to Wailoaloa Beach approximately a block from Queens Road. The canopy of the huge mango tree provided shade from the intensity of the tropical sun at noon. As I waited for the bus to Nadi Town a group of women in silk saris and children in punjabis were talking in rapid Hindi. Two dark skinned Melanesian men were laughing and speaking in Fijian, a language filled with double consonants, harsh to my ear.

All the softness of Rarotonga was behind me now...the vowel rich language, the easy fluid laughter, the evocative double rhythm of the drums.

The ancient windowless bus rattled to a stop. The driver was perched high on the driver's seat on the right side of the bus with an open cash box containing tickets of many different colors. The fare depended on destination. It was thirty five cents one way to Nadi Town.

I hurried to a seat before the driver changed the huge gearshift and the bus lumbered off.

We passed a small clothing factory, a Chinese store, patches of cane fields, homes made of corrugated metal or woven bamboo walls with thatched roofs. I wondered, as we passed, how the people lived there, curious to know what their daily lives entailed. There were also modern brick or concrete block two-story homes that would not have been out of place in California. As we neared town we left the scattered rural development, crossed a bridge over the Nadi River and turned onto the main street, which was a continuation of Queens Road.

Nadi Town reminded me a bit of Mexican border towns, dusty and commercial, but a bit more orderly.

Morris Hedstrom was a thoroughly modern supermarket. Nadi Craft Shop was bright, clean and well stocked. Gelato Ice Cream Parlour was outstanding with sparkling clean blue and white décor. Ice Cream was homemade on the premises. A delicious, well-packed double vanilla cone was $1.30. The Hot Bread Shop next door emanated aromas that would have made Grandma's kitchen jealous!

I exchanged money and picked up a pineapple and dates at Morris Hedstrom, then crossed the street to catch the bus back to the hotel. The return bus was crowded. I watched nervously in this unfamiliar place for landmarks which would help me recognize my stop

After washing my clothes in the sink, I went downstairs to ask the maids if I could borrow their clothespins and lines for drying.

It was completely dark when I wakened from a nap. I quickly dressed and went downstairs to find Felix. They told me that he had gone to the airport to meet a plane, so I ordered a pot of coffee and waited in the lounge by the pool.

When Felix returned he was wearing his uniform, a flowered red and white shirt, white sulu and red elastic cummerbund, sandals with bare legs. He is a large man and I was surprised how completely masculine he looked in what Westerners would consider a wrap skirt. He came directly to me, said he had to shower and we would leave in half an hour.

Two young women at the next table asked if I wanted to join them. Renee, from a small town in northern Minnesota, was teaching at a community college in a boomtown in Northern Alberta. The town, prospering from the exploitation of tar sands as an energy source, had grown to a population of about thirty thousand. There she met Cynthia, from Illinois, who had lived in the North Country for twenty years and had watched the effect the sudden growth has had on tribal village society. They have taken a year from teaching to travel. Their trip began in Peru where they took the rugged bus trip to Machu Pichu. Bolivia was easier for two lone female travelers. They said, "Fiji is a totally different experience!"

When Felix returned wearing a shirt, pants and sandals I introduced them and explained that we were going to pujah.

Felix Ashok in uniform
at Nadi Bay Motel

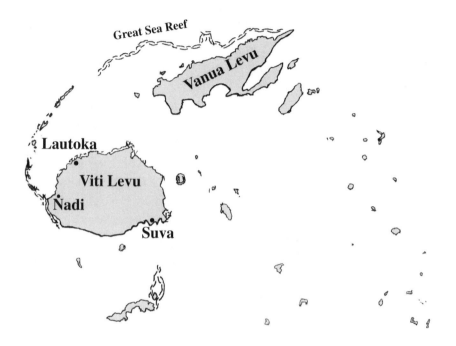

Fiji is a group of islands about 1500 miles west north west of Rarotonga and about 1500 miles almost due north of New Zealand.

The scale on this map is approximately 50 miles per inch. Viti Levu is about 60 miles from east to west. From the southeasternmost islands to the Great Sea Reef is nearly 250 miles.

Chapter Thirteen

Pujah

I had neglected to bring a flashlight and the night was dark. We walked down Wailoaloa Beach Road; then we turned onto Queens Road toward Nadi Town. English style, we walked on the narrow right hand berm facing traffic.

Felix mentioned again the accident that had killed his parents. Although he had siblings, none of them was able to care for him.

I had no idea where we were going. The darkness was broken, intermittently, by the lights of speeding taxis. Perhaps we had walked a mile when we turned into a driveway and found pujah in progress. The temple was a large pavilion on poles. The ceiling was draped with pink and gold and orange muslin. The supporting pillars were covered with split, braided palm fronds encircled with twinkling electric lights and decorated with a garish blend of tinsel and marigolds. A dozen men were behind the altar, one chanting into a loudspeaker, others accompanying him on modified Indian musical instruments, the sitar and tabla adapted to this different time and place.

The women and children were seated under the canopy toward the altar, like a garden of blooming flowers in their colorful saris and punjabis.

I slipped off my sandals and, leaving Felix, found a place on the mat among the women. Grateful that I had worn a full skirt, I tucked my legs under, a very slim pretext of grace and modesty.

The chanting continued as mosquitoes feasted. I regretted that I had not brought repellent. A child, dark eyes kohl-rimmed, scooted closer to me. She reached out a tentative finger to touch my skin then scooted back to the safety of her mother. I could feel curious eyes shyly cast in my direction, then quickly away. One hour passed, then two.

A festooned cradle swung above the altar. The sermon followed in Hindi. It seemed like Christmas with a different cast. Fire was lit in an oil pan set on a tray with a bowl of ochre. Women and children went forward two or three at a time and took the pan in their hands.

With arms extended, one at a time, they moved the pan with the flame in a circular motion over something on the altar. Each person ran her hand over the flame in a circular motion and "cleansed" her face with the purified hand; then put a coin through the flame in the pan, dropped it on the tray and touched the bowl of ochre with a finger which was used to put a tikka on her forehead. The men who were singing and playing instruments grasped each other's arms to make one line. With joined, extended arms they repeated the motions the women had over the flaming pan.

Music and chanting resumed. Afterward, the women and children were each given a piece of stiff paper larger than a dinner napkin. Boys and men came with bowls and pots of delicious, familiar Indian foods. Women eating first and being served by men emphasized how much the culture had evolved and adapted during the third and fourth generations after their migration from India.

After serving the women, men gathered with their food by the huge tub where yaqona was being mixed from crushed kava roots. Although Felix and I had eaten together, he went with the men, so I followed the women, who were still unsure who I was or why I was there, into the house.

The house, built of corrugated metal, had linoleum on the floor. Around the perimeter of the room, green vinyl covered couches and chairs were in continuous rows against the walls. A large trunk was set on the couch nearest the door. Awkwardly, I found a place to sit beside it, while the women arranged themselves in a circle around a large mat that was placed in the center of the room. Each of the women had brought a small round rolling board on short legs and a rolling pin. A poinsettia-print plastic tablecloth was set in the middle with a huge silver tray in the center. Large masses of dough were brought from another room and torn into smaller pieces. Two women rolled these pieces into strips one to two inches in diameter and cut them into pieces, which were tossed to girls who rolled them with their hands into floured balls. These were tossed in front of the women who expertly rolled the balls into smooth, thin rounds. The puri, which was ready to cook, was borne away on the tray by boys who returned the silver trays over and over again to be filled by the busy women.

I envied their grace as they sat cross-legged on the floor rolling hundreds of puri for the next day's feast. It seemed a humble task for women dressed in gorgeous silk!

At first they ignored me. I wished for Felix to come and intervene; to introduce me, to explain my presence or to take me home, but I didn't know where he was.

Shyly, a young woman in a blue sari came to me and asked, "Did you come with Felix?"

"Yes, I'm staying at the hotel where Felix works." But there remained a broad gap in their understanding my presence. I found it hard to explain why Felix, who was younger than all my children, had brought me.

She then brought me to Felix's sister, a quietly beautiful woman in her late twenties who strongly resembled Felix. She smiled warmly and asked me, skeptically, "Have you come with Felix?"

My answer seemed far from adequate.

"Would you like to see where they are cooking?"

I eagerly followed her away from the busy circle of women in the living room, through a hallway with beds in recesses on both sides. We went through the kitchen where dough was being mixed and down three plank steps into the backyard. There a dozen men were busy stoking a wood fire in an elliptical-shaped hole in the ground over which the oil in a large black pot, at least two feet across, was kept bubbling. Puri, a delicious flat Indian bread, delicately puffs while frying in deep oil. Some of the men were more dedicated to the task, while others were holding a bilo, a polished half coconut shell, drinking yaqona like men might be drinking beer around a barbecue back home.

The men were laughing and talking in rapid Hindi mixed with English and Fijian. It was smoky work. The following day would be the Feast of the Nine Days to celebrate the birth of Lord Krishna.

It was hours since I had seen Felix. I knew it was well past midnight and I had no idea how to go home. I made excuses and went outside in search of Felix. He rose to meet me and introduced me to two Indian men who, he said, would bring me home because they were leaving and would pass by that way.

Several of the men invited me to the following day's feast. Felix said that he would come with me at 10:00 a.m. I was grateful for their acceptance and promised that I would come.

My ride home was in a huge, ancient taxi, but they would accept no fare.

When I awoke there was no water. The hotel was full and I knew that when the other guests began to stir an emergency would quickly follow.

I found Moses, a young man who appeared to be a blend of Indian, Oriental and Caucasian. I suggested that we dip water from the pool and place buckets in the bathrooms for flushing. We gathered up empty oil drums and placed them in strategic locations, filling them and providing buckets for dipping. Then I walked to the Chinese store for a few bottles of soda for drinking. When I returned I found that the emergency had brought staff and guests together into a cheerful sort of chaos.

Before I arrived in Fiji I had been warned repeatedly about not walking as freely as I had on Raro. Only half believing, I asked the Fijian maid about the parameters of safety.

"Is it safe to walk to the beach?"

Without hesitating, she said, "No."

"The five kilometers to the airport?" I persisted.

"If someone stops, tell them you want to walk. They might take you somewhere else...or charge you a lot of money. The traffic is heavy and fast along Queens Road. There is no footpath." She continued thoughtfully, "If you take a cab, they might charge you too much." Her advice was, basically, to take the bus.

When I looked from my window, the view of the sea in the distance was hard to ignore.

I joined Cynthia and Renee for coffee in the lounge. They invited me to walk with them to Wailoaloa Beach. I leapt at the chance to go in their company.

The dusty walk down Wailoaloa Beach Road passed cane fields and clearings where horses and goats were tethered. Chickens scratched and clucked beside simple houses. Men carrying bush knives, called sele levu, passed us.

Sele levu is the all-purpose tool of the Fijian villager. Meaning, "big knife", it is used for cutting cane, clearing land, gardening, house building, gathering and opening coconuts.

Wailoaloa Beach was farther away than it looked from my window. Without their company I would have turned back as I was feeling engulfed in an uncomfortable strangeness.

In a clearing near the beach, a yaqona party was in progress. Though it was still early morning, their raucous laughter suggested that they had been drinking all night.

As we turned down the beach along the line of coconut trees, which looked so inviting from my window, Cynthia began telling me about their experience of the previous day.

About mid-morning they had been walking along this beach. A Melanesian man approached them, smiling and motioning to the palm trees. He asked if they would like a drinking nut. They agreed and he climbed a nearby tree. He chopped the top off the nut with his sele levu and handed it to Cynthia. After she had taken a cool drink, he said, "You owe me $60."

Shocked, she said, "I don't have $60!"

He persisted, growing rude and abrasive, then threatening. Renee took $5.00 from her pocket and gave it to him.

"You're lucky I don't hurt you for giving me so little." he said angrily as he let them pass.

It was a warning confirmation of all that we had heard before, a variation of the extortion practiced by the sword sellers of Suva. As tourism becomes more important, the government is moving to stop these offences. On the yellow leaflet passed out before leaving the plane, "Bula. Welcome to Fiji" was followed by "tips for enjoying your holiday in Fiji." It concluded with the warning, "Don't allow sword sellers, touts/carry boys or taxi drivers to hassle you." But a large man carrying a sele levu can be quite intimidating.

Boats were moored at buoys in the shelter of the bay.

We met a young Air Canada hostess and walked with her to the Traveler's Beach Hostel where she frequently stayed on stopovers and holidays. Its long, dark corridor seemed drab to me. The party atmosphere and isolation also seemed, to me, negatives and I was doubly happy for the choice of hotel I had made.

As we walked back, we saw two more groups of men around makeshift tanoas in clearings along the beach drinking yaqona, perhaps because it was Sunday and a holiday.

At the hotel, I waited for Felix, but he was nowhere to be found, so I walked alone to the temple. Pujah was in progress when I arrived. This time the women smiled as I slipped off my shoes and sat among them.

When the long service was over, a program for the children involved lottery drawings and the passing out of gifts. A sumptuous feast followed. Again, the men served the children and women first.

I asked if I could take pictures and they eagerly accepted the offer, arranging themselves in family groups as I took nearly two rolls of film. After I returned to the States and had them processed, I sent a package of pictures to Raj and asked him to give them to his friends who had attended the feast. It was late afternoon by the time I left.

The following morning Felix told me that it was his day off.

"Would you like to go to the market in Nadi Town?" he asked.

Another couple staying at the hotel asked if they could join us and walked with us to the bus stop. Before the bus came, Felix flagged down a running taxi, which was returning from the airport. He negotiated the price with the driver. $1 for the four of us.

The fragrant mound of red and gold spices at the market, stirred a deep nostalgia for India. Colorful pyramids of fruits and vegetables filled the main room under the galvanized metal roof and spilled out under tents of blue plastic awnings stretched between poles. The large back room was devoted entirely to kava roots and was doing a brisk business. Table after table presented their product, which to my eye was all the same. Some were selling samples, dipping bilos of yaqona from galvanized tubs. It was a murky, colorless liquid. The older roots make stronger yaqona, they told me; the cleaner the roots the finer, less earthy, the flavor. A bundle about 2 feet tall and fifteen inches around was priced at $150.

I walked between neatly ordered rows of women selling dalo roots, slim purple eggplant, okra, cucumbers, papaya, beans, oranges, coconuts, watermelons.

I left Felix in the market with friends and wandered through the stores on the main street. Perhaps because I walked quickly with a false certainty no one hassled me and the smiles seemed genuine. Or perhaps I didn't look prosperous enough to bother.

As the bus passed the temple site I was surprised to see that it was simply a huge open carport without decoration.

Raj, the competent young manager of the hotel was one of the men playing instruments behind the altar. I learned that the temple was at the home of his parents and his father was the leader at pujah with the loudspeaker.

"You went where very few tourists have the opportunity to go." Raj said.

"I know."

An older resort hotel nearby, the Dominion International, had a pleasant poolside dining room. It was an easy walk down Queens Road toward the airport past a pricey Japanese restaurant, past the newer Westgate Hotel and the Sandalwood Inn. A friendly staff and moderately priced Sunday brunch drew me back.

To get a complete view of the range of Fijian hotels, I decided that I should visit the Regent of Fiji, an up market resort near Nadi Town. At the sign that indicated the road to the Regent I got off the bus.

A professional looking Melanesian woman was among the people waiting at the bus stop. I asked her how far off Queens Road the hotel is located. She answered, "A very long way, too far to walk." She introduced herself as SiSi. She was also on her way to the Regent where she was the executive housekeeper. Her husband was also employed there as training manager for the restaurants.

A cab slowed and she stooped to the open window and asked the driver, "How much to the Regent?"

She told me to get in, that it would be 35 cents. She explained to me that this cab is returning empty from the airport.

It was a long ride and I was grateful for her advice and help. She told me that if I have trouble finding my way back, to have the hotel page her and she would help me find a cab, although the bus also runs.

I said "Vinaka" and we parted.

The Regent of Fiji was a posh self-contained resort hotel. Continental breakfast on the Ocean Terrace, exactly the magnificent setting the name implies, was $14.70 with tip and tax. It included a fruit plate as pleasing to the eye as taste, watermelon, star fruit, guava, a banana. A pot of fresh Fijian-grown coffee and an exquisite basket of assorted mini-Danish came with service that was formal, but friendly. With all its opulence, I missed the warm informality of Nadi Bay. The comparison is a clear example of the difference between vacation and travel. Travelers, especially solo travelers, need the easy camaraderie of hostels and budget hotels because of the extended periods of separation from the familiarity of home and friends, while the vacationer loves to be dazzled and pampered for a time.

The Regent is located on "village land". The lease was purchased in August, 1990, by a Japanese firm.

I walked to the adjacent Sheraton Fiji. Shiny new, there were impressive expanses of tile in white and beige décor. The lobby was spacious, open air, furnished with square, modern geometrically designed chairs, tables and art, relieved by shimmering fountains.

The restaurant overlooked a seaside pool. Sailboats at moorings rode gentle swells like appropriate props.

I walked nearly to the gate, a long walk through a dusty construction area, when a cab stopped. He agreed to my offer of fifty cents for a ride back to the bus stop on Queens road.

Graders and trucks were preparing ground for construction of another new hotel, which will be built by the same Japanese company. At the time, I read that of 200 resorts in the Fijian Archipelago, only two of them are owned by indigenous Melanesians.

The cab driver told me that the Village of Narewa owns the land. Akulau Island offshore is also village property. Uninhabited, its inviting sand beaches make it a tourist's delight for day trips arranged at the hotels. He mentioned, offhand, that the island is home to great numbers of fruit bats.

By that time, I felt absorbed into the life of Nadi Bay Motel. Quite at home there, I had forgotten that I didn't really mean to stay in Fiji.

In the afternoon, I walked with Felix to his sister's home, a modern, Western style ranch. While we talked over tea, Felix relaxed on the couch watching an Indian video with all the sex and violence that would have caused it to be banned in the India I knew of 20 years before. At that time, there was no TV broadcast on Fiji's islands, but videos could be watched in some homes.

We returned to the hotel early because the Nadi Bay Tigers were scheduled to play the soccer team of the Nadi Police. I was invited by the maids and desk clerk to go along. It was my first soccer game, a rough and tumble one which we watched from the grassy hillside. The Nadi Police wore smart green and white uniforms. Beside them, our team looked a bit rag tag. Because the game was both played and cheered in a mix of the local languages my confusion lasted throughout the game. Raj, the hotel manager, played the second half, a wild, rough game. Our team won 4 to 2, celebrated by a horn blaring, tire screeching ride through town before we returned home.

The airport accommodated one hundred eighteen flights a week, sixty eight of them international. Most of the international flights were met, as mine was, by Felix. The flight path was directly over the hotel, so the roar of low flying jets and incoming and departing passengers became part of the rhythm of our days.

Renee and Cynthia have flown on to Australia. Barbara, an attractive, active English woman about fifty was then in the room next to mine. She told me about her favorite place in Bali near Monkey Forest Road. Much like Are Renga, there was an easy, constant exchange of travel information.

"While traveling on Viti Levu," Barbara said, "look for a little red sign above the cab's license plate, front or back. It tells what city a cab is from. If a Nadi taxi is in Suva, or visa versa, make an offer because the cab may have to return empty." It was a broad expansion of what SiSi and Felix had taught me on a more local scale.

I awakened to the harsh sound of scrub brushes on tile mixed with laughter. All this was happening at daybreak. Moses was there and Sanjay and a half dozen cooks and waiters. It seemed more social than hard work, with the tanoa of yaqona at the side. So, that's the secret that kept the pool area and lounge spotlessly clean!

Scott, a backpacker from Sydney was on his way to the U.S. He invited me to split cab fare downtown with a couple "kids" who flew in today. One was a farm boy from central England (one hundred Holstein cows and grain) and Janet, a French teacher from Montreal.

We went to Chopsticks, a Chinese Restaurant upstairs above the downtown bustle of the main street in Nadi Town. Scott was recovering from a bad cold and was due to fly out near midnight. A huge bowl of Long Soup was a nourishing, economical choice, a rich chickeny broth packed with vegetables. Scott is a photographic lithographer whose father, a hot air balloonist, died a year ago in a balloon accident. Scott was running away from a consuming grief.

When we returned, Barbara was deep in conversation with a young Fijian woman. I joined them, but quickly realized that their conversation was personal. I made my excuses and went upstairs.

Barbara later told me that they had been discussing Fijian marriage customs. The young woman shyly explained that, as daughter of a chief, her marriage to the son of a chief had been arranged. They had not met at the time of their marriage. She was just seventeen and after the ceremony she was nervous and trembling. His family put a sheet of heavy paper in the bed to test her virginity. A curtain was hung beside the bed and for four nights his family sat, listening, outside the curtain. When they were sure the marriage had been consummated and her virginity proven, the lali drum was beaten. Its booming sound announced the good news of the union throughout the village. The couple was given the sheet of paper proving she was a virgin.

In Fiji, tribal village culture still predominates and the purity of chiefly lineage remains paramount.

Chapter Fourteen

Pam, Eirin & Lucas

Pam was traveling alone with her two sons, Eirin, who was nearly three, and Lucas who had just turned six. We went together on the bus downtown and I showed them the market. Eirin begged for a cob of corn, roasted in the husk, and ate it greedily even though it seemed to be strangely pickled or fermented. Pam bought a small sample of powdered kava root for her husband, Dan.

They had spent the winter traveling in New Zealand. Before leaving Alaska, they had sold their home in Cordova, but kept their fishing boat. For years they had worked as a fishing team, quite successfully, it seemed, because Lucas said, "Sometimes I'm knee deep in fish!"

Part of their fishing season was spent in Cordova and part in a cabin on the rugged cliffs above Bristol Bay near Egegik, where they had another fishery. Both Lucas and Pam had grizzly bear stories. Once, Pam said, when they had skinned a seal that had died, they spent the day scraping the hide before tacking it on a board to dry. When they went to bed, they thought the skin, left downstairs, might attract bears, so Dan got up and moved the fur to an empty cabin next door. In the morning they found that a bear had pushed the door down during the night and had eaten the fur, tacks and all.

Dan had left them on Rarotonga and returned to Alaska for herring season. Pam came on to Fiji with the boys to wait until he had a house for them. She knew a woman who had been a Peace Corps volunteer in Fiji. The interesting stories she had told Pam made Fiji her chosen destination, but a cyclone was in progress in November when they came. They had to overfly Fiji and go on to New Zealand. She would pick up a fax from Dan at the American Embassy in Suva in a week or two to learn whether he had gotten a house. It was too cold in March to bring Eirin north to Alaska. His small chest, misshapen since birth, had three large scars from as many surgeries, an attempt to correct a congenital heart defect...a heart with three chambers. Often he would be cyanotic from minor exertions, so she backpacked him most of the time, her long lean frame carrying him tirelessly with the ease born of love.

When we crossed the bridge into Nadi Town, we noticed that a Hindu festival was in progress. In that religion with myriad gods, many days are set aside to celebrate or appease the deities.

We walked from the main street to the festival grounds near the Nadi River. In the first shrine, the officiating priest, wearing only a dhoti, welcomed us warmly and gave the children handfuls of apples, bananas and pears from the sacrificial altar. The grotesque god-statue was festooned with marigolds and tinsel.

The only Westerners, we sat at a picnic table under a large pavilion and watched the procession of about twenty worshippers, while everyone else watched us. Barefoot women in the procession were dressed in saris and carried individual offerings of fruit in colorful pyramids. Men and boys bore platforms on poles with floral arches and canopies. Three times the shrine was circled by the worshipping procession. The attending priest ceremoniously burned incense before the altar of a different god-idol.

Food, in very large pots, was cooked over a fire of burning logs, stirred by men with paddles. A ceremony and drama were to be held before the feast. We overheard someone say there would be fire-walking. Everyone, they said, was welcome.

After Eirin's nap, we returned to the site of the festival, but everything seemed to be finished and the crowds had diminished. We had come chasing a false rumor. Later, we were told, some penitents would be skewering their cheeks, but we felt more repulsion than curiosity. Lucas was very disappointed, so Pam made a few quick phone calls from our hotel. At Hotel Mocambo they were having a fire-walking demonstration at six thirty.

We quickly caught a cab and arrived after most of the spectators were seated on a row of folding chairs on the verandah. We sat on the steps, as there were no chairs left. For the first time I felt like a tourist with cameras flashing all around us.

Fijian men, wearing heavy "grass" skirts, which looked like they were made of highly flammable dried corn husks, were moving rocks, which had been heated in a pile over burning coals. With heavy poles and long curly vines, they caught one rock at a time, pulling it around with the vines, their actions accompanied by loud shouts. The rock moving and shouting continued about an hour until the large stones were in a fairly level heap. Boughs of green leaves were scattered around the periphery of the hot rocks. One man sat regally at the head of the scene on a rock. Another man moved around and around the fire pit giving commands.

Six men suddenly appeared from the darkness and sat in two rows a little distant from the activity. They began rhythmically pounding lengths of heavy bamboo rods against the earth. Did it all have meaning or was it done for dramatic effect? One by one, a dozen men walked about five feet quickly across the ashen rocks, toes curled protectively upward. It was a made-for-tourists spectacle that left us wondering why we had paid $11 each to watch the famous firewalkers of Beqa.

Pam and I were using the same guidebook. While Eirin and Lucas swam, we compared our individual, loosely planned itineraries. It was the last day in March. I had decided to stay in Fiji and to go on to other islands in the Archipelago. She was committed to stop at the American Embassy in Suva. She had circled the resort of Tubakula, which was on Queens Road on the way to Suva. I noted in my guidebook that Tubakula had been recommended by a Swedish couple I had met on Rarotonga.

Just then a couple from San Jose joined us. Bob Walsh and Phing Tjoe were returning from her home in Indonesia where they had been visiting her family. They had just come from Tubakula and gave it their enthusiastic approval. They suggested Unit 6, an A-frame right on the beach. Pam called ahead and made a reservation for April 2. We agreed to split the rent of F$37.

Because of the children, Pam wanted to take a cab, but the difference in fare was significant, so we compromised on taking a taxi to the depot next to the market in Nadi Town and we took the bus from there.

I had repacked my necessities into two small duffle bags, vowing that is all I will ever carry on future trips! My garment bag, briefcase and additional duffle were strapped to the wheeled aluminum frame and stowed in the locked storage room at Nadi Bay Motel for $2.00

a day. I bought some stamps in town and withdrew F$300 on my Mastercard (US$199) because I did not know what I would find once we left Nadi.

The bus fare from Nadi to Tubakula was $3.30. Pam stowed her huge blue canvas bag in the open luggage rack below the bus and we climbed into the already crowded bus. Helpful hands passed my duffles overhead until we found places to sit near the back. Two men cheerfully volunteered to move so we could sit altogether.

Queens Road wound through low, dry mountains inland until at Cuvu we caught a sweeping view of the sea as we descended to the coast.

We were having trouble with the ancient, heavily loaded bus smoking and were reduced to a crawl as we labored up the mountains. At Sigatoka we were delayed before being transferred to another bus to resume the trip.

Pam exclaimed excitedly as we looked at the colorful crowd on the platform, "Now I feel like we're in Fiji!" Without the tourist trappings, the homogenization that happens in urban areas, we were immersed in the sounds, smells and sights of a truly different culture. I sat on the platform with Lucas, among the laughing, chattering groups of Fijians while Pam backpacked Eirin to the bank and grocery store on the main street.

Beyond Sigatoka the landscape changed. The cane fields and arid Western Highlands were behind us. We were running nearer the coast through lush tropical forests. Passing the villages of Nayawa and Korotoga, the beginnings of the Coral Coast, tourist accommodations were evident. Just beyond the Reef Hotel, around the corner, our bus stopped.

The office of Tubakula was located in a large frame building where we were told a video was shown each night in the lounge. Credit cards were honored. Our luggage was put in a large wheeled cart pushed by a congenial Fijian man named Mohammed Yakub. We followed a path toward the beach, passed a row of five A-frames nicely spaced with a grassy strip dividing them. A grove of coconut palms was the only thing between the apartments and the beach.

Our A-frame was on the end next to an open field. There was a large combination kitchen, dining room and living area, a bedroom and bath downstairs. A steep, un-railed stairway led to the loft with four beds. Double windows in the front and back made the fan unnecessary as the ocean breeze swept through. The front second floor window provided an unobstructed view of the lagoon; outside the rear window a large frangipani tree was filled with blossoms. A covered lanai on the seaside, with tables and benches, provided a small outdoor living area.

Pam and the children settled into the bedroom downstairs and I chose the bed by the ocean-side window from which I heard the constant muted thunder from the distant reef. That very distance would become a source of terror!

I wakened early, slipped out past my sleeping family, and walked to the Reef Hotel, which had seventy two rooms with a pleasant dining room. The rooms all had balconies or patios, which shared my ocean view and breezes, but for twice the price. Free amenities for guests included a nine-hole golf course, tennis, superb reef walking, kayaks, horseback riding and opportunities for fishing. The in-house travel office offered a smorgasbord of well-packaged tours...commercial, touristy and safe.

When I returned, Pam and the boys were swimming in the lagoon marveling at the exotic sea life they found there. It is the same ocean they see from their cabin in the far North at Egegik.

Eugene Burdick, in *The Blue of Capricorn* wrote "The Pacific is enormous...the most active, unpredictable, mercurial and surprising of our oceans. The Pacific covers 64,186,000 square miles, one third of the surface of the earth, as much as all the land masses of the world combined."

Our experience in the lagoon at Tubakula was polar opposite from the frigid ruggedness of the North. That wild, untamed, near-Arctic splendor made the soft warmth of Fiji's shores a magic place in contrast.

Tubakula was more than I expected. Of twenty two A-frames, 1-11 had ocean views; six in front, with five staggered behind in a second row. Units 12 through 22 were poolside and slightly less expensive. Hammocks were scattered in the shade around the pool.

The dormitory "clubhouse" had eight bedrooms, with three beds in each and wall hooks for hanging clothes. Down the hall were toilets and four clean tiled shower stalls in a row. There was a large well-equipped communal kitchen. If I had been traveling alone, for $8.00 a night it would have been a superior choice. The guest in the "clubhouse" provided his own sheets and towels. For those situations, the American Youth Hostel (AYH) sleep sack was very useful. The very lightweight "sleeping bag" rolls into a small cloth sack. For member information: American Youth Hostels, 1332 "I" Street N.W., Washington, D.C. There is a reduced rate for senior members.

In the main building, a schedule was posted for the shopping bus to Sigatoka, four miles away, for $1.00 round trip. There was also a Suva shopping bus; seventy eight miles east for $32 per person round trip. The regular commuter bus, which we took from Nadi, passed every half hour in each direction with a scheduled stop across from the Reef Hotel.

Pam had heard about a weekly Fijian feast and meke held each Tuesday night in the bordering village of Malevu. It was dusk when we turned down Queens Road toward the village. I felt like the cowardly lion on the yellow brick road to Oz in search of courage. Pam, Eirin and Lucas were my unlikely companions.

Tall, rocky cliffs on our left had been cut away to build the road. As we rounded a curve, the sea lay on our right. We entered a small fishing village with thatch roofed, traditional Fijian homes on both sides of the road. Fishnets were strung on poles to dry and outriggers overturned above the tide line.

Farther into the village, a small sign pointed the way up a footpath to the Fijian feast. We walked up a short incline, at the top of which stood a large bure. Woven bamboo walls of the bure were topped by a thickly thatched roof. Its steep pitch came down from the massive center ridgepole. Windows were wood-framed openings in bamboo walls. The path led to an open door. I hesitated and a large Fijian man invited us inside. He told us to leave our shoes at the door. The springy pandanus mat felt like silk as we walked barefoot into the dimly lighted interior.

Kerosene pressure lamps cast dancing shadows on the ceiling as we were led to the far side of the spacious room where village women reclined on mats, propped up on elbows. A collection of exquisite seashells was priced at $1 or $2 each. After purchasing one from each woman, we joined the kava ceremony at one end of the village meeting hall.

As we sat around the tanoa, I determined to put away my Western sensibilities and enjoy this commercial opportunity to experience a near-authentic taste of Fijian culture.

The host sat cross-legged (a posture I painfully tried to emulate) while another man brought a galvanized pail of water and began pouring it gradually into the bowl. The host kneaded a bag of pulverized kava roots in the bowl with his hands causing a gray, milky fluid to ooze into the water. After it was mixed to sufficient strength, a coconut half shell, a bilo, was offered to the first guest who clapped his cupped hands once before receiving it and three times afterward...the traditional cobo. Yaqona is drunk all at one time, holding the bilo in both hands.

In the very informal atmosphere questions were answered without offence. He said kava roots, which are pounded to powder, should be as big around as your thumb, at least three years old. Five or ten years old would be better. In times past before pails were available, the water was contained in tubes made from bamboo. In those days, the roots were chewed before mixing with water, as they still are on Vanuatu.

Village women were busy cooking and preparing the long banquet table for the feast. They placed a plaited coconut frond "skirt" on the long row of tables and covered the top with large green leaves.

After the kava ceremony, we put our shoes on and followed our host into the back yard, a barnyard with goats and chickens ranging free. It was some distance away from the bure where the earth oven, in Fiji called a lovo, was being opened. A covering of banana leaves was removed. The roofed fire pit was used to cook food, chicken, pork and prawns, which was put in plaited green coconut frond baskets. Palusami, taro leaves in coconut cream, a dish that seems to be common throughout the South Pacific, was wrapped in aluminum foil, then banana leaves and tied with magimagi, string made of the fiber of the coconut husk, which is called sennit in Polynesia.

After food was placed on the feast table, guests helped themselves. Forks and knives were dispensed with, so we all ate with our fingers, Fijian style. Benches were set along the walls for guests who were less comfortable on the mats. Villagers mingled with guests, bringing their plates of food, and conversation was easy and natural. We were quick to forget that this was a commercial endeavor by the village. Our $10 fee seemed to replace the sevusevu, the gift required by custom when visiting a Fijian village.

I asked, casually, if an Indian would be welcomed to the village. I was surprised that the answer came so vehemently and without hesitation, "He would not dare to come!"

Fiji is not a melting pot of assimilated cultures, but a patchwork of carefully retained traditional cultures existing uneasily side by side, cultures which are very slowly being modified by the floodtide of change sweeping the Pacific.

An armed conflict between the two ethnic groups resulted in a coup in 1987 when the election of an Indian as Prime Minister was nullified and a Melanesian man was put into that office replacing the elected Indian. Beneath a seemingly tranquil surface, this unresolved conflict was still boiling and is sure to erupt in violence again.

Tables were cleared and moved away. Meke, the traditional dance, began. Musical instruments consisted of a drum and many hollow bamboo tubes about three inches in diameter and of various lengths, which were pounded against the earthen floor. Some were played from a sitting position, some kneeling, some standing. Melanesian dance is more formal and stylized, quite unlike the fluid, joyful abandon of the Polynesian drum dances.

Early morning walks to the Reef Hotel for breakfast was the delightful beginning of every day. A sign announced that a feast and meke would be held at the hotel Wednesday night. The price was

$20. It was the same village group, Matanisigh, which means Sun's Face, which had entertained us in the village for half the price, giving us a much deeper look into village culture.

From the entrance of Tubakula you can see the sign of Kula Bird Park. A ten-acre natural rain forest, it is accessed through the Reef Estate Golf Course, either by a short walk, or, for fifty cents per person, in a blue canopied wagon drawn by a patient, plodding pair of handsome draft horses.

Steve Perrin, the managing director, introduced us to his pet parrots. He told us of conservation efforts of the park to preserve endangered indigenous species like the colorful Koki parrots whose nests are frequently robbed of young for pets. Besides the tropical gardens and cages of beautiful, unusual birds, there was a worthwhile display of Fijian seashells. The aquariums of tropical fish were a tantalizing preview of what could be seen reef diving.

Near Kulukulu Village, just south of Sigatoka, there were undulating sand dunes up to one hundred forty feet high. Protecting coral reefs were absent, so massive surfers' waves roll up to the beach. Nearby was a small, rustic backpacker's resort. It is about four miles off Queens Road, too isolated for any but the most enthusiastic surfers. We were warned to stay together and to watch our gear because the huge dunes leave a lone traveler in total, vulnerable isolation and there have been incidents of attacks and thievery.

Archaeologists have discovered skeletal remains and lapita pottery in the dunes, which link the early settlers of Fiji to the flow of eastward migrations.

On the Coral Coast, packaged tours are a huge and growing industry. Coral Coast Railway? Day trip to Beachcomber Island? Highland Tour? Suva? Wilderness? Orchid Island? Schooner Cruises? Garden of the Sleeping Giant? Beqa divers? Kalevu Center, a built for tourists Fijian village?

After our Mocambo fire walking experience, compared to the Malevu Village Feast, we decided to avoid the cleaned-up, orchestrated, polished-for-the-tourists presentations and venture as far as our courage could take us.

When we went to Malevu for the village feast, I had noticed a small clapboard Methodist church nearby. On Sunday morning, I retraced our steps into the sleeping village, past the thatch roofed houses, the nets drying on bushes, outriggers, all seeming more familiar and less daunting in the morning light. Like wild things, the village goats were precariously perched on ledges on the rocky face of the roadside cliff, ledges discernible only to the sure-footed goats.

I climbed the incline, walked past the bure village meeting hall and found the small church a bit further down the path. Walking through the open door, I realized that, although it was nearly ten o'clock, I was alone.

I chose a pew about halfway down on the right. RAMBO was carved in the back of the rough wooden pew in front of me. I wondered why the worst face of the West is found everywhere.

Children began drifting in, singly and in groups. Most were barefoot. The girls wore dresses and the boys were dressed in neatly pressed shirts and shorts. Some of the older boys wore sulus. Each child came to me, shook my hand, told me his or her name; then they sat on the other side giggling or talking quietly, like children everywhere.

A Fijian man, hair graying, came to sit beside me. He wore the usual dress gabardine sulu, white dress shirt and sandals. The glasses he wore made him look even more distinguished. He smiled and asked, "Where are you from?"

"The United States," I answered. "Have you always lived in the village?"

"Yes," he said, "I have no money to go anywhere else."

I told him that the location of Malevu village is as pretty as any place I have ever seen.

"Have you a family?" he asked.

"Yes, I have six children and thirteen grandchildren."

He said, "Thirteen?" His brow furrowed. "Where is your husband?"

This was a question I was asked so often in Fiji, I realized that the policy of New Tribes Mission, which had been such a disappointment to me, was well founded. I was tempted to say, "He has passed on," without indicating to whom or what, but his sincere concern required an answer.

"He has remarried," I said.

He clapped his hand to his cheek and said, with passionate dismay, "But WHY?"

Silence lay like a cloud between us.

"Does he give you any money?" he asked, deeply concerned, trying to reach for understanding.

"No," but quickly, lightheartedly, I added, "I live with my children, so it's o.k."

He looked pained, doubtful. Then slowly, forcefully, said, "It may be o.k. for you, but not to God!"

He persisted, "Do your children give you any pocket money?"

I probed my mind for an answer that would be encouraging.

"No, but they pay me rent."

Again, he put his palm to his cheek, signifying amazement, and shaking his head slowly, "That's strange, that's VERY strange!"

His voice trailed off into the cultural chasm that lay between our understandings. He knew nothing of mortgages, auto expenses, utility bills, taxes. The puzzled look on his face begged me to explain how COULD a parent charge rent? I looked at the thatch and tin roofed houses built by villager's hands of native materials on communal land. I tried to explain, "That is their way of helping me without letting me feel that they are helping me."

He asked if my father is alive, still searching my fractured life for some anchor of support.

"No," I said, "my father died when he was ninety two."

"Ninety two? Ohweee!" A cry of surprise mixed with grief and sympathy for my abandoned state.

"How old are you?" he asked, more intimately, leaning toward me, but I had no time to answer. I had been unaware that other parishioners had come in as we spoke.

A stern man came forward and took me very firmly by my elbow.

"I will show you where you will be sitting," he said as he guided me to the front of the church where there was a bench along the wall near the pulpit.

Across the small church from me, also in front, small boys sat on three rows of benches facing my solitary seat. I had unknowingly sat in the men's section and was being reproved.

The deep, resonant sound of the lali summoned worshippers. The huge slit log drum was housed in a thatched structure beside the church, which resembled a shaggy haystack.

An old man climbed laboriously up the steps to the pulpit. Chief Demuru, eighty six years old, delivered a masterful, fiery sermon. He was a true orator. I wished that I could understand Fijian. His notes fluttered in the breeze coming through the row of glassless windows, down from the pulpit to my feet. I picked the sheet up and walked half a dozen steps, handing it to the pastor, the chief, who took it in his weathered brown hand and smiled kindly at me.

The man who was my warden came forward during the sermon with a stick to berate a squirming boy in the front row across from me. The boy was led back down the short center aisle by a twisted ear and out the door. A few minutes later the child returned, cheeks tear-stained, and he sat quietly as I was sure to do under that deacon's watchful eye.

After the sermon, Sunday school certificates were handed out. Boys up to their early teens bowed to the officiating deacon, a friendly, smiling man who shook hands with each one as he received his honor. Each boy turned to the congregation and repeated the bow. Girls receiving certificates curtsied. Each child was shy, proud, embarrassed. I could tell that this was an important community event.

Pastor Demuru slowly descended the pulpit steps, smiling, and walked directly to me. He apologized for his lack of English and gently escorted me out the door indicating that I should stand beside him to shake hands with the departing congregation.

Two young men in sulus and dress shirts who were in the congregation walked me home from church, escorting me to the entrance of Tubakula before they turned back toward the village.

Chapter Fifteen

To the Edge of the Reef

I awakened from a nap in time to see Pam and the boys playing in the shallows of the lagoon. Massive coral heads protruded from the shallow water and at low tide the reef looked like the top of a massive red wall.

Coral is very sharp and coral cuts are prone to become seriously infected in tropical climates. In lieu of reef-walking shoes, I put on my Minnetonka Mocs and hurried to join them. By the time I reached them, Pam, with Eirin in his backpack, and Lucas, were busy studying sea anemones in a tidal pool.

Having neither snorkeled nor scuba-dived, reef walking at low tide was a way to see the colorful coral and strange sea creatures. There was pink coral, red coral, white coral with phosphorescent green snowflake designs; bright blue starfish, sea urchins, chiton and sea cucumbers. Tiny fish whose colors would grace any aquarium came to nibble at us. Eels and sea snakes and stingrays added to the adventure.

Lucas and I went ahead walking on patches of dead coral heads, like rough fragmented sidewalks. Between them we jumped onto the sandy floor of the lagoon, with water about to my knees. Excitement of discovery drew us on, closer and closer to the reef.

The edge of the reef, where waves break with a thunderous roar, looks like any rocky shore. But the far side of the reef can go to canyon depths. Sharks, lurking just beyond the reef, outside the protected lagoon, patrol the waters.

We were not more than fifty feet from the edge of the reef when I realized to my horror that the tide had turned! Water was pouring over the reef into the lagoon like the wall of water in a flood. When I looked back at the shore I realized how broad the lagoon was. We had come perhaps half a mile or more.

"Lucas," I shouted over the din. "Hurry!" I grabbed his hand as we stumbled and waded as rapidly as we could through the deepening lagoon. A nonswimmer, I was aghast at the awesome peril into which

I had taken Lucas. He showed no panic and I tried to make it a game, only twice looking back at the in-rushing tide. Why had I not remembered sooner the Maori fishermen on Raro, nets stretched across the openings in the reef, while fish were being swept over the coral wall? Or the legend of the Passage of Plaintive Calling? I had been warned frequently about the danger of tidal surge and suction.

By the time we reached Pam halfway to the beach, the coral of the reef was no longer visible, obscured by the foaming tide.

"Pam, I'm sorry I worried you!" I apologized.

She casually answered, "I knew you'd turn around. The water was coming in for about twenty minutes before you saw it, but you couldn't hear me over the surf crashing."

They continued to play along the beach. When Pam and the boys came in for lunch she mentioned the shells they had found. I went to look at them, opening the door to our small lanai. I was startled by the unexpected presence of a Melanesian man at the door, inside our lanai.

"I just came to rest on your porch," he said, improbably, answering my unspoken question. He seemed flustered and as surprised by my presence as I was by his. Although the breeze was cool, there were beads of sweat on his forehead.

I followed his gaze to Pam where she was standing by the stove. The T-shirt she wore barely covered her brief bikini. The guidebook's warning had obviously been understated: "Swim wear on the beach can be construed as an invitation." Even though we were at a resort and she was with her children, perhaps he had misunderstood, or worse. Social interaction across cultural barriers is often like playing the same game with two entirely different sets of rules.

"We must get the children's lunch and put them in bed for their naps," I explained as I closed the heavy wooden door and bolted it. Pam was suddenly shivering as I reminded her of the admonitions in our guidebook against wearing swimsuits. Melanesian women go into the lagoon fully dressed to swim or gather seafood. A former Californian, living in Alaska, Pam was eager for sunshine so she could get a bit of tan! This was a resort beach and it should have been o.k. but the guests were a mix of Melanesians on vacation and international travelers. In addition the resort beach ran uninterrupted into the village of Malevu.

A sign in the kitchen warned guests not to bring locals to the bungalows. I had thought it a precaution against theft, but we were carrying very little of value. Perhaps incidents were common?

Pam described the near-intruder to the man at the desk, not indicating why she wanted to identify him. He was an athletically built, good looking Melanesian about thirty. She was told that he is a frequent guest, a policeman on leave from Suva.

I felt that Pam's security might be at risk.

"Let's leave tomorrow, Pam. We can go on to Ovalau."

She agreed, anyway, that she was anxious to see if the fax had arrived from Dan. After the children were asleep, we talked for a long time. Tearfully, she told me that Eirin is facing his fourth surgery when they get home, but time would prove that he would endure the surgery twice more, the fifth time in Switzerland. We took out our guidebooks and discussed the road ahead, deciding to avoid staying in Suva if possible.

The next morning, when we told the children our plans, Lucas warned me seriously, "If a sword seller asks your name, don't tell him!"

With a population of about eighty thousand, Suva seemed too large a city for us to deal with. We decided to purchase a Patterson Brothers bus/ferry/bus ticket in Suva and travel on together to Levuka on the island of Ovalau.

For $1 a cab delivered us, our luggage and children to the thatch roofed shelter across the street from the Reef Hotel where the buses stop.

Sunbeam Express stopped, half empty, but we waved them on. We had ridden one of their buses, which had chugged reluctantly up the mountains as far as Sigatoka. When the Pacific Transport bus stopped it was full. They somehow cheerfully made room for us. It was an express bus to Suva ($4.35). We left at nine, a bit after the scheduled departure time of eight forty five.

We rattled over mountains and valleys, through jungles and past Coral Coast hotels, but we saw nothing that compared to the location we had chosen with Tubakula Beach Resort, Malevu Village, Sigatoka, Reef Resort Hotel, Kula Bird Park and the Dunes. It had offered a rare combination of experiences.

Suva came as a surprise! A beautifully situated city on a bay, it was a real city with attractive suburbs in a lushly tropical setting. David Stanley wrote in the South Pacific Handbook, "Suva is the pulsing heart of the South Pacific, the most cosmopolitan city of Oceania." Rob Kay in Lonely Planet described the city with the same affectionate generosity, "Suva can lay certain claim to being the largest and perhaps the most livable city in the South Pacific outside New Zealand or Australia."

The bus deposited us at a depot in Suva. All the stories I had heard on Rarotonga about Suva sword sellers and extortionists came to mind. I was cautious when an Indian cab driver asked if we needed a ride. We asked the fare to the American Embassy where Pam would pick up her fax. Would he wait, and then take us to the Post Office? The guidebook said the Patterson Brothers bus boards across the street from the Post Office.

He said the fare would be $3.00. When he learned that we planned to take the Patterson Brothers bus he said that we must have a ticket in advance purchased at their office.

Pam's fax had arrived. We took the children to the bathroom at the Embassy while the driver patiently waited. The Embassy seemed to be staffed mostly by Fijian nationals. We felt comfortable leaving our luggage with the driver in the cab. He had mentioned no additional fee for the stop and wait at the ferryboat office while Pam ran upstairs and purchased our tickets. When our errands were finished, the fee the driver asked remained $3.00 in spite of all the extra things he had done for us. Sunil Sharma created an excellent first impression of Suva. He owned and operated his taxi, Blue cab BH 088.

The bus started loading at twelve thirty and by one we were on our way. Our assigned seat was a wide one near the back of the bus, which allowed Pam and the boys and me to all sit together. At first out of Suva the road was surfaced, but as we encountered construction, the road narrowed. We wound through the mountains. One detour after another made the trip a rough and difficult one.

At Korovou, about ten minutes before we reached Notovi Landing, the bus made a half hour stop at the Patterson Brothers Agency. More knowledgeable travelers purchased snacks and sodas and used the bathrooms. We later learned what they must have known.

There were no food concessions on the ferry and no water in any of the facilities to either flush or wash.

It had been suggested that we carry a bottled beverage, such as mineral water, because the water on some Fijian islands can be a problem. After that, I frequently made use of the collapsible quart container, a parting gift from Cynthia and Renee, which allowed me to easily treat water with potable aqua or iodine solution when I couldn't boil it. Some travelers make the mistake of using ice cubes or brushing their teeth with untreated water.

In spite of detours and horrendous driving conditions, we boarded the Ferry Ovalau, bus and all, about three thirty as scheduled. We left the bus and went upstairs to the passenger cabin.

Pam and I spoke of our plans after Ovalau. She had decided to go on to RukuRuku Resort. It sounded simple in the guidebook. "This modest resort is good for families. There are six bures, which can accommodate four people each. The resort has a van which leaves from the bus stand in Levuka every morning at nine a.m. The fare is $1.00."

I was uncertain what I would do. I would look at Levuka first to research available lodgings. I had read that it was the historical center of power and the capital of Fiji until 1883.

Pam articulated what I had frequently thought.

"I'd love to go to Vanua Levu."

Her friend's Peace Corps tenure had been spent on that island, the second largest in the Fijian Archipelago. Vanua Levu was covered by seven pages of the *Lonely Planet Guide*. It spoke of the gorgeous setting of Savusavu Bay on the south coast where it listed a few tourist accommodations. The *South Pacific Handbook* said, "It is much less touristed" than Viti Levu. It was recommended for off the beaten track travel, but sketchy information was limited to three pages.

I told Pam about *Changes in Latitude*, which I had read just before going to Rarotonga, The author, Joana McIntyre Varawa had gone to Fiji on vacation and had married a Fijian man. I showed her on the map approximately where she and her husband, Mali, live on tribal land, Vedrala Island in Ngaloa Bay near Lekutu. In my wilder moments while still traveling in my armchair I had planned to go by ferry to Nabouwalu, then by bus to Lekutu to try to find her. But the reality lay somewhere on the far side of fantasy and now I was looking no further than our arrival in Levuka.

We had no reservations, but innocently planned to stay at the Royal Hotel, a clapboard Victorian built in 1850. For two generations it had been run by the Ashleys, a kind, gracious family who are locals. Our guidebook stated that they were part-European.

Sitting there on the ferry it all seemed quite straightforward and well planned.

I left Pam and the boys and went outside. It was a smooth passage. From the deck rail I could see small swells and little whitecaps and, in the distance, the green hills of Ovalau.

As I stood at the rail, face to the wind, a Melanesian man approached me. A handsome man with a broad smile and neat moustache, he was wearing a blue dress shirt, gray pants, gold wristwatch and carrying a briefcase. He impressed me as an urbane, sophisticated man. His voice was deep and well modulated; his English diction was impeccable with little accent.

He introduced himself as Tom Valentine, a name that struck me as more Western than Fijian.

"For a long time I have been watching you," he said. He asked where I am from.

"The United States."

Almost immediately he asked, "How do you like Fiji?"

Remembering Tubakula and Nadi and most particularly, Felix, I said, "I love Fiji!"

I told him that I had met a young Christian Indian; that Felix had been involved with a group called Youth With a Mission. Suddenly embarrassed to be praising an Indian to a Melanesian, aware of the deep conflicts, I simply said, "I have a soft spot for Indians," then changed the subject quickly.

"My son nearly joined Youth With a Mission years ago. They were going to the Philippines in a ferro-cement boat. But instead of YWAM, he chose to attend a Bible School, Christ for the Nations."

He just smiled through my awkward monologue. Then said, "My daughter, Molly, plans to join YWAM in Nadi soon." Pausing, he added, "I have read all of Gordon Lindsay's books."

I was momentarily overwhelmed at this thread of coincidence. That a Fijian man, casually met, had read the books written by the President of an obscure Bible College in Texas which was attended by my son long ago! Equally astounded that all this information was exchanged in a three-minute conversation between strangers.

Tom told me that he had come to Ovalau to see a government minister about buying some crown land.

"I am returning on Thursday. Would you come home with me to Vanua Levu to meet my family?"

Without hesitation, I said, "I would love to meet them."

"We live on my wife's tribal land," he said. He explained that he had been a plumber-welder in the city and they had everything there, but they chose to return to the bush to minister to the Indian tenant farmers on the tribal land and in the surrounding villages.

A minister! That explained the deep resonance of his voice and his warm, almost amused, smile when I spoke with him about Felix and my son.

He said, "An American woman lives on an island near us. She wrote a book."

Amazed, I said, "Joana McIntyre?"

"Yes," he said, with surprise.

I told him that I had read her book, *Changes in Latitude*, just before I left home.

It began to seem much more than coincidence.

Ovalau was coming closer. I excused myself and went to find Pam. How could I explain what had happened in those few minutes on the deck?

Lucas, Eirin, and Pam

Chapter Sixteen

Ovalau

When I told Pam about the strange series of coincidence, that I would be going to Vanua Levu in a few days with a stranger I met on deck, she was surprised, but less so after introductions when Tom included Pam and the boys in his invitation. She declined because of Eirin. She didn't know what we might encounter on Vanua Levu.

As we said our temporary good-byes, I told Tom that we would be staying at the Royal Hotel.

The crossing to Ovalau was completed about four fifteen. The bus was boarded again and we began the last leg of our journey to Levuka.

The road was barely more than a single lane, un-surfaced, with deep ditches on each side to handle run off from the torrential seasonal monsoons. We held our collective breath as the bus lumbered over rudimentary plank bridges, which we felt could not possibly bear our weight. Heavily loaded, we moved like a ponderous, swollen animal.

Lorries, carrying loads of workers from the fish-canning factory, met us and scraped by with inches to spare, sometimes mingling paint. A roar of delight went up from the passengers of both vehicles when the impasse had been successfully negotiated. I looked down into the roadside ravines and wondered on what precarious, uncertain ledge the outside tires moved.

The fish-canning factory was the major employer on Ovalau and we were meeting what constituted rush hour traffic. Each mile brought new challenges and shared suspense as we met trucks, earth moving equipment, lorries, meeting each in turn, clinging to the edge of the road. Tumultuous cheers rose each time we passed without tipping. A small grass airstrip witnessed that there was an easier way, but we were seeing Fiji, feeling its life as mile after mile of mountains, cultivated patches, cows, villages and people passed our windows.

The bus stopped at Patterson Brothers Agency and disgorged its passengers onto Beach Street, Levuka's main thoroughfare. The Koro Sea lay on one side. On the other, Levuka was nestled beneath high, rocky bluffs and low mountains.

We collected our luggage and inquired about the Royal Hotel; then joined the throng of people waiting for the Royal Hotel van. It filled quickly and we waited for its return. When we got to the small hotel, the lobby was crowded and before we reached the registration desk we learned that it was fully booked.

I told Pam to wait with the children in the lobby and I would check out the second hotel listed in our guidebook.

Darkness comes quickly in the tropics and by then a light rain was falling. When I asked directions to the Old Capital Inn, they sounded vague and it seemed far away. I ran past shuttered shops in that direction, block after block, desperate to find a place for the children to stay. I turned down a cobbled lane, slippery from the rain, with open gutters on either side carrying the surface water toward the sea. Shaking the rain from my umbrella, I stepped inside.

"Yes, this is the Old Capital Inn Restaurant. The hotel is next to the Royal."

I didn't wait for directions. I knew the way all too well and hurriedly retraced my steps in the drizzling rain.

A short walk led through a picket fence to a simple white clapboard building with peeling paint and a white galvanized metal roof. Bermuda shutters shaded the windows of an enclosed porch. Inside, I walked through the porch lounge into a wide corridor. A young girl showed me a room, which was vacant. It had three beds, one double for the children, with mosquito nets. The windows had no glass, but Bermuda shutters. There was a fan and dresser. Small, crowded, it was $16.90 for the four of us including breakfast at the Old Capital Inn Restaurant.

"Do you know where it is?" she asked.

Grateful for a place to stay, I went to get Pam and the children.

After getting settled, we walked into town to see if we could find a restaurant that was still open. The Paak Kun Long served a big bowl of long soup full of vegetables for $1.50.

I awakened early. It was not yet eight o'clock when I was moving along with a stream of people on their way toward the village center and the fish cannery. Beach Street wraps the waterfront with turn of the century buildings whose facades are reminiscent of the American Wild West. Uniformed students walked quickly, singly or in groups, to school.

A slightly fishy smell was brought off the water on a stiff breeze reminding me of some of my favorite places: Gloucester, Nassau, Bombay, the Chesapeake, colorful places where life is anchored firmly to the sea.

Ovalau is the center of the Fijian Archipelago, both geographically and historically.

The first European encounters with Fiji by the early navigators were mainly accidental. In search of the fabled, but elusive, southern continent, Abel Tasman sighted land, probably Taveuni, in 1643, but having skirmished with Maoris on New Zealand, they made no attempt to land. More than a hundred years later, in 1774, Captain Cook recorded landing on Lau, leaving some nails and a knife after the people fled without contact.

As master of the *Resolution* during Captain Cook's third Pacific voyage, Captain Bligh had seen Fijians and heard of their fierce reputation from Tongans. The mutiny of his crew on the *Bounty* in 1789 left him helpless in Tongan waters in a small open boat with 18 fellow officers. They had no choice but to sail toward Timor, the nearest European settlement they knew because their boat was too heavily loaded to travel against the wind. Their course was through the uncharted reefs of the Cannibal Islands. In spite of the difficulties, he recorded his discoveries in great detail. Maps still record the area through which he passed as Bligh Waters.

The nineteenth century began a savage chapter in the history of Fiji when opposing forces of greed and Christianity met on her shores.

Again, it was an accident that began it all. The American schooner, *Argo*, was wrecked on Bukatatanoa Reef near Lakeba. One of the two seamen who survived the shipwreck, the massacre, and the deadly illness brought ashore by the crew, Oliver Slater, spent nearly two years among the Fijians. He went on to Mbua Bay by canoe where he was later rescued by a passing ship. While at Mbua, he had seen some trees called yasi dina by the natives, known as sandalwood, treasured in the China trade. Sandalwood (santalum yasi) is actually a root parasite which thrives on the roots of other trees.

Those early contacts set the scene for years of bloody intertribal warfare fueled by the lust for wealth, which brought guns to Fiji by Europeans as trade goods. Tribal conflicts raged after acquisition of firearms. Along with traders, beachcombers came. Europeans often took multiple wives from chiefly families for power, prestige and protection. Many remained in the islands. By 1814 the sandalwood had been depleted. European contacts continued through trade in beche de mer.

In 1835 the first European missionaries came, also to Lakeba, Wesleyans David Cargill and William Cross. The missionaries came with their wives and slowly made an impact, although they were sometimes tormented witnesses to cannibal feasts and killings. Both men and their wives died young. William Cross died in 1842 after a long illness. Rev. Cargill, who was suffering from fever and guilt and depression after the death of his wife, died by suicide.

Cross and Cargill were replaced by the Reverends Lyth and Calvert and Hunt who, with their families, came with equal dedication.

In the midst of all this, the U.S. Exploring Expedition sent six sailing ships to the South Seas in 1838. *Voyage to the Southern Ocean* recounts, through letters of a young seaman, Lt. William Reynolds, to his sister, the first sighting of Antarctica. The letters also chronicled the Expedition's experience charting the Fijis.

Ratu Cakobau, through ruthless intertribal warfare, consolidated his power and declared himself King of Fiji, making Ovalau the center of power. By 1870 there were six hundred whites living in Levuka, two thousand Europeans throughout the islands. Levuka had become a lawless outpost of seamen and traders, which had attracted an assortment of rough and shiftless drifters and fortune hunters.

In 1874 the high chiefs of Fiji pleaded again with Britain for protection, offering to her Majesty "the government of the islands, but not the soil of the Fijian people."

It was on the streets of this historic capital that I walked.

The buildings of Levuka were mostly of white clapboard and corrugated metal with false fronts, which reminded me of my hometown in Minnesota in the 1930's. The sidewalks were roofed with posts along the curb side for support. Across the street, a treed grassy swath ran to the concrete breakwater at the sea's edge. Faces were both Indian and Melanesian and a rowdy maritime atmosphere still prevailed.

Levuka is one of three official Ports of Entry in Fiji. Suva and Lautoka, the other two, are both on the main island of Viti Levu.

A long dock extended into the sea to accommodate huge ships that docked at Queens Wharf. All night the mammoth Russian ship in port was lighted from bow to stern and the work of unloading the voluminous catch continued. Pacific Fishing Company (PAFCO) was founded in 1964 by a Japanese firm. The cannery was opened in 1976, a joint venture with the Fijian government.

When I returned, Pam and the children were ready, so we walked through the town to the restaurant where we had our free breakfasts of fried eggs and toast. After going back to check on the van to RukuRuku, I left them to explore the town. When we asked about the van, we were answered by shrugs or blank stares or promises that it would be at a certain place. It never was and we began to wonder if the van and RukuRuku existed at all.

On my way back I met Lisa, who was also staying at the Old Capital Inn. While staying on Rarotonga she had sustained a serious moped burn on her leg, which had become dangerously infected. Muffler burns occur so often they are jokingly called Rarotonga tattoos. I walked with her to the Levuka Hospital, a building very much like the Old Capital Inn. Both functionally and architecturally, it seemed from another century. Above the registration desk in the entry hall there was a row of assorted bottles. The sign stated, "It is wise to bring a clean bottle with you to the hospital for your mixtures." My impression of the hospital was one of caring and empathy, peeling paint, worn benches and myriad glass bottles on a shelf in the emergency room containing unlabeled mixtures. However, some very effective medicine is practiced throughout the South Pacific using traditional native plants.

An Indian doctor very patiently cleaned her wound, medicated and wrapped it. He also prescribed medication for her hands which were turning as dark as liver spots around her fingers, a problem that worried her more than the infected burn. The staff seemed competent enough with their limited resources and supplies.

I did not have a contact point at which to inform Tom Valentine that we had been unable to stay at the Royal. I thought the opportunity to go to Vanua Levu might have been lost, but on our way back from the hospital I found him waiting on the bridge by the Royal Hotel.

The government minister he had come to meet had been called away to settle a land dispute on another island. He said, "Can you be ready to leave tonight?"

Without hesitation, I agreed, so we walked to the Patterson Agency office to purchase my bus/ferry ticket to Nabouwalu. As we walked he explained that he and his brother Martin, and son, Benjamin, were taking a truck load of beche de mer to Nabouwalu where they were to meet a Chinese middleman to whom they would sell their cargo if a fair price could be negotiated. I heard faint echoes from the history books and through my mind sailed the schooners of the China trade, a reality still, even though the ferry was a far less romantic ship than the schooners with their billowing sails.

"Would you mind taking the bus to meet us at the ferry landing?" he asked, adding that the beche de mer smells so bad that none of them would ride in the back of the truck.

The young man from whom I purchased my ticket (F$26), Tom said, was the son of the chief of all of Ovalau.

My course was set.

I hurried to find Pam and the children to tell them of my change of plans. When Eirin understood that I would be leaving them, he sobbed heart-wrenching sobs.

"Pam," I said, "Arrange my flight back to the States along with yours. I'll meet you in Nadi in two and a half weeks."

Swept along on a tide of circumstances I would never have anticipated, on a tide of tears from a three-year-old fellow traveler, my departure date from the South Pacific had been determined.

While Pam continued her fruitless search for the van to RukuRuku, I wandered around taking pictures of Levuka. The Levuka Public School was built in 1879, the oldest public school in Fiji. Many of the leaders of Fiji are graduates of this school tucked away on the hillside, pale yellow against the tropical greens. School and grounds were well kept and three crosses adorned the peaks of the three wings of the building.

At Café Levuka I ran into Pam and the boys. With cake and ice cream, unaccustomed luxuries, we celebrated our last afternoon together for a while. A young woman named Kathy, who was from San Francisco, owned Café Levuka. She delighted the boys by letting them play with her pet iguanas, long, very green, very large lizards.

I packed slowly, reluctant at the thought of leaving my young companions. Pam tucked a precious gift into my luggage. An orange and some biscuits (cookies) she had been carefully hoarding since New Zealand. The gifts that pass between backpackers on parting help define the lean austerity in the life of the traveler. Things taken for granted at home; the paycheck, a well-stocked closet, the supermarket and overflowing cupboards, are half forgotten symbols of another world. It is partly a matter of economy, but more than that awareness that whatever you bring along tends to reduce your mobility.

After saying good night to the children, I joined the other guests in a loose congregation at a big table in the center hall dining room. It was a friendly place; maps, ideas, guidebooks, coffee shared across the table.

There were communal facilities for kitchen and bath; two stalls for showers, two for toilets. The concrete floors reminded me to bring rubber thongs on my next trip.

Posted on one of the toilet walls, the *Toilet Testament* told the story better than I could. Its author is unknown to me:

Bless this room, O Lord, we pray
Make it sweet by night and day.
Bless the seat and bless the flush,
Bless the early morning rush.
Bless the nasty little brat
Who pulled the chain and drowned the cat.

Bless the girls who lock the door
Reading books an hour or more.
Bless the phantom with the feet
The prints of which are on the seat.
Bless the fiend whose favorite caper
Leaves you stranded with no paper.
Finally, with love and kisses,
Bless the bloody fool that misses.

Traveling "bottom end" is a mixed bag that requires both flexibility and a sense of humor, but most of all, a love of people and human interaction.

Although you travel alone you never need to be lonely.

Ferry to Nabouwalu from Levuka

Chapter Seventeen

The Ferry to Nabouwalu

My night was short, my sleep restless and I was awake before the alarm, which would have rung about three a.m. Quietly, I got up and dressed in the dark so I wouldn't waken the children.

With an emotional hug, Pam and I said good-bye. I shouldered my duffles and walked out into the dark and silent streets of Levuka. An occasional dog barking broke the stillness, accentuating the silence.

The bus stop was a bench near the waterfront across the street from the Patterson Agency. Because it was deserted, "What ifs" leaped up in my mind like little ghosts, "What if this isn't the right place? What if I missed the bus? What if Tom won't be at the ferry landing?"

My uncertainty was partly allayed when two Indian women in saris came sleepily to join me. Their nephew shouldered a trunk and carried a large flashlight.

Although it was a soft night, the breeze was a bit fresh off the water. A crescent moon was visible through wisps of clouds.

When the young man asked me where I am going I realized that I didn't know. Nabouwalu first, but then? I did not know the name of the village that was our destination...only that Tom knew Joana McIntyre, so it must be near Galoa Island, which was not on my map. I realized, too, that I had met Tom just two days before...a Fijian...a stranger...in a land so different. It seemed beyond coherent explanation, but from inside it felt God-led and right.

About fifteen sleepy passengers had assembled by the time the bus arrived. We left at four forty a.m. and passed through the shuttered main street of Levuka. Two early fishermen sat on the quay. A dog, sleeping in the street, moved reluctantly away. Our bus screeched to a halt to pick up a roadside passenger.

From the front seat I had full view of the seemingly impossible road ahead. The road hugged the water with neither guardrails nor berm. Sharp blind curves veered around rocky cliffs, but at least this time of day we had the road to ourselves.

The bus thundered on, laboring up hills. Yesterday's heavy rains made the road more difficult, eroding the edges and creating puddles and ruts that were not there the day before.

We passed through a sleeping village, then another. Palms bent to grace the narrow road and huge mango trees canopied it. The bus sideslipped and wallowed through a low muddy spot. Three horses moved slowly out of our way. Village after village was still asleep in the early morning darkness. We passed bamboo thickets and pandanus as we bounced over ruts. Narrow plank bridges with no guardrails were barely above the streams that were swift running from the night's rains.

Turning left we found the sea again. On the miles of winding road I saw no place wide enough to meet the smallest Volkswagon, yet two days before, we had met trucks and lorries full of homeward bound cannery workers. Tree limbs sometimes brushed my face through the open window. Nauvalova Village. We began to climb. A barefoot man ambled along to his morning bath wearing only a sulu, carrying a towel.

Every gear was used up the steep inclines. Suddenly, the sea was on our left again, lights twinkling across the water. It was twenty minutes before six a.m. In the beam of the bus's headlights I saw Tom standing at the ferry landing. He and two men beside him were anxiously searching the faces on the bus, which turned around and backed into the yawning mouth of the ferry.

As I stepped off the bus, Tom wrung my hand in greeting.

"I'm so happy that you came!"

Like Tom, the two men with him extended their hands in a warm welcome.

While Martin and Benjamin secured the truck, Tom brought me to another part of the ferry's bowels into which vehicles were driven. He showed me fourteen plasticized rice bags full of beche de mer, explaining that they are big sea slugs. They had been gathered over months of deep diving the reefs. For market they were boiled in salt water, then split open, dried and smoked.

Benjamin and Martin knew that the shrewd Chinese man would inspect the lot and they were anxious to learn the price. It should be $4,000 to $5,000, which was no small amount in the island economy. The effort those bags represented included not only the work, but often the risk of life itself.

The crossing to Notovi Landing on Viti Levu was smooth. We discharged a bus and passengers bound for Suva and picked up a bus from Suva going to Vanua Levu; then continued on to Nabouwalu. Halfway across, we began to roll a bit, but beyond the cross current we moved comfortably again.

Tom was surprised to find his cousin among the passengers that boarded at Notovi. Sissy was returning from Suva, where she had attended a women's meeting for two weeks with a church group. Her husband works for Comtrac (Caterpillar) in Labasa.

Martin and Benjamin settled inside the cabin to watch a video and rest. Sissy provided Tom and me with snacks from an ample lunch basket she had brought.

It was exciting to see one set of islands after another recede into the misty horizon...Ovalau, Laluvia, Thangalai, while the broad, high island of Vanua Levu spread across the water before us. The Fijian Archipelago is made up of 300 islands, about one hundred of them inhabited. Lofty peaks folded into velvet green slopes. Coconut groves were at the water's edge as we neared the long dock.

Nabouwalu. We joined the crowd exiting the ferry. A long line of cars and trucks jostled their way to the ramp, honking, impatient to board the ferry, while an equally impatient group tried to exit.

Tom went to a small Indian-owned grocery while Martin and Benjamin did their business concerning the beche de mer.

Sissy and I went to a small restaurant and ordered tea, while Tom went to see if the clan's lorry had arrived. The lorry driver, Tom's nephew, seemed less welcoming. The older man accompanying him took my hand in both of his, warmly welcoming me in Fijian. He climbed into the back of the truck, which had a bench along each side of the covered truck bed. Tom tossed my duffles in back and Tom and I climbed, against my protest, into the cab. I was embarrassed to be leaving the older man riding alone in the back.

The road from Nabouwalu toward Labasa was unsealed, though even at that time the government was planning to make it a macadamized highway. The logistics of road building in a country of islands, scattered over a broad expanse of ocean, make the problem an expensive and difficult one.

Rivers from the mountains ran swiftly under narrow bridges. I was not aware of any road signs or markers, but I knew we must be passing the infamous Sandalwood Bay and the unnamed villages might be Bua or Lekutu.

I was concerned for the older man sitting on bare benches in the back as the truck bounced mercilessly over ruts and rocks and left a dense dusty trail in the air.

When we reached Nassarawaqa Village, after about a three-hour ride, they said we were almost home. A few miles beyond, we turned right onto a narrow road with deep ditches. The embankments were so ruddy they reminded me of the Mesabi Iron Range of northern Minnesota. Leaves of many plants were a deep blue/green, which might give additional clues to the mineral elements in the soil.

After driving a few miles through crown land, we reached what they called clan land. In Leonard Wibberly's *Fiji-Islands of the Dawn*, the author emphasized that the British colonial rule has always been directed at protecting the Fijians from exploitation by the whites. He wrote, Fijians are among the few islands in the South Seas where people are permitted to continue with communal tribal life they developed through the centuries.

He explained that the first Governor to Fiji was a Scotsman who understood clan and made sure that the Fijian people would not be alienated from their land by initiating laws that assured that most of the land would be held in perpetuity by the clan and could never be bought or sold.

The tribe to which Tom's wife belongs had fifteen hundred acres, some apportioned to family members, some in dense forest, five hundred sixty seven acres of cleared, flat, fertile farm land. It had been cleared under a government agricultural scheme some time ago in an abandoned attempt to raise pigeon peas. Some of the land was leased to Indian tenant farmers. The rest of it lay fallow.

We turned onto a lane of neatly clipped grass between rows of blooming hibiscus bushes and young frangipani trees. At the head of the lane stood a galvanized steel structure about twenty feet wide and fourteen feet deep. The wooden board door, with a metal bolt, stood open. On each side of the door, wooden shutters, hinged at the top, were pushed out with a pole to reveal unscreened, glassless window openings. A similar window was on each end of the house.

Momentarily I was seized by panic. Where am I? How do I live here? How do I go on from here? It was all jumbled into a single startling thought.

We walked around the side and entered a wood framed addition with one side open from about waist high up. The opening led into a room with a dark, very weathered wooden floor. In one corner there were two closed doors, painted red. I assumed that one went into the main house. In the other corner a fireplace, shoulder height, was made of the same corrugated iron as the walls of the main house. A large aluminum kettle was boiling over a small fire of sticks, smoke drifting out through a wall opening.

As we entered, Tom's wife was standing on a battery turned on its side, which functioned as a stool for cooking. On one wall an antique glass front cupboard held dishes, tin plates and cups.

Tom's wife came and welcomed me, a stranger, uninvited, by holding both my hands in hers, eyes sparkling. She impressed me as a very kind, confident, self-possessed woman who was enviably comfortable with herself and her life.

Salote introduced me to her two daughters, Melisha (Molly) and Patina (Tina). Molly, a little shy, with soft manners, had the same grace and charm I saw in her mother. Tina, a beautiful child of eleven, an angel-imp with a radiant smile, had a playful, beguiling nature. Benjamin and two older children, away from home, complete the family.

The driver, so taciturn during the drive, had gone on about other business.

Salote offered me tea and Molly opened the door to the main room. They were all barefoot, so I slipped off my sandals. Molly laid a cloth on the floor and we sat on the mat around its perimeter. Tea was served and luncheon plates were laid out. Bowls of a white boiled root, canned corned beef with onions and curried potatoes were set in the center of the cloth. Each bowl was offered to me first, then to Tom and Tina. Molly sat fanning the food gently with a towel if flies came. Salote poured tea and served. I asked them to eat with us, but they declined and ate later.

While on the ferry, Tom had explained that his great, great, great grandfather was one of twin brothers who came from America. One had married thirteen daughters of high tribal chiefs and in doing so amassed great amounts of land and prestige and founded a vast family. Tom said that whenever Fijians heard his name, they would ask, "Who is your grandmother?" to determine from which tribe he comes. Lineage remains very important in Fiji.

In Fiji's Times it was written about Charlie Savage, another American who had many wives of chiefly rank, "any son born to Savage would have been a vasu and would have held almost unlimited power. As a political safeguard, the Bauans made sure his sons were stillborn, although a few daughters were allowed to live."

Raised Western, Tom had little knowledge of tribal life before they decided to move back to Salote's mataquali to minister.

Salote's "share" of the clan land was an island just off shore. They had no boat and no money, so life was very hard. Tom worked with hand tools to clear the dense forest of mangroves that lay between the mainland and the island's rim. He cleared spaces, slash and burn, to plant young papaya trees and oranges, limes and bananas. He erected a house there.

The rhythm of their lives was tied to the tides. When the tide was low they could wade across the intervening expanse of water. After three months on the island, they decided to go to her father, the chief. He was the man who met me at Nabouwalu and endured the rugged trip in the back of the lorry.

Her request required certain ceremony. The Vaka Viti, the Fijian Way, required that she bring a tabua, a whales tooth, and on her knees plead for the arable land they needed. Joana McIntyre, in *Changes in Latitude*, explained that much of life in Fiji is conducted with ceremonially good manners making communal life possible, comfortable, secure.

Following her request, there was a meeting of the tribe, the mataquali. Thirteen acres next to the chief's property was surveyed and everybody agreed and signed. It was still clan land, not freehold, but their continued use of it is assured, although, of course, it cannot be sold.

The galvanized iron house was moved from the island to its present location. Their oldest daughter, who now lives in New Zealand, helped sink the corner post. It was a coconut tree log so heavy it nearly toppled and crushed her.

As we sat after lunch having tea, a voice called from outside the open front door. Tom answered and several conversational exchanges followed in Hindi. Permission to enter was granted. The Indian man bowed as he entered and crawled across the mat, presenting himself to Tom. Salote poured him a cup of tea and he sat next to Tom discussing business. His tone was respectful, somewhat reverential. Their business involved transporting one hundred watermelons to market in the tribal van.

Before he left, three men came into the room through the kitchen...Benjamin and Tom's brother, Martin. The third man, tall and quiet, was introduced as Waibute, Salote's brother. Molly and Salote brought fresh bowls of food and tea and they sat among us to eat.

In the main room there was a double bed and desk on one side. The desk was piled high with books and papers, the desk of a scholar. A backless chair sat, like a stool, in front of the desk. A curtain was strung on a light rope, affording privacy. On the other side, two cots with aluminum frames were hung with mosquito netting. This area was also curtained, but the curtain was pushed to one side.

Tom carried my two small duffles to one corner and indicated which bed would be mine. I looked questioningly at Tina, knowing that it was hers. She smiled and said, "I like to sleep on the mat."

At the appropriate moment I asked Tina quietly, "Where do you go to the bathroom?"

She giggled and led me down a curving path through flowering bushes to an outhouse complete with a carved moon on the door and toilet tissue! It was set in a grove of trees, lending privacy. She waited halfway down the path; then showed me another path to the well where water was brought up by pails. She was my angel and guide through the cultural labyrinth, making it all seem easier. Because I had grown up in a village in northern Minnesota before REA had extended electric lines to our community, my own long ago experience made the transition easier.

It seemed that she perceived my next question, which remained unspoken. Laughing, she ran before me down a wide mowed path through tall stands of mission grass. As I went around the bend, I saw her slip off her blouse and shorts and in her underwear dive into a pool of water. She came up, still laughing, shook the water from her hair and reached for a bar of soap on the planked dock. Sitting on a barely submerged log, she soaped her body and dove into the pool again, then jumped out and quickly dressed.

The bathing place was made private by a dense screen of mission grass on both sides of the stream, obscuring the house and kumala patch on the nearer side and whatever might lay across the stream. Upstream was a thick stand of pandanus, each trunk held high above the water on a fibrous teepee of roots. From this, I guessed that the stream was lower than usual, a fact that Tom later said was worrisome.

On the way back to the house we talked about school. She said that she was studying Hindi. She was already conversant in Fijian and English as most young children are. In the days that I was there, I did not see either her or Molly go to school and I wondered if my presence hindered it.

The school was eight miles away. I wondered at the relevance of what she would learn there, beyond literacy, to her survival in the bush or village. However, her two oldest sisters had both married and gone on to New Zealand. I wondered how Molly and Tina would get to school. I guessed that money for gasoline for the truck was scarce and that the trip to meet me was made at great sacrifice to the tribe.

Tom and the chief had brought two big bags of tuna they had gotten from the cannery in Levuka. Tom boiled the fish in a big pot over a wood fire in the back yard; then he smoked the pieces of boiled fish, tending them on a rack for hours. This delicious fish was served either cold or in lolo (coconut cream) with cold, boiled kumala for breakfast, lunch and dinner while I was there, as staples. From their garden, bananas, papaya and watermelon were added. Sometimes we also had corned beef and potatoes, but I felt they were an expensive, imported luxury.

Tom's determined plan was to show me three islands in the lagoon, which were part of the clan's property. It was decided that the trip would be made on the following day.

The big aluminum teakettle was always on the grate. Throughout the day, as people came and went, tea was served, sometimes black tea which they had bought at the Indian store at Nabouwalu, but more often lemon grass tea from their garden. Sometimes we sat around the kitchen floor, sometimes on the mat in the main room. Except for the furniture I have mentioned, there was none.

After eating, the dishes were removed to the table in the back yard where Molly washed them with water she carried from the well.

When all the work was finished, Salote said, "Come have a stretch." Everyone relaxed on the mat, stomach down, propped up on an elbow. Their single benzine lantern cast flickering shadows on the walls. When Martin, Benjamin, Waibute and his nephew came home, I excused myself, exhausted from my long day of travel that had begun in the middle of a near-sleepless night, and I went to bed.

I pulled the curtain and changed into my nightclothes. The dimness provided as much privacy as the thin curtain. Slipping into my sleep sack, I quickly drifted off to sleep with the sounds of five Fijian men laughing and talking at the foot of my bed. With the exception of Tom, all of them had been strangers the day before. In the company of these gentle Melanesians, the anxiety I had felt about coming to Fiji seemed a travesty.

Tina, Salote, and Molly at home in the bush, Vanua Levu, Fiji

Chapter Eighteen

The Far Side of the Lagoon

I awakened sometime after 3:00, took my small flashlight and crept over sleeping legs to the open door where the lighted lantern hung. I startled a cane toad twice the size of my fist that had hopped inside. The sounds of sleep continued undisturbed as I slipped out into the night and began my search for the elusive path that Tina had shown me in the afternoon. Unable to find it on my first try, I walked back to my starting point casting the thin beam of the light left and right to keep on the narrow path. Each time, I arrived at the well. Finally, I walked around to the back door from which Tina had shown me the way.

Slowly I pushed the outhouse door open, flashing light into the dark corners. From living in the North Woods, the Arizona desert and Florida wetlands, I knew about bears and coyotes and alligators, but among these unknown jungle sounds there was no anchor of familiarity. There was no moon at all, nothing to illuminate the deep night. Returning to the house, the pale glow of the lantern made a welcoming pathway to the door.

Shyness made the bathing place the greatest challenge while staying in the bush. I decided that it was the perfect time to bathe, before the family wakens. Quietly, I gathered my clean clothes, toothbrush, treated water and a towel and followed the mowed swath to the river. Though the night was warm, the water felt cold as I dropped cautiously onto the slippery log. A nonswimmer, I was concerned about the depth of the pool beyond the log. Carefully, keeping one hand on the dock, I soaped and, using my cupped hand as a dipper, rinsed.

Wild pigs were rooting and grunting upstream in the stand of pandanus. Only darkness and ignorance kept me from panic as I was then unaware of their mean dispositions and I had not yet seen their hideous curving tusks that Fijian men wear as trophies.

When I had finished my bath, the pale light that precedes dawn revealed dim outlines of trees and grass. Suddenly, the stillness was broken by the sound of soft Fijian voices raised in praise. Ukulele and guitar harmoniously filled in the spaces that might have been given back to silence. Then the voices lifted again in song, this time in English: "We thank you, Lord, for shoes on our feet, fine clothes to wear, good things to eat..." Each morning before dawn their worship began in praise and humble gratitude for their multiple blessings.

Tina, Molly and Tom were sitting in the kitchen, cross-legged, heads bowed in an attitude of prayer. I slipped in quietly to sit beside Tina. I wondered where Salote was.

The sun was well above the horizon when Molly rose from prayer to light the fire for tea. Tears washed my cheeks, moved by their reverence, their gratitude for what seemed to me so very little. I realized then that poverty and wealth are matters of spirit and attitude rather than circumstance. My life was forever changed by their example.

"Tom," I said sincerely, "yours is the richest family I have ever known."

From the small room off the kitchen, I could hear racking sobs. Tom went in to where Martin and Benjamin had been sleeping. Sobs were lost, muffled, in a nearly incoherent flood of repentance as Martin found his way back home to the family of God.

I remembered things Leonard Wibberly had written in *Fiji-Islands of the Dawn:*

"Christian missionaries, in many ways splendid men, earnest and devout, prepared to sacrifice their lives to convert the most fearsome cannibals of the South Seas. They came in fear and trembling. But they came anyway. The first Christian missionaries to arrive in the Fijis were not European, but Tahitian. Hanea and Alai had been sent to Tonga by the London Missionary Society on their way to Fiji. It took them four years to find a ship that would take them to Fiji. In 1830 they went to Oneata in the Lau group in the company of Takia, a chief who had been to Tahiti and Sydney."

I earnestly wished those good men could know that their lives and deaths had made an eternal difference in those islands. Most died before they had completed a decade in the islands. They were young men who, with their wives, gave the ultimate sacrifice in that strange and terrible place.

Lotte returned from her father's house, where she had gone early to request the use of a borrowed bullock team to harvest kumala for market.

I overheard them speaking of going to Labasa early the next day. I still did not know where I was, but recognized Labasa as a city and remembered that an airport was located there. If they were going there anyway, perhaps I could ride along. I had become aware of the sacrifices the family was making by my presence, certainly not by anything they said, but by an intuitive awareness.

If this was to be my last day with them, Tom was intent on taking me to the islands and went off to make arrangements.

One of the nephews arrived with a light team of bullocks, brown with irregular white patches on their flanks. Row after row of kumala was turned over with the plow. Molly and Lotte joined the half dozen men gathering the roots into piles, which were put into large gunny bags and piled at the edge of the field. It seemed light work filled with joking and laughter.

Tina, Tom and I began the three-mile walk to Salote's oldest brother's house, the man who will be chief when her father dies. The trail led between tall stands of ubiquitous mission grass. I have read that the mission grass was introduced by accident when it was used for packing ammunition cases during World War II. Since then, it has spread rapidly over the island making the work of farmers ten times harder, especially so because there is little mechanization of farming. Everything is still accomplished laboriously with hand tools.

Our walk was leisurely. Tom told me that a few years ago he felt the time had come for the ceremony of mata ni gone, presenting the children to his great grandmother's village. Pigs were purchased, bolts of cloth, tabua...about $3,000 worth...to present to the chief of the village. Unaware of the importance of the occasion, they arrived a day late to find people from 200 villages waiting for the great feast and ceremony to begin.

Until then, he had not realized how high born his great grandmother was.

"All the people in these villages were subject to the turaga, the powerful chief, in my grandmother's family." Tom said. "When the ceremony was over, people came to me, fell to their knees and begged me to come back to claim my land and hereditary position as vasu. 'Whenever you want to claim it, it is here', they said."

Slowly, Tom added, "I should know more of our tradition."

Salote's brother was sitting on the spacious covered porch when we arrived, a handsome man in his fifties, I would guess, with closely cropped hair. He was barefoot and wore only a faded red sulu. He rose to greet me with a broad smile, his large hand extended. Tina lovingly picked up a small cousin. I couldn't tell if it was a boy or girl.

A six-year old boy followed them out to play.

Lotte's brother is a minister. His wife, after preparing and serving us a cup of milo, hurried away to meet Lotte for a scheduled women's prayer meeting.

The house was the same simple structure as Tom's, but larger. An old refrigerator stood in the corner, near a working surface with jars and bottles on top and a blackboard covering the side. I guessed that this large open porch might be the kitchen. We did not go inside.

I didn't know exactly why we waited. I was like a child being taken by a parent somewhere, knowing neither the reason nor the destination, just trusting. The time passed quickly with lighthearted conversation and laughter as Martin and Benjamin joined us. Martin, barefoot, wore only a light cotton sulu in a yellow print, Benjamin jeans and a T-shirt. Each man wore a wristwatch, which seemed curious because time was never of the essence in this land with few schedules or appointments. Everything was accomplished in its own time in nature's cycle of light and dark, rising and falling tides.

The mystery of our delay was solved by the arrival of Kolomi. He was a sturdy, muscular young man who wore brown shorts, yellow T-shirt and a colorful striped visor. Tom introduced him as Brother Kolomi and I sensed the love of sheep to shepherd that passed between him and Tom.

Once more, Kolomi went down the path into the forest and returned indicating to Tom, "Not yet."

Ominous gray clouds were gathering and I began to wonder if a storm would preclude our going. After Kolomi returned the third time, we set off together down the path.

I cringed as they walked barefoot over sensitive grass, a strange prickly little ground-hugging creeper that folds its fernlike leaves at the slightest touch. I had seen it first on Rarotonga. Kolomi led the way, single file, as Tom and Patina followed and I hurried along behind them. There seemed to be a strange sense of urgency now in our mission.

About twenty minutes later, the land began to change as the soil beneath our feet became spongy, then wet. Suddenly, in a narrow clearing, the boat was before us. Red and yellow paint marked the water line. A square cabin topped the bright blue hull of the heavy, wooden, flat bottom boat. Kolomi pushed it off from the mud flat and with a rope, began pulling it through a channel of murky black water.

High, arched roots rose from the muddy banks holding the bole of the mangroves and the dense green foliage above the high water line. Tom began pushing the boat, while Tina played happily around them. My feet were bare in Minnetonka Mocs, which are made of soft deerskin and had already survived reef walking at Malevu. As I stepped into the ankle deep muck I felt it ooze between my toes.

About a quarter mile into the mangroves, the water was above my knees. Kolomi told us we could get into the boat, which he poled skillfully, avoiding the tangle of roots on either side. Mangrove limbs arched the narrow channel giving an eerie impression of half-light, a vault of gloom exacerbated by the low scudding gray clouds that spanned the horizon above and beyond us.

The boat seemed like a smaller version of the African Queen. Out of the mangroves, as we entered the lagoon, the boat glided over a transparent sea that revealed a colorful garden of corals, bright blue starfish and vividly colored, darting fish.

In the lea of the island, Salote's island, which had been their home, lack of wind falsely promised an easy trip in spite of the gray sky, but as we steered for the distant islands, clouds above and whitecaps below, threatened a different sort of day.

The boat was powered by a laboring fourteen horsepower Johnson outboard motor. Kolomi had brought a yellow slicker, which he held up with his left arm to deflect the stinging salt spray, while he deftly handled the motor with his right arm. Waves began breaking over the bow, then over the cabin. Kolomi tried to give me the slicker, but I insisted he keep it because in his position he took the worst of it.

Over the roar of waves and engine, Tom yelled at Patina to go down below into the cabin as the boat lurched over growing waves. Tom and I stood in the cockpit behind the cabin. With my left hand I grasped the cabin roof, while my right arm extended above the cabin and clung to one of the two supports, which ran in parallel rows front to back over the top of the cabin.

I shouted to Tom who stood beside me, "We don't have to continue!" I felt my being there had caused all our lives to be put in jeopardy. Himself unsure, Tom turned to Kolomi and said, "Is it okay?" Kolomi nodded, continuing to keep his eye on every swell, every breaking wave.

Each time Kolomi veered the boat to cut into a breaking wave, Tom put his arm firmly around my waist as a support, withdrawing it as soon as the danger passed. His voice rose above the engine's roar in a steady emotional outpouring of Faith. "The disciples came to Jesus when the ship was covered with waves saying they would perish, but Jesus rebuked the winds and the sea and there was a great calm. They marveled that even the wind obeyed him."

Tom continued in this way, telling and retelling every story about walking on water and stilling waves, his deep voice a buoy of confidence.

Only once, the thought crept in. If the boat goes down my children will never know what happened. Even I had no clear idea where I was. I had not written to anyone since Tubakula. Even if they knew I was in Fiji, there are three hundred islands and to Tom and his family, I was just a stranger passing through their lives.

At the place we were crossing, the lagoon appeared to be more than ten miles wide, perhaps twenty. There was nothing by which to define distance there. I believed that we were in Ngaloa Bay, but none of these features or islands appeared on my map.

The cross current halfway to the first of the two distant islands became treacherous and again I asked Tom if we should turn back and again we acceded to Kolomi's judgment and continued.

Closer to the island, in shallower water, Tom went forward to watch for coral heads and rocky outcrops and guided Kolomi around the island where he anchored the boat in a sheltered cove. During the dark history of Fiji, during the last century, countless ships were lost on these uncharted reefs...Nantucket whalers, East Indiamen, schooners and trade brigs. First they were drawn in their search for whales; then for cargoes of sandalwood and later beche de mer. They risked shipwreck and massacre to barter iron nails and trinkets and later muskets for cargoes worth 400 times their investment. It was in these waters, on these very islands.

A breathtakingly beautiful island lay before us. Beyond a few clumps of mangrove stretched a broad golden sand beach edged by coconut palms. In the higher center of the island, huge tropical hardwood trees formed canopies over grassy clearings. Every element of a dream island was there and not a footprint in the sand!

We went over the side of the anchored boat into the clear water, which gently lapped the beach giving no hint of the ocean's fury spent so savagely nearby.

I laid my shoes by a clump of bushes, my bare feet reveling in the soft warm sand. We walked and ran and played like children while Kolomi foraged for some coconuts. One swift blow of his sele levu opened the husk, another the green nut which he passed first to me to drink. Cool and slightly sweet. Refreshed, I passed it on.

Kolomi opened a watermelon, which he had brought in the boat and he cut it into wedges. He went to the high ground where he carefully planted the seeds, which he asked us to save. Papaya was growing there with large fruits nearly ripe, oranges, bananas and nuts of types I had never seen before. Kolomi cracked them between two rocks and handed me the sweet delicious meats, similar to macadamia.

Tom explained that Martin and Benjamin dive for beche de mer on the reefs beyond the further island. They sometimes spend six months there diving, living off what they can glean from the island and sea, coming home only on weekends.

A lean-to shelter was under a canopy of trees. Nearby were racks on which, after cooking, they dry the beche de mer to preserve it and prepare it for market. If these islands were located near Sanibel Island in Florida, they would have made Florida developers salivate in greedy anticipation of their market value.

Reluctantly, we waded back to the boat. I asked Tom if I could take his picture. He said, "Wait a minute," and went back to the island to pick frangipani blossoms to put behind each ear.

While on the island it was easy to forget the fury of the sea. The crossing to the farther island was still rougher but the distance was not as great. That island was a little smaller. In half an hour we walked around the perimeter on beaches as beautiful as those of the larger island.

The three islands are clan land, historically used for making copra, fishing and gathering beche de mer, that strange but still lucrative source of cash from international trade. Tom waved a hand in the direction of still another island. "That's where Joana McIntyre lives. She has been very good to that family. She and Mali are away in Hawaii now."

The sky was growing still more threatening so we shortened our stay and boarded the boat for the trip home, a distant line on the far horizon. The roughest leg of the return journey was from the larger island to the one on which Tom and Lotte had lived. Once we were out of harm's way, I realized that my arm was raw, bleeding and bruised from holding on so tightly to the brace on top of the lurching cabin

When we stopped at the island nearest shore, I followed them barefoot to the island, but I could not continue with Tom and Kolomi all the way into the bush where they and Patina walked so easily in bare feet.

They checked patches of ripening fruit and on the way back, Kolomi cut a large bunch of bananas. They were unlike any I have seen, green with just traces of yellow, fat with blunt, not tapered ends. He hoisted them to his shoulder and walked on.

Retracing our steps from the boat through the mangrove swamp was a lighter journey because, safely back, I knew the end of it was a cup of tea in Salote's kitchen.

Tom said, admiringly, as we walked, "Kolomi is skillful. Did you see him cut into each breaker? If caught in a trough broadside, a flat bottom boat like that can easily be rolled."

I marveled at how life in the islands is lived with what seems like total abandon or total faith. There, laughter comes so easily through it all. Perhaps they have learned a key to joy that eludes us in the West where we take ourselves too seriously and cautiously insist that everything be insured, even life, which seems the ultimate foolishness.

When we returned to Salote's brother's house, Kolomi placed the bunch of bananas at his feet, like a gift or offering. On the porch there were several freshly woven palm leaf baskets, like large fat envelopes secured with magimagi, which is called sennit in Polynesia. He caught my curious gaze and untied the cord of one, removing a large, shiny smoky blue crab for me to admire.

The story of our journey to the islands was told and retold. I think it will be for many years to come.

Pushing the boat through the mangrove channel. See page 129.

Chapter Nineteen

Isalei, the Sweet Pain of Remembrance

Lotte and her sister-in-law were sitting on the kitchen floor mixing a very large pan of dough. She looked up and saw my mud and salt soaked skirt and offered to wash it.

"No, thank you, Lotte. I saw the brush on the dock. I will do it."

When I returned after bathing, Molly was sitting on a mat outside the kitchen door baking roti on a grid set on four empty aluminum cans above a fire of sticks. Baking roti is a time consuming task requiring patience as each small ball of dough is rolled on a board and is baked on the grid, one side until delicately brown, then the other, all the while tending the rapidly consumed fire of sticks.

How strongly the Indian influence has permeated Fijian diet! We had a feast of dahl, curried potatoes, fish in lolo, kumala and the delicious stack of fresh roti Molly set before us. After dinner, we enjoyed lemon grass tea with long life milk, which can be kept without refrigeration. Even on the islands where grocery stores exist they are few and far away, so except for a few purchased staples, life-sustaining food comes from the land and sea.

After Molly had cleared away the dishes, Lotte invited us to have a stretch. In the lantern's light Molly and Tina, Salote and I, friends now, talked easily. A huge cane toad hopped through the door, across the mat, casting a grotesque shadow. Salote squealed as Patina took a towel and redirected its route back out the door. Cane toads were introduced in 1936 from Hawaii to help control slugs and beetles and millipedes, which grow several inches long in the tropics. The toads, which have a gland on their neck that contains a deadly poison, have grown to be a serious nuisance in Fiji.

The next day promised to be a busy one with good-byes and an early morning departure to Labasa. We slept early. It seemed that I had barely fallen asleep when, in the darkness, I heard Tom's voice quietly call, "Molly, Buta, Lotte, Tina." He persisted gently until he had aroused each family member. Sleepily, for there was no hint of dawn, they rose, found their guitars and ukuleles and began their quiet praise, which gradually swelled into worship. Martin and Benjamin joined. From deep inside his soul, Martin poured out a prayer for five minutes, ten...and praise continued until it was fully light.

It was Friday and the plan was to leave early to get the watermelon and kumala to the Labasa market. The truck carried Martin and Benjamin to the main road where they would catch the bus retracing our route by bus/ferry/bus back to Levuka where Martin lived on Ovalau.

Then Salote's two nephews, sons of another brother who lived in the house beyond the chief, were going with Waibute to pick up the Indian tenant farmer and his watermelon. Afterward, they would return to load the kumala. With so early a start we could be in Labasa before eight o'clock. An hour passed, then two, with no sign of the returning lorry.

I was packed and Tom felt the responsibility to provide transport for me to Labasa. He went out to the road and looked in vain for some sign of the returning lorry. A cloud of dust signaled an approaching vehicle, rare on this road that goes into the bush. His heart sank when he saw that it was the truck of an itinerant used clothes merchant. So that was the source of Reebock T-shirts and Yankee baseball hats...used clothes imported for resale. I had read in a book about life in the bush of Togo in Africa, second hand Western clothes are referred to as dead yevo clothes, for who would sell such good clothes. They must be dead it was assumed.

Tom asked me to go inside and stay out of sight while he tried to negotiate a ride for me to the main road. The price, he said, would soar if they saw me, a Westerner.

The merchant was not going back that way, so it became a waiting time once more.

I was wallowing in uncertainty over what would be best. I had convinced Tom and Lotte by now that I could take the bus; that I had taken buses and ferries all over the South Pacific. I felt that I had, unwittingly, placed them in a difficult position. If the lorry was having mechanical trouble, would they feel compelled to repair it quickly at whatever cost? Would they leave for Labasa this late in the day if I weren't there? The sun was high and it was getting very hot.

In the distance, we could see two men walking and went to meet them. Waibute was with one of his nephews. They told of the truck breaking down after they had dropped Martin and Benjamin at the road before they got to the Indian's farm. They had tried pushing the truck to get it started, but to no avail. They had finally given up and the other man walked to get a mechanic in Nassarawaqa.

Already hot and exhausted, they began the five-mile walk home. Waibute lay on the mat, clearly spent, while Molly prepared cold fish in lolo and roti left from the day before.

I reassured the family that it was no problem for me to walk to the main road in time for the noon bus. I had told them before that I had walked the perimeter of Rarotonga, 20 miles, in three days for pleasure, so they were reluctantly convinced.

Waibute sat up. "I will walk with you. I will eat and have a swim and I will walk with you."

Nothing would dissuade him, although it would mean an additional walk of ten miles, round trip, to the road.

Molly said, "I will walk with you." It was decided.

An hour later, good-byes were said to Tina, Salote, Tom and the chief. We started down the road, Molly carrying one duffle, Buta the other. We walked in comfortable silence to conserve energy because they had twice as far to go as I.

Sometimes I would ask about a tree or flower, so different from familiar forests of North America. Molly mentioned that there are a lot of wild pigs in the bush, which can be dangerous. I remembered my predawn bath in the river and the rooting, grunting pigs so near. We passed great distances with neither houses nor crossroads.

Buta suddenly stopped. I had heard only the sounds of the bush and our footfalls on the stony road. He took the duffle from Molly and told her to run to intercept a truck which he heard coming from a side road in the distance.

We caught up with Molly who had stopped the Indian mechanic. "Yes, it's all fixed," he told Buta.

I didn't want to further compromise their plans, forcing a trip to market so late in the day, so I said I would take the bus anyway and accepted a ride with the mechanic who had offered to drop me at the road.

We talked of India; how beautiful it was in 1970 when I had visited. It stirred nostalgic curiosity in him for a place he had never seen; a culture whose modified fragments exist in these islands among the third and fourth generation immigrants where Indians can never feel really at home.

When we came to the main road, he said, "I will take you into Nassarawaqa village."

He had picked up an old Indian woman in a white sari who had been waiting with an assorted group of Indians by the roadside. She must have been a widow, as white is for mourning. She spoke to the driver in Hindi, but as we rode, side-by-side, in silence, we sometimes exchanged a glance or smile.

The driver suddenly pulled into a carport. "I will have my bath now," he said, leaving us for about twenty minutes in a van into which he had transferred our things. When he returned, refreshed, he said, "O.K. we will go now."

When he left us on the porch of an Indian store in the village, he seemed to expect nothing for the ride, nor did I offer it. He told me that I could catch the bus there and showed me from which direction it would come.

It was both store and ANZ bank branch with windows barred for security. The storekeeper, a woman, asked if I would like to use the bathroom, which was in her home in back of the store. It was a modern home, indicating a far more than average level of prosperity for a village. I was grateful for her offer as the ride to Labasa might take two hours.

I bought a large bottle of soda. Using a glass, I gave the bottle to two young Indian men, also waiting. They looked at me curiously, "Are you a missionary?" one asked.

"No," I responded, "I was just staying with the family of Tom Valentine."

There was spontaneous, generous praise for this high born Fijian man who had come to serve and love the poorer Indians. They told me that Tom has a thatch and bamboo church in which he ministers to the Indians. In these young men I saw the love and respect they feel for Tom. I felt so lucky that our chance meeting on the ferry had brought me there.

Just before the bus was due, the lorry rumbled to a stop outside the store. With much cheering and laughter, they claimed me back.

Salote hopped out and I climbed into the tall cab. A young child, about three years old, stood next to the driver peering through the back window at her father. I scooted over and picked her up to set her on my lap making room for Salote. As the child turned to see me, she let out a scream of terror, her eyes like those of a frightened animal.

I had not looked at a mirror since leaving Tubakula, so my first thought was that something terrible had happened to my face.

She leapt from my lap and buried her head in Salote's shoulder, refusing to look up. Her bloodcurdling screams continued.

The driver shifted gears and we roared off, but the sound of the engine couldn't drown out the uproarious laughter coming from the men in the back of the truck.

"Louisa, Louisa," Salote was saying gently. I tried to reach the frightened child to pat her reassuringly, but Lotte stopped my arm and put her finger to her lips begging my silence. "It's a long way to Labasa," she said.

The driver, the same man who held such reserve toward me the first day, smiled and comforting me in my pained confusion, said, "She has never seen hair like that."

I was bewildered and not at all soothed by his comment. I put my hand up to my curly white hair to smooth it. More bluntly, Lotte said, "We live in the bush. She has never seen a white person before."

During my days in the islands, I had somehow forgotten that I am different and could easily be mistaken for a trevoro or a ghost.

About thirty miles later, Louisa, quiet at last, sneaked a cautious peak at me, then quickly looked away again.

We stopped at a roadside grove. I bought two bags of oranges, one to share with the family and one to bring along.

Salote said this grove had bought the trees from her mother who had raised large quantities of oranges to ship. Since her death, the grove had fallen into a state of neglect.

I regretted that I had not met the matriarch of this remarkable family. Tom, with enormous respect, had shown me where she was buried, wrapped in masi (called tapa or siapo in Polynesia). Her grave was beneath the large mango tree beside the road across from the chief's house.

After crossing the Labasa River, I noticed a sign for a hotel on Nasekula Road. The lobby of Takia House was on the main floor, the rooms above main street businesses. I told Salote that I would appreciate their dropping me off at the hotel when they had delivered their produce to market. No hurry, I added, because I would enjoy seeing the market function as an "insider".

Labasa was a modern city of about 6,000 with a heavy overlay of Indian culture. The market was the active commercial center of the city, sprawling, clean and friendly.

We delivered several bags of kumala to their regular buyer and the grandfather's kumala to Tima, Salote and Waibute's sister who lived in Labasa and had a booth at the market.

The Indian man had been going from stall to stall checking the price of watermelon. He came back smiling broadly and reported that the price would be $3.00. The truck was moved and the watermelon unloaded. Waibute circulated, greeting friends, teasing the market girls with easy banter. In spite of being a very handsome man he had never married.

A big, smiling woman, Tima embraced me like a long lost relative. I instinctively felt that she embodied all the saintly qualities Tom had attributed to their mother.

It was late afternoon when Molly walked me into the hotel lobby. Her cousin carried my duffles. They waited until I was registered and there we said good-bye...a hug from Molly and a warm handshake from her cousin whose response to me had grown quite different from our first meeting when he drove us home from the ferry at Nabouwalu.

I wondered if Tom would have taken the bus as Martin and Benjamin had in returning if I had not been there. The truck, the gasoline and benzine for the boat were all communal assets expended generously for a stranger Tom had brought home.

Knowledge of the family's financial constraints had come to me slowly, in oblique ways.

Tom had urged Lotte to tell me about their family prayers. Shyly, she told me that anything they need, anything at all, she emphasized, like flour or oil or shoes, they write on a list, which they put in the Bible. They put their hands on the Bible, each family member, one hand on top of the other. Then they pray, expecting their prayer to be answered.

She hesitated. Then, with Tom's urging, she told me about the chicken. They had been given a beautiful laying hen. One day it was missing. For days they prayed for the chicken's safety. If someone had stolen it, they prayed that his heart would be softened so the chicken would be returned.

A few nights later, in the middle of the night, the penitent thief came to their door with the chicken in his hands.

I related this story not so much as an indication of their faith as to give the reader awareness of their financial circumstances compared to our own. Yet, there was no trace of a spirit of poverty in their rich, joyful lives.

I ascended the long, wide flight of stairs from the hotel lobby to the upper floor, where the rooms and bar and restaurant were located. The carpet was a bit frayed, the hallways dim, but the rooms were clean and bright.

Fatigue washed over me like a wave. I ran a bath and sank into its warmth to my neck, reveling in the luxury...my first bath in three and a half months of travel during which even a warm shower was not always a given.

By the time I had reluctantly climbed out, the water had grown chilly. In my robe, I laid down across the top of the bed. When I wakened from a deep, intense, almost painful, sleep it was dark. Friday night revelry had taken over the street below, music blaring, horns honking. The streets were full of groups of noisy celebrating pedestrians.

I found my way down the dim corridor to a swimming pool, closed for remodeling, then to the bar and to a restaurant, which was still open.

An Indian girl sat cross-legged on a banquet table along the wall, joking with a Melanesian girl who stood nearby. The restaurant was otherwise empty.

I glanced at the menu. Dinners were $6.00 to $8.00. The Indian girl took my order for fish and fries and went into the kitchen. Twenty minutes later, she brought my dinner and sat across the table from me, drinking tea.

"I'm Moonie," she said.

I welcomed the conversation as I began to realize how much I missed my new Fijian family. Dinner was delicious. I tried to remember where I had heard the name of the fish, walu. Yalu? Was it a corruption of spelling? Somewhere I had been told that yalu was the name for moray eel. Never mind. It was delicious.

Back in my room, I looked in my glossary. Walu: a kingfish. That made sense. "a lean, dry fish served as steak similar to salmon". I had eaten eke (octopus), ika mata (raw fish marinated in lime juice) and many nameless, unrecognizable things at the Maori's umukai and the Fijian lovo and the Indian's Feast of the Nine Days. The only thing I had seen eaten, but would not, was "spaghetti" on Rarotonga. In a certain brief season, a substance that looks exactly like its namesake is extruded from a sea creature and is eaten raw with great enthusiasm in the lagoon where it is found.

I slept soundly, comfortably, long. It seemed like no time at all before I was back in the dining room. Moonie greeted me enthusiastically and I was glad for her company. We talked over tea for some time before she asked me if I wanted breakfast. She was not only the waitress. She was also the cook. It was Saturday and I had nothing particular to do, so I stayed and talked, as there was no one else in the dining room.

Tom had asked if I would be going to Taveuni. He knew some property that was freehold and "for sale" and he wanted me to look at it. Taveuni, the Garden Island of Fiji. Why not? The young diver from California who had carried my notes from Rarotonga kept telling me not to miss Taveuni. The beauty was not limited to the reefs, he said. Kools. $8.00 a night. Nice people. Not fancy, but adequate. Taveuni had been the high point for him during several months in the South Pacific.

My guidebook said there was a road, a three-hour drive over the mountainous hump of Vanua Levu from Labasa to Savusavu on the south coast. The bus ran four times a day, it said, for $3.00 one way. Twice a week the ferry Ashika sailed from Savusavu to Taveuni. After considering the possibilities, I opted to go the easier route and fly. I inquired about the Sunflower Air Lines office.

Walking through the streets of Labasa, unlike Nadi, I saw no other white person, but passersby showed little curiosity or interest and I moved among them anonymously and quickly.

The flight to Taveuni would be $38. I also booked a flight for Friday from Taveuni back to Nadi for an additional $98. It seemed so long ago that I had left Pam and the children in Levuka with the promise that I would meet them in Nadi sometime before the flight we were to share to LAX on the 22nd of April. Just ten days distant.

I ambled along with the Saturday morning crowds, walking back from the airline office, relaxed now that my course was determined.

The street seemed like a social center, with groups gathered on street corners and in doorways, visiting. I stopped at the ANZ bank to get an advance in Fijian dollars on my Visa, not knowing what to expect on Taveuni where the map showed small villages, but nothing that seemed even remotely like a city.

I found Waibute waiting on the step when I returned to the Takia. He seemed like a treasure lost and recovered! I invited him to come up to the hotel and have lunch with me.

When we stopped in my room he removed his shoes at the door and sat cross-legged on the carpet ignoring the presence of furniture. I sat beside him and we talked for the first time, one on one.

"What is it like on the other side?" he asked.

How could I encapsulate the enormous differences between life on Vanua Levu and in the States. Where would I begin? My answer seemed vague, inadequate.

"Do black people and white people live together?"

Hard questions. Again, I gave him meaningless, evasive answers. Empty answers.

I showed him the small album I carried. There were photos of my tall, blonde Scandinavian son and his petite Vietnamese wife. Their beautiful children, more Oriental than Caucasian, would have looked quite at home on Tahiti. The other children were typical American mixtures, Irish, English, Navajo, Jewish, Scandinavian, German. But that still didn't answer his question, because at that time I hadn't plumbed the depth of it.

"I could get a job on the other side working on a farm," he ventured.

Instant panic! How could he think of leaving tribal land with security and position and independence? The drudgery of a farm laborer, a migrant, was something I could not begin to explain, so I went the other way around.

I spoke of the inherent wealth of their tribal land. Who in America owns 1,500 acres of prime farmland with no encumbrance of mortgage? And what price would be put on three pristine tropical islands situated in a lagoon so beautiful it defies description?

I had tasted tribal life where work, communally accomplished, seemed more like play. The tribe provided a net of security in mutual cooperation. The land itself provided wild pigs, coconuts, papaya, bananas, kumala, mangoes, all requiring little effort. Crabs were there to be gathered. There were abundant fish in the lagoon. They had all this, without selling ones time for pay, without mortgaging 30 years for shelter. In Fiji there was time for laughter and stories and worship unhindered by scheduled obligations and responsibilities. How could I put it in a balance that was fair and honest, that Buta would understand? My responses left him dangling and left me feeling helpless.

At Tubakula I had asked a man if Sigatoka was east or west. He looked at me blankly. "We don't know east and west." Was it that way for Waibute? That the only direction that matters was the sea and what lay beyond it on the other side?

I suggested that we go to the dining room for lunch. When he hesitated at the door, I said, "Should you put your shoes on?" It was an instinctive response from having lived in all those places where signs at the door said, "No shoes, no shirt, no service." Then I kicked myself for having said it. This was his country, his culture. For the first time in my travels I was the one caught in the frustrating cultural warp, not knowing what was appropriate.

In the dining room, I saw that Buta was fully as comfortable as when he was barefoot in the bush. He was a man caught between two worlds and more than equal to both of them.

I recommended the walu. The Melanesian waitress was a distant cousin of his from Lekutu and there was a flirtatious interaction between them.

After lunch I walked with him the short distance to the market. Tima was at the stall selling kumala. A glowing personality, she introduced me to the other market women. When I turned to leave, Buta said, "I will pick you up tomorrow for church."

I suggested 8:00 so we could have breakfast first. I took a long walk through the city, feeling unsettled and alone for the first time in my travels, like I was leaving with something unfinished.

At dinner, Moonie and Buta's cousin sat with me. I asked the girl from Lekutu whether the soil in that area had been checked for mineral content. I told her that it seemed so red, like the areas in Minnesota with iron mines. I also mentioned the color of the leaves, wondering if that was an indication of copper in the soil.

She said that sometimes men have come to dig holes in the bush checking about this.

I asked her if she thought this was good or bad. She said, "Sometimes it's good because wild pigs fall into the holes when the boys are chasing them." Then she added, "But sometimes it's bad because the boys fall into the holes."

Leave it alone, I thought, as I imagined how mining could savage their land.

As I was finishing dinner, four Australians came in from the bar. They were bricklayers who were working on a lengthy construction contract at the sugar mill. In two weeks they would be going home. Ken, about fifty, had an outrageously funny sense of humor. George, about the same age, was more conservative. "Specs" and Marty were younger. Marty left the dining room to call his wife and he returned moody and depressed. His young wife, five months pregnant, had been crying on the phone and he wanted to go home. Ken raced into the kitchen and carried Moonie over one shoulder, laughing and protesting, back into the dining room where he ordered another round of beers.

Except for a nun I saw one day on the street, they were the only white people I saw while I was in Labasa.

I awakened early, dressed and began waiting for Waibute. 8:30 passed, a quarter to 9:00. I left a note on the door saying that I had gone to the dining room, then wondered if he reads English, which was, after all, his second language. Throughout breakfast I wondered if I had done something to hurt him...asking about his shoes? Or had I misunderstood? In my confusion, I realized how important they all had become to me so quickly. I returned to my room.

Suddenly, he was there at the door. I thought, what a kind, handsome man he is, and for a fleeting moment I wished there were not so many years between us.

I left the door open. This time he sat on the bed and I sat on the bed across from him. We talked again about "the other side", but there was no way I could explain the difficulties of life in the West that too often outweigh the pleasures...with a climate so rigorous that it requires sturdy houses and clothing for four seasons. A life so scattered and demanding that cars have become a necessity. Where lawsuits are so prevalent that insurance is a prerequisite. And everywhere, the temptation is fed by advertising to acquire things that soon begin to own us. He made me look at my culture, my life, through an unfamiliar lens and nothing has ever been the same.

It was almost time for church, so we went outside. Tima was there, at the curb, in an old car driven by an Indian. In the back seat, a young woman with a baby and two Indian girls, all organdy and ribbons, made room for me. Waibute was left on the curb and I was carried away as if by a torrent of flood which swept me up. I asked helplessly if Waibute was coming and Tima said, "He will be coming along later." I watched in the rear view mirror as the image of Waibute, still standing by the curb, still watching us drive away, receded in the distance.

At the edge of the city, a few miles away, we stopped at an Assemblies of God Church. The Indian man who had driven us wore a smart Western business suit and seemed to be a deacon or pastor of the small church.

I sat beside Tima and her daughter as the congregation drifted in. I was the only European and Tima and her daughter were the only Melanesian Fijians.

Through the open windows I watched groups of sandal-clad Fijian men in sulus and dress shirts, carrying Bibles, walk past this church and on to another somewhere.

I could have been in a Hindu temple until the sermon began. The dress, the music, the marigolds, were all very Indian, but as the sermon began I knew that these were fundamental, born-again, Christians.

The children were gathered outside after church under some great overhanging trees.

They sat on a double row of benches set in a semicircle. My chair was put before them and I was asked to speak to them. I felt inadequate and totally unprepared, an imposter, half distracted, as I looked down the road on which Waibute should have come.

We went to Tima's home for lunch. It was a Western house of brick that would have easily fit in any modest city suburb in the States.

The Indian man and I sat rather stiffly trying to make conversation while Tima and her daughter prepared lunch. The children ran to their home across the street and returned with their Mom who said it was time for their lunch. Just then Tima announced that lunch was ready. I sensed a conflict for his presence based on the fact that I was there and to fix the awkward situation, jokingly, I sent him home with his wife.

The table in the dining room was formally set. It was a banquet, with a place set for the man who had just left and another empty chair for Waibute.

Lunch included lamb shanks in lolo, curried crab, taro, kumala, jello and canned pears for desert. I saw the expense and effort that had gone into this special lunch. I hadn't understood.

It was very hot, but my feeling of uneasiness contributed to my discomfort as I felt that I was committing one social faux pas after another.

After lunch, her daughter cleared the plates and gathered the mass of food that was left over. Tima asked me to come and meet her other daughter. We went into a room beyond the kitchen. There, in a crib, lying in a fetal position as helpless as a baby was a twenty four year old woman. My heart broke for this gentle, cheerful woman who had lovingly borne so great a burden for so long.

Tima's husband had started the church we attended. When he died of a heart attack, she would have chosen to go back to their tribal land but for the care of her youngest daughter, so she was carrying on in the church and in the market, a blessing to everyone she meets.

We returned to the living room for tea. It was late afternoon when I walked back to the hotel.

My sleep was restless. I awakened early, bothered that I had not seen Buta again on Sunday. The parting was too sudden, without explanation or good-by and I felt that I must try to see him again.

My flight was scheduled to leave about 11:00, so I wrote a note to him and put it in an envelope with some orange seeds I saved from the grove grown from his mother's trees. I encouraged him to begin the groves again, to make use of the land and prosper there.

Because of the holiday, the early morning streets were deserted. I walked in the direction of Tima's house, but had not paid attention when I rode there on Sunday. I missed the street again and again. I asked passersby, "Do you know a Fijian woman named Tima?" Each time the response was negative as I turned down one street after another.

The sun was getting high when I was forced to give it up. I had met a Fijian man and asked, "Do you know Waibute?" He smiled and said, "Yes." I handed him the envelope and said, "Will you please give him this?"

When I reached Nasekula Road, the main street, it had been cordoned off. A smartly uniformed policeman stood guard. His uniform was a navy blue shirt, white sulu with sharply serrated hemline, red cummerbund and sandals.

The way back to my hotel seemed blocked. It was the celebration of victory in an international sports tournament, the Rugby 7 National Holiday. Uniformed school children and every club and organization in Labasa were marching at attention in parade dress. I hurried down the street along the parade route toward the Takia, which was on the other side of the parade.

Suddenly, there was Waibute! I couldn't conceal my surprise and delight as I told him I had been looking for Tima's house so I could say good-bye to him.

When we got to the hotel, Moonie was in the lobby waiting for me. They both came up to my room to keep me company while I packed.

"Next year," she said firmly, "you will come and I will travel to New Zealand with you."

Next year seemed too far away for me to think about, but I told her, "Maybe."

They waited with me on the street and walked me to the cab. I gave Moonie a hug, took Waibute's hand in both of mine and reached up to kiss his cheek.

"Isa, Buta. Isalei, my friend."

Tom, Tina, and Waibute at morning prayer, Vanua Levu, Fiji

Cottages at Tubakula

Chapter Twenty

Somosomo

The airport is a $6.00, twenty-minute cab ride from Labasa. We passed through cane fields from the edge of town over country roads in spectacularly beautiful foothills and valleys.

The airport consisted of a group of small buildings with a covered, open lounge beside grassy runways.

A few passengers had gathered when a cab arrived carrying three well-dressed Melanesian businessmen. They had what I have come to recognize as chiefly bearing.

The younger man began conversation with the usual questions, which, in Fiji, always quickly got around to "Where is your husband?" and "How old are you?" with the predictable responses. They seemed highly distressed to see an older woman traveling alone, unprotected.

The young man said, pointing to one of his companions who was checking luggage, "His name is Tui. He is a chief."

Tui and the other man joined us. Tui apologized that he had not known that I was going to Somosomo.

"I would have arranged a home for you to stay in," he said.

The Sunflower Airlines plane had 18 seats. The young Melanesian steward who buckled me in asked where I am from. He said that he had been in Los Angeles last week on his way home from Germany.

We rose above green, cultivated slopes with the sea behind us, and rugged mountains ahead. Fifteen minutes into flight clouds shrouded the mountains and obscured the dense rain forest below us. Responding to air currents, the plane sideslipped a bit, then held steady. Ridge after ridge of mountains, with occasional cultivated plots, passed beneath us with grassy meadows in the valleys. Then, just outside my window, at our wingtip, a rock mountain towered above the plane.

Green lower slopes sheltered small villages where palm trees lined the shores. From the air it seemed like so much land and so few people. We reached the sea again, but a land mass lay close beyond, defined by a very irregular coastline. The massive bulk of the island wrapped around a deeply indented bay, which nearly split the island.

As we passed between parallel ridges, turbulence played with our small plane. Suddenly, across the last ridge, the sea spread before us with a smorgasbord of islands on the horizon in every direction. Shining ripples barely ruffled the calm cobalt blue sea below us. In landing mode, we crossed the beach and overflew crops in neat rows, skimmed treetops and settled onto the narrow strip of macadam.

I felt the confusion of landing in a strange place. I had come to Taveuni on an impulse and had no clear idea where I should stay. From the air I had observed small villages scattered along the coast, but no sign of any commercial center.

The manager of a lodge approached me, but hearing the rates, I apologized and told her that I am traveling budget.

Sukh, a taxi driver who overheard me, suggested Kool's. It had been recommended. I had circled it in my *Lonely Planet* guide, so I felt comfortable with that.

Somosomo is an eleven mile drive from Matei Airstrip over an unsealed road that leads through wildly beautiful countryside. Precipitous cliffs plunge to the sea as the narrow strip of road hangs precariously on the edge.

In some places we passed through gently rolling land with small villages and fields of taro and bananas. We crossed a fast running stream where a dozen women stood washing clothes on rocks.

Kool's is on the far side of Somosomo. Anil, a neat, shy Indian teenager showed me two available rooms. There were six units in a row in a single building constructed of corrugated metal painted a saffron shade of gold. The first room he showed me, in the middle of the row, was $8. It had a single window on the back wall looking at dense bushes, which separated Kool's from a too-close neighbor's house. I chose the unit closest their house, bright and airy, with windows on three sides for $13.20 including tax.

Returning to the cab for my duffles, I paid the $10 fare, then settled into my room. The walls, painted bright blue, were plywood with slats trimming joints. A green cotton spread covered the bare mattress, with curtains and pillow covers of matching material. A mosquito net hung above the bed in voluminous, dusty folds, a necessary protection where windows are not screened. A kerosene lantern was on the dresser even though a single bare electric light bulb hung from the ceiling.

Chitra appeared at the door, an Indian woman in a pretty pink Western-style cotton housedress. During the following days I noticed how blended the cultures seemed to be on Taveuni where there was an easier mix of Europeans, Indians and indigenous Fijians.

She showed me the communal bath in a separate corrugated building across a coral-gravel, covered patio from my door. Three doors led to "his," "hers," and a concrete floored shower room where there was no pretense at anything but cold shower utility. In the third building beside the bath, a few feet away, three doors opened into a double, connected communal kitchen. Four legs of the food cabinet were set in dishes of water to discourage ants.

I followed Chitra into the office to register and paid the four nights lodging in Fijian dollars, which would have been impossible to obtain on Taveuni where banking is limited. Chitra became my guide, cook and advisor in the days that followed, which more than made up for the stark simplicity of the lodging.

I shopped for basic groceries across the street at Kaba's Supermarket. While I was putting the groceries away, Chitra came to tell me that she and her husband and son were going to their garden plot and would pass the Garden Island Resort which was owned by an American woman. Would I like to ride along?

Kulle also had a cab and was at the airport when I arrived. Chitra said he and Sukh are friends as well as rivals for the limited cab fares on the island.

Although it seemed worlds away from Labasa, the holiday that had brought life to a rowdy standstill there permeated life on Taveuni as well. We passed families picnicking and fishing and playing like families everywhere on a holiday.

In less than two miles, we pulled into the Garden Island Resort. It was modern and beautifully landscaped and seemed to exist in utter contradiction to its wild setting.

As a travel agent, Lela Prym had been coming to Taveuni on holiday for six years. In the 1988-89 Christmas season she learned that the resort, part of the Castaway Group, was in receivership in the bank's possession, a victim of the plunge in tourism during and after the 1987 coup.

She and a partner decided to buy it although 50% local ownership was required. It took four months to acquire it. They took possession of it in August, 1989 and she brought into management all the savvy of the former owner of a Washington D.C. travel agency.

The sea view from the lounge, dining room and poolside focused on Korolevu Island. The small offshore island had spectacular snorkeling and an inviting sand beach to compensate for the mostly rocky shoreline of Taveuni. The $10 round trip by hotel launch provided an hour or all day on an island all your own.

Just 20 minutes away by boat, Rainbow Reef was reputed to be one of the prettiest underwater gardens of coral in Fiji.

Lunch was lavish by a backpacker's standard. I had grilled walu, fries, banana cake and ice cream, topped off with coffee grown on Taveuni.

In spite of the moderately upscale atmosphere Lela and the staff made me feel completely at home. Reluctantly, I left the friendly comfort of the Garden Island Resort and turned back down the road toward Somosomo. I passed a large wharf where a government gunboat was docked; passed a coffee plantation, a copra shed, picnicking families, a lone fisherman. A boy, carrying a young sibling shoulder high, smiled shyly.

There were boys in groups returning from swimming, men carrying bags of fish from the sea, nets over their shoulder, a man with a sele levu in one hand balanced a bunch of bananas on his shoulder with the other.

I had forgotten, again, the serious and repeated admonitions against walking alone in Fiji.

Suddenly there were footsteps pounding behind me, coming up alarmingly fast. I whirled around expecting an assailant. Instead, I saw a smiling young American wearing a hat with the University of Minnesota emblem.

"I'm from Minnesota, too!" I exclaimed. His unbelief was palpable. "Pequot. Pequot Lakes." I continued.

"You are from Minnesota!"

His amazed response was understandable. If distance can be measured by culture, climate, life-style, we were light years from Minnesota.

Bob had arrived in November to do a Peace Corps stint as a teacher. He had been assigned to one of eleven government high schools where pupils coming from distant islands were boarded. He lived and taught at Bucalevu Village.

As we walked into Somosomo I asked if he knew that an American woman owns a resort just a mile and half down the road from his village. His amazed response made me realize the degree of his isolation.

"No," he said, "I haven't been away from the school in five months except to run into Somosomo for a soda occasionally."

It was partly a matter of budget, living on a Peace Corps stipend. But I guessed that it was more than that. Perhaps it was the enveloping strangeness of the culture which prevailed on Taveuni. Isolated pockets of resort development were grafted improbably onto the traditional tribal society. There was no urban center except for Somosomo, a chiefly village with a history of power.

"Would you like to go to dinner tomorrow night at the resort? I will introduce you to Lela."

He would be finished with school at 3:30. When I told him I would walk to the village to meet him, he showed me a fork in the road by a small store.

"If you take this road you can avoid going through the village. It's a bit farther."

Scraps of information under etiquette in my guidebook came to mind. One does not show up in a Fijian village uninvited. A sevusevu is first offered the chief and his permission and protection is sought.

We set the time and place of tomorrow's meeting. I stopped at Kool's while he continued on to Kaba's store. The name Kool's comes from Harnam Singh's nickname, Kulle. Kool's had been apartments owned by his parents until a few years ago when they were adapted by Chitra and Harnam to serve transient budget travelers.

Labasa. Was it just this morning? It seemed a very long time ago. I put my AYH sleep sheet on the bed, covering the pillow with the flap and crawled into it.

In the twilight of half sleep I remembered the things the missionaries had written about Somosomo and their midnight flight from its terrors. The rhythmic double beat of ta bili was all around me. Thud THUD Thud THUD. It filled the late afternoon with echoes from the past, lending darkness, a depressing aura of mystery I had not felt on the other islands. I fell into a hot, restless sleep with the stereophonic sound of iron rods pounding kava roots into powder for yaqona drinking around dozens of tanoa throughout the village.

I awakened with a start. The diesel generator shuddered into life at 7:00 and lights turned on in every corner of Kool's compound. I lay there for a minute to get my bearings; then to escape the overhead glare of the ceiling bulb and to get in touch with the reality of this new place, I gathered my soap and towel, showered, dressed and went into the kitchen to make a cup of tea.

All the lights throughout the compound were connected directly to the generator without the benefit of switches to make the light optional.

A traveler was finishing a plate of rice and curry at one of our communal tables. He said Chitra would prepare dinner for $3.00 if an order was placed by 2:00 p.m.

I had wondered about the "Beware of the Dog" sign on the front gate. A nondescript brown and white spotted dog came to wag his welcome. With the smallest encouragement he climbed on my lap with licks and wiggles. The older dog, Scooby-Do, less demonstrative, seemed no greater menace. Kitty completed the family, which quickly enfolded the guests as part of it.

With my tea, I sampled one of the papayas left on the bench outside the kitchen door for guest's free use.

At 9:00 Kulle came out to tell us that at 9:30 the generator would be turned off. He placed a kerosene lantern on the table and in the dimmer light we continued our conversation. Taveuni had no general electric supply, so expensive imported petrol was used sparingly for the few privately installed and maintained generators.

My long, restless late afternoon nap made sleep come slowly. I awakened at 5:30 to the sound of the lali from the Methodist church and was waiting for dawn's light when Kulle came at 6:30 to unlock the kitchen.

My neighbors were stirring. Their shrill conversations in Hindi caused a feeling of strangeness to creep over me again. Gloom and isolation are twin specters which stalk the lone traveler. It is a mood not to be played with, one I never allowed my self, so I quickly showered and walked to the Garden Island Resort for breakfast.

The road around the rim of Taveuni was as beautiful as any I had seen. The second time, with predictable turns and familiar scenes, the walk to the Garden Island Resort seemed shorter.

The aroma of coffee and bacon, mingled with fresh fruits, met me. I settled into the dining room, grateful that this much of the West had crept into this island, beauty on beauty, like an exquisite hybrid grafted onto a strong native root.

Lela entered the dining room, smiled, and brought her coffee to my table. She had compiled a comprehensive five-page list of suggested scenic trips, tours, tourist activities and cultural experiences. Unlike the Coral Coast of Viti Levu, which bombards the visitor with commercial, slickly packaged tours, on Taveuni you must search them out. The bonus is a sense of discovery without the hype and tourist hordes.

Buoma Falls...a perfect half or full day trip. With guide, taxi and village fee, $55, less if shared, an hours drive. I made a mental note to do that the next day.

On Lela's list were Warrior Burial Cave, bird-watching at Des Voeux Peak, Lake Tagimaucia with its exquisite flower of that name which myths claim can grow nowhere else; the Blowhole at Navakau, literally at the end of the road. Plantations and beaches and the sign at Waiyevo marking the International Dateline where you can stand with one foot in yesterday. For avid hikers there was the Tobu Vei Tui Falls or Waitavala Waterslide. I was beginning to wish I had more time on Taveuni.

For history buffs, Wairiki Mission had a story to tell of the tide-turning defeat of thousands of attacking Tongans. The French missionary priest who advised Taveuni's warriors on fighting strategy, was rewarded by the grateful Fijians who built the large mission.

Lela promised that Bob could come to use the pool anytime. She said, perhaps a little wistfully, that she could understand his feelings of isolation, which can be part of living so far from home.

The coffee plantation was not on her list, but she thought I might find it interesting. Her Fijian husband, Waqa (pronounced Wonga) managed the project, Delaiweni Estates. She thought he might be at another plantation, but I could talk to Peter, his assistant, or Philo, his secretary. She called to make a 10:30 appointment for me.

As I left, she mentioned another American lady living just beyond Matei Airstrip. Her name was Audrey.

It was a hot, dusty walk, which seemed more than a mile and half and took me longer than I expected. I turned in at the sign, which indicated that the plantation is owned by the Carpenters of Australia.

The road leading into the Plantation passed a residence on the left, turned sharply and narrowed, passed another residence on the right, then led up a steep hill between head high coffee bushes in bloom. I saw no one around. Past a large barn-like factory where coffee beans were processed, I continued uphill to a level area where coffee beans were lying in large flats for sun drying. Vats and machinery for roasting beans told me that a lot of effort lies between the bush and neat cans of vacuum-sealed ground roast in the store.

There seemed to be no one in the buildings on the highest level so I walked back down to the factory. A man there told me that the first residence I passed was the office.

By then, I was quite late for my appointment. Philo brought me to Peter Vakaoqotabua who provided a wealth of information on coffee from production to marketing with the help of wall murals depicting each phase of growth and processing.

There were four divisions for production in various parts of the island. They grew two strains of Arabica coffee...Robusta from New Guinea and the Ivory Coast of Africa and Catura, which is a smaller plant in two of the divisions.

In the beginning they had problems with twig borers and cherry borers, but the healthy acreages of bushes gave clear indication that those problems have been solved.

The coffee cherry is picked when red. A machine called a pulper removes the red skin and the bean breaks in half. The beans ferment in a vat for 36 hours; then go into a hot air dryer for four hours. The drying is finished on large plastic sheets in the sun. A small machine tests the beans, which should register 7% moisture. The huller takes off the thin skin. The next process mechanically separates and grades the beans which are classified into four grades AA; A-1; A-2; A-3 and triage, which are broken pieces, usually thrown away.

Except for the amount used for domestic consumption, the majority of the product was exported to Australia. Production can be 100 tons, but varied because of cultivation schedules. Every six years, on a portion of the plantation, the plants are stumped; that is, cut down to 12" to encourage new growth.

The climate on Taveuni is consistent and hillsides provide necessary drainage. Mountain climate is not prerequisite for coffee production. You can successfully plant coffee down to sea level. Chemical herbicides are used to control weeds. In January, Catura is picked, Robusta in June and July.

I will forever have a greater appreciation for a fine cup of coffee!

Fishing village at Malevu, Fiji. Next to Tubakula

Fijian Policeman in full uniform at Lambasa, Vanua Levu

Chapter Twenty-One

The School at Bucalevu

By 2:30 I began walking back to Bucalevu Village to meet Bob. I remembered that he had cautioned me to turn off the main road between two blue buildings, one of them a small store. That road would lead me directly to the school.

Suddenly, when they learned that I was looking for the American Peace Corps teacher, seven children of assorted sizes, who volunteered to be my guides, surrounded me. The boys wore tan shorts and white shirts. The girls were dressed in lavender uniforms. Anna Kinoi said that the father of Kilimo, the youngest boy in the group, was Principal of the school where Bob teaches and he would take me all the way.

Although I could see the two blue landmark buildings, the children turned down a trail, which led through a dense forest and up a steep hill. Suddenly we were at the edge of the village, a scattered cluster of about 50 houses. Curious eyes followed me, hostile eyes. We walked directly through the village past a group of men working on a rusty old truck, past cooking fires, past other groups of men and women going about their daily chores. The deeper into the village we went, the closer the houses were to the path. I could feel the resentment; the anger directed toward me for rudely intruding into their village. I knew that I was going where I should not be, where I would not have dared to go alone.

The village was built on a steep incline up from the coast. The elevation afforded a sweeping view of the sea. Buildings and homes seemed randomly scattered. The rambling path brought us to the center of the village, to the women's meetinghouse. I looked through the open doorway where about twenty women, barefoot, in western style blouses and skirts or dresses were sitting on mats. In the center, a dozen women were busy with the design of a huge tapa. Tapa is a cloth made by beating the fibrous damp pulp of the inner bark of the paper mulberry tree with little wooden clubs. When it is beaten into a large piece of thin cloth a traditional design is made with stencils cut in banana leaves. Dyes are made from lampblack mixed with coconut oil and reddish earth. Tapa is used in ceremony. It is worn by both the bride and groom in marriage or to wrap a body for burial. It is a traditional gift sometimes used for wall hangings. It is arduously made and very expensive.

Boldly, I asked if I could take their picture and I was surprised at their enthusiastic response as they moved closer to the center so they could all get into the camera's view, which took two frames because of the size of the group.

The women's house, or community center, had glass louvered windows and a metal roof with pandanus floor mats.

Gradually, Ana Kinoi and the others drifted off along paths leading to their individual homes. With Kilimo's guidance, I found Bob at a staff meeting from which he excused himself.

The school is very impressive with about 200 boys in attendance. Two thirds of the students were boarders from other islands. The school included a one hundred ten acre farm. Mornings and afternoons the boys work on the farm. Their food staples were dalo (taro) and casaba. They had a dairy farm where cows were milked by hand. Once a week a pig from their piggery was butchered to feed the students.

The principal's home was large and looked quite modern in stark contrast to the traditional thatched bure with a high ridgepole, which was just down the hill beside the classrooms.

Bob's house was a small compromise between the two. He had a kitchen and combined sleeping-living room. Behind them was an empty room. I suggested that he sweep the dirt floor and put down dried coconut leaves and a pandanus mat as Salote had done. The sasa covers the dirt floor and cushions the mat, making it more comfortable for sitting and lying upon.

His cold shower was in a separate shed-like building outside the house. A houseboy delivered a quart of fresh milk to Bob each morning.

After showing me the school and introducing me to some of the students, we walked down the steep hill on the longer road that avoids passing through the village. At the main road we saw a bus and hurried to catch it.

The launch to Korolevu Island had quit running at 4:00, so we weren't able to go snorkeling. We settled into the dining room and began a conversation that lasted until they were ready to close the dining room at 10:00.

At the next table there was a couple from Wyoming with two small children. They lived in Suva where he taught at the main campus of the University of the South Pacific. University students in Suva come from islands throughout both Polynesia and Melanesia. It has several branches throughout the islands including Samoa and Rarotonga. With so much in common, their conversation was intense and ended with an exchange of addresses and invitations to visit.

"This is the first time in five months I have left the village at night." Bob confided. "My whole life has been the school and the children."

"Did you know that another American lives on the island?" I asked.

He seemed surprised. I told him about Audrey and determined to meet her the next day and let Buoma Falls wait.

"She makes cookies which she sells at the airport."

"I wonder if she makes chocolate chip cookies?" he said wistfully.

Throughout dinner, live music from the adjoining bar added to the pleasure of the evening. The string combo, with outstanding vocalists, had begun their evening's performance with a set of hymns. Like so many island musical instruments, the bass was homemade of a big box for resonance with a long, tautly stringed stick, giving a very professional sound.

Because of the ethnic tensions, few taxis ran after "lights out", so we arranged to take the employee's van home.

After closing the dining room, the tanoa was brought out, yaqona mixed and bilo after bilo passed around. From then on the night and the music belonged to them, jamming just for the fun of it.

The sound of the van rumbling past sleeping dormitories seemed magnified by the silence. We dropped Bob off and I felt like a naughty teenager coming past Chitra and Kulle's window. While I fumbled with the gate in the dark, I was grateful that the dogs met me with silent tail wags.

In the morning I rode with Kulle to the airport for $1.00. He routinely went to meet the morning plane looking for possible guests. I went simply to meet Audrey. Kulle pointed to a path beyond the airstrip, which went into the jungle.

"She will be coming," he said. Then in answer to my doubtful look, he assured me, repeating with emphasis, "She will be coming."

Audrey Brown had grown to be a legend on Taveuni. On the appointed path, she came sweeping out of the jungle carrying a large basket-tray full of bags of homemade cookies and candied nuts. Wearing a pink Indian gauze dress with matching enamel earrings, she exuded a simple elegance that was magnetic. I walked home with her and before we arrived at her house we were no longer strangers.

From California, she came to Taveuni first in 1983 when her brother had found property on the island. She and her husband returned home nursing a desire to return. It seemed to them an idyllic place to retire. Four years later they moved to Taveuni and began building their unusual home which could grace the pages of any House Beautiful Magazine.

Her home consisted of two spacious hexagons joined by a long, airy dining room. It had dividers that lend some privacy and definition, but no walls. The lavish use of Fijian dakua wood was impressive...four inch tongue-in-groove. Every wall had great expanses of arched louvered-glass windows to maximize the garden and sea views.

The house stretched across a low ridge overlooking the road and, beyond the road, a grassy field of palms just fifteen meters from the sea. The Village of Naselesele owned three small rocky offshore islands. Village goats were kept on the islands where they survived on the sparse vegetation and natural rainfall.

On the slope from the ridge to the road, a garden of hibiscus and frangipani, ginger and Lady Fletchers lend lavish color and fragrance. The deck, which wrapped the sea view side of the house, was a shady haven where Audrey served an extraordinary dessert smorgasbord.

Her success was born of an instinct for survival when her husband went back to California on business and didn't return. She had grown to love Taveuni, but needed an income, so she began baking cakes for the resorts to serve their guests.

Nothing is easy on Taveuni. A permit to bake and a hawker's license were required. The first cake she took to the Garden Island Resort on an open island bus in the rain. The icing was still so soft there was no way to cover the cake. The next two she took to Maravu Plantation Resort in two taxi trips because she had to hold them on her lap during transport. Joe Kloss, another expatriate from California, was her third customer for guests of the pricey Qamea Beach Hotel. Jo's shopper came to Taveuni on Tuesdays. After picking up the cake she took a taxi from Audrey's to the boat dock near Somosomo for the twenty five minute launch trip to the island resort. When you get away from the simple traditional life-style in those islands everything from electricity to water to acquisition of supplies and transport becomes complex.

From this beginning, Audrey started baking cookies. Referring to her daily walk to the airport to sell cookies, she said, "No one else can know you're a bowlful of jelly on the inside." Her manner and smile reflects confidence she had not yet begun to feel. "Some days I still wake up and think that I cannot face the people at the airport again...that I can't face the rejection if no one buys my cookies."

We talked about the feelings we had in common, about the painful insecurity inherent in finding yourself cast adrift, alone, past 60.

"In the Fijian language," she told me, "there is no word for alone."

Language is the mirror of any culture. That explained the reactions I had experienced from Fijians when they learned that I was traveling alone...anxiety, despair, pity...and when they learned that I was over 60, "Ahweee!" with the hand to head gesture that indicated amazement in addition to all of the above.

She explained that life is communal in the village. Their circle of relationship and interaction is small. A newly married woman coming to her husband's village may not go a mile away to shop, may not even move freely about the village.

When I mentioned how lucky she was to be so near a village, she said that in the four years she had lived there she had been to the village only once when she was invited to a wedding. For the wedding they built a lovo and killed a beast (cow). Weddings are held in the bride's village and the guests stay in the bride's compound four or five days. I remembered Barbara's story about the groom's family sitting outside the bridal curtain waiting for four days until the marriage was consummated. I wondered if that was an exception or a common part of the union.

The bride wears a masi top and slim masi skirt. The sulu the groom wears is also masi, but fuller. The bride's hair is sprinkled with sandalwood dust for fragrance and cosmetic appeal.

I asked Audrey about her immigration status. She said that her residency was good for three years. To obtain residency status there were three requirements: 1) You must be able to pass a physical exam. 2) You must be able to prove income. A house in another country is considered as income. Mortgage, if any, was not deducted. 3) You must have no police record. A $100 fee was required to process residency. For renewal she had to fill out a form declaring that things were the same. She had to go to Suva to file, although sometimes it could be taken care of by mail.

Visitors were allowed to stay up to six months, having their passport stamped each month. After six months the applicant was required to leave the country for at least 24 hours so there was an exit and entry stamp on their passport.

Audrey's delicious dessert smorgasbord consisted of fresh island coffee, iced tea, orange juice or lemonade from her groves served in a tall pitcher. She served two varieties of cookies, which she called, New Zealand style, biscuits. They might be chocolate chunk or chocolate filled coconut or sesame seed/coconut/almond. You could choose fudge cake topped with a kahlua truffle or homemade lime tarts. The limes were also fresh from her trees.

The reef was distant, creating a broad lagoon. The beach was golden sand with a clean lagoon bottom and clear water. Giant turtles swam there and dolphins came to play. Beyond the reef, whales could sometimes be seen.

Audrey Brown had the soul of a pioneer. She sent me off with a delightfully satisfied sweet tooth and the feeling that I would love to have this remarkable woman as a friend.

Chapter Twenty-Two

Dive Taveuni

I walked back down the road along the sea, retracing our steps, but kept to the road rather than turning onto the trail, which led to the airport. The road climbed gradually and I lost the sea view, as it turned a bit inland to avoid rocky headlands.

I had heard of Ric Cammick from several travelers I met on Rarotonga, but it was his wife, Do, who answered my knock at the door and welcomed me. I slipped off my shoes at the door and to my acute embarrassment realized that road dust mixed with sweat had become mud. I asked Do if I could rinse my feet somewhere. Her easy answer was nonchalant. "Just step into the shells." By the door there were two giant clamshells, foot-size, side by side, with a water tap that solved the problem that was apparently not unique with me.

She was in the midst of an important interview and I had arrived unannounced. She poured me a glass of iced lemonade and handed me a copy of a recently published article from a New Zealand magazine about the beginnings of Dive Taveuni.

Do was five months pregnant when she and Ric moved from Auckland in 1974. Their home was high on a bluff above Somosomo Strait. It overlooks a vast rainforest and coconut plantation on the broad slope running down to the sea.

For seven years after arriving on Taveuni they had no source of water except run off of rain from their small corrugated iron roof. Three times a week Do drove fourteen and a half kilometers to do their laundry with the village women on the rocks in the stream at Somosomo.

At first they were inundated with friends and friends of friends who wanted to dive. So Dive Taveuni grew from its simple beginnings into a first class dive resort with modern accommodations.

As close as the sea seems, it is a twenty four kilometer drive over the rough, unsealed road to the wharf where Ric's dive boat is kept. This takes a heavy toll on the truck and much of his time is consumed by maintenance of the truck and their moody generator. So don't call it Paradise! But Ric is a man doing what he loves. Over and over again I had heard that he is the best diver in the South Pacific.

The article stated that once he discovered Rainbow Reef and the White Wall he was hooked. The compelling appeal of diving is the adventure as well as the beauty.

Leonard Wibberly (*Fiji-Islands of the Dawn*) described his experience diving: *The sunlight strikes down from above, illuminating the top of the coral outcrops, shedding light like a cascade of satin down the side of the reef, and leaving the underparts in dark and nervous shadows. There is the sense of being watched...the desire to look behind and below and above you for the watchers. They are all around, silent, coldly observant and invisible.*

The most difficult thing for Do was separation from their two sons when they were in New Zealand attending school.

I asked them the question I always put to expatriates, "Would you have done it differently?"

I have always gotten the same answer, emphatically and without hesitation, "Never!"

It was much further than I expected to Valentine's Campground across the road from Prince Charles Beach. Tom's uncle, who had put the freehold property up for sale, owned the campground. It was eleven acres, partly low ground with palm-covered slopes on the hills behind the coastal plain. The beach was adequate, the best on the island, but small, with coral outcroppings. Beaches are not the main attraction of Taveuni. The gardens and rainforests, waterfalls, reefs and diving are the focus of tourism.

I began to realize that it was a long way back to Somosomo and the eleven o'clock bus must have passed long ago.

It was the second time that Paula in his blue taxi came along and rescued me. When he stopped, knowing that he was returning to Somosomo empty from the Airport, I asked, "A dollar?" Of course, he knew that I was desperate, but he smiled and I climbed in to ride back to Kool's. He knew what I did not...that on Wednesday there is no afternoon bus. He could have charged me anything! (Paula-Bale, Box 4, Taveuni, Fiji Islands).

Both Chitra and Lela had told me about the falls at Buoma.

Chitra said, "Iona, you must see Buoma Falls," and although Kulle runs a taxi, she added, "You can take the bus in the morning from Somosomo." On Taveuni I never encountered any of the greed and harsh competition that usually blossoms with the growth of tourism.

As I snuggled into my sleep sack for a nap, I thought, Tomorrow. Mataka. Mataka is the essence of Fijian life, a more relaxed version of manana. I think it has evolved as a necessity in the torpor of tropical summer.

I awakened slowly from my nap to the sound of school children laughing as they walked past on the road. Quickly, I gathered three bags of cookies which I had purchased from Audrey and began the walk to Bukalevu. This time I was engulfed by a larger group of children, but somehow I belonged to Kilimo. The glances were both less curious and less hostile as we hurried through the village. Bob was in a teacher's meeting, so we talked briefly as I handed him his cookies.

"Chocolate chip?" he asked, with child's eyes, sparkling.

The letter he wrote to me in May was in contrast to our conversation a month before when he expressed his doubts about being able to continue because of his feelings of isolation. He had returned from term break, which he had spent with other Peace Corps volunteers immersed in traditional Fijian culture in a village on Viti Levu. After a few days in Suva, he wrote, "I was happy to get back to my own house, bed and life-style. I realized how much this is my home now."

Several other volunteers had come to Taveuni for the second week of break. They had hung out together doing touristy things, going to Buoma Falls and snorkeling off Korolevu Island. He said two of the volunteers had gone diving and were very impressed.

"I just finished talking to another American tourist from Wisconsin," he wrote, "who confirmed that the quality of diving is better than the Great Barrier Reef." He added that he has a new sense of appreciation for Taveuni after seeing it through the eyes of tourists.

An alarming letter from Bob in March, 1992, told of a serious accident with his lantern fuel the preceding October. He had been flown, by the Peace Corps, to Hawaii for treatment of second and third degree burns. After nearly a month in Hawaii, he returned to Taveuni for a short time before being transferred to an Indian school near Pacific Harbor on the Coral Coast west of Suva. He added enthusiastically, "I love the food, like the kids, have a great house and the staff is friendly." He referred to the joy of living a near-normal life with electricity and indoor plumbing. But he appreciated the beauty of Taveuni and the more complete Fijian experience he has had having also lived in a Melanesian village.

Chitra's rice and curry made a delicious dinner. I shared the table with several other travelers who had by then filled all the rooms. There were Canadians, Europeans and an Aussie, but seldom other Americans in "bottom end" accommodations.

Chitra told me that the bus would leave Somosomo station between Kool's and Kaba's at nine o'clock or a few minutes before.

We rolled through Somosomo, around the sharp corner over the stream where Do had joined the village women washing their clothes. The fare to Buoma Falls was $1.85. The ride was worth the price; the waterfall was a bonus.

The incoming tide was churning on the rocks below the narrow road. There were places I would rather not look down from my window seat, where the sheer cliff face fell sharply down to the sea, but the blind curves ahead were just as unsettling. Clouds of dust signaled the presence of other vehicles ahead. We stopped briefly at the airport. Audrey was there with Lela. "Audrey," I shouted from the window, "Bob loved your cookies!"

She smiled and waved in response as the bus lurched away.

I had not gone beyond Audrey's house, beyond Matei Village, before. A sea wall protected low-lying fields. Near the shore there was a galvanized iron smoke house. Beside it was a pile of coconut husks for fuel. We passed impenetrable jungles. In a sandy cove, mangroves lined the shore. There were rocky islets and porous lava rock. Every scene was a sensory overload. An extensive copra plantation flanked the road on both sides. The coconut trees appeared to be about fifty years old with no young plantings, reflecting the drop in copra prices. In small villages, bougainvillea arched doorways and climbed over walls. Large bushes bloomed with masses of coral-pink flowers in lilac-like clusters.

At ten twenty the bus reached the end of the road and all the passengers left the bus. Some went to the village; others took the ten-minute walk to the falls. Veiled cascades of the lower falls descended into a large pool with a sloped gravel beach creating an easy access for swimmers. On the sides were diving rocks. The return bus would leave at two thirty. I realized that I had brought no insect repellent, food, or water.

The park opened in February, 1991, just a couple months before my visit. The waterfall development was a village project funded by New Zealand...$43,000. The second falls, which was not quite as tall, but broader, than the lower falls, was accessed by three hundred seventy six steps. The project was well done, with changing rooms for swimmers, toilets, rest areas and appealing landscaping. It will include a restaurant.

On the day I arrived in Taveuni I had made arrangements for Sukh Lal to pick me up on Friday for the trip to the airport for the return flight to Nadi. Apologetically, I explained that to Chitra. She laughed and said that's o.k. It seems to be a game that Sukh Lal and Kulle play with a fine spirit of friendship.

My last evening, I took out my *Lonely Planet* to appraise what I had seen and what I had missed in a visit far too short. If I had planned my trip throughout Fiji, I couldn't have achieved as perfect a balance of experience. In Nadi, I had been involved with the Indian community, on Vanua Levu I had lived with an extraordinary Melanesian family. On Taveuni, through the eyes and experiences of expatriates, I had come to understand Fiji in a far deeper way than before.

I once heard a priest say, "If you just take the next good step, He will always be there to lead you." Throughout the trip, I had simply taken the next good step.

On the way to the airport Sukh Lal loaned me a dog-eared copy of *Islands*, dated February, 1990. The article had featured his island tour, just $90 a day for cab and driver.

As I waited for my nine fifty five flight, Audrey arrived, and I spent my last hour on Taveuni with her.

There were eleven passengers and the familiar crew on the same Sunflower Twin Otter D HC-6 that had brought me to Taveuni.

A carton of cookies had been loaded, but after a hurried conversation among the flight crew, they determined that there would be no flight to Savusavu until the following day, so Audrey's cookies were hastily off-loaded just before the flight.

In flight, we left Audrey's house and Goat Island behind. From the air the island view spread out revealing villages and plantations and the familiar narrow ribbon of road running along rocky ledges beside the sea. We passed Somosomo, Garden Island Resort, the coffee plantation and factory, then the plane swung out over Somosomo Strait.

Near the southern side of Vanua Levu there were massive coral beds. Irregular, parallel strips of white foam defined breakers smashing against coral reefs. Layers of wispy, smoky clouds created shadows that lay like ink blots in patches on the pale lagoon.

Sky, sea, clouds merged on the horizon to my left...the mountainous landmass of Vanua Levu on my right. Below us was an enormous reef and turquoise-green lagoon and beyond the reef lay moana, the deep blue sea.

Huge lagoons lay around small islands. At ten thirty five we sighted Ovalau and by ten fifty Ovalau lay behind us as we approached Viti Levu. We were flying low over the north coast. A network of natural channels through the mangroves reached the sea, like the one through which Tom and Kolomi and I had taken the boat. Cane fields lay below us in neat strips, green alternated with earth brown. A broad silver river snaked its way to the sea.

From the air, Lautoka seemed to be a handsome, modern city, a reflection of the prosperity from sugar cane production, which comprised half of the nation's exports. Before tourism, sugar was the single economic anchor of Fiji.

We landed at eleven twenty. The flight of less than an hour and half gave a splendid overview of the beauty and diversity of the Fijian Archipelago.

There was no one to meet me, so I wandered into the tourist shop, where I admired the baskets. The Fijian sales girl proudly told me how they are made. "When the coconut fronds are brown," she said, "they fall off the tree. Cut out the center rib from which you can make a broom. Under pandanus, over the coral sand, put tambakous, the soft center leaves..."

It seemed no problem to hop on the bus back to the hotel. Shouldering my duffles, I left the bus and walked down Wailoaloa Beach Road. I felt like I was going home.

Pam had not yet returned, but it was four days before our Air New Zealand flight was scheduled to leave for Los Angeles.

On Sunday morning I wakened early. One of the many hotel cats sat on the thatched roof of the pool lounge watching, with me, the layered peach and gray horizon beyond the cane fields lighten into dawn. When I had arrived on March 22, my plan was to transit Fiji. I traveled as a circumstantial tourist and in thirty days my experiences had led me to seven islands among people I would never forget!

Thirty days! My visitor's permit had expired! I was not scheduled to fly out for two more days. Panic sent a chill through me. I had unwittingly become an illegal alien. Not knowing what to do at this hour on a Sunday morning, I went to the front desk to explain my dilemma and seek advice. Very seriously, she said, "You must go to the police."

In shock, I went to the deserted lounge to see if Sanjay could get me a pot of coffee. Their concern enveloped me.

I related my problem to a young Canadian who joined me.

"No big deal. Forget it," he said. "My brother came out of the jungle in Costa Rica two weeks after his permit expired. They just put him in jail overnight, stamped his passport 'No return' and put him on the first plane out."

Panic turned to horror, horror to despair. Sanjay and the desk clerk conferred. Together they came to the table to tell me that they had learned that the Immigration Office at the airport was open.

"Just go to them, admit your problem."

For $1.00 a couple from New Zealand let me share their cab to the airport. I tried to make light conversation but my mouth was too dry to talk.

At the airport on my way to immigration I found myself walking beside two young women wearing badges that identified them as staff of the Immigration Office. There on the sidewalk, I blurted out my anxious confession as we walked.

They smiled.

"No problem!" one girl said.

The other added, "After seven days we issue a notice to the police and they would pick you up."

Sweet relief. At my request, she signed a note stating that I had come to immigration the morning my visitor's permit had expired to prove good faith.

I walked to Felix's sister's house. While I was gone, Auntie Usha had died, one of the three women dressed in white in the picture I had taken at the Feast of the Nine Days. The men had taken her body for cremation by the sea. The body of the deceased is prepared by friends and relatives. Felix had told me that the greatest insult from a relative or friend is, "I will not touch your body when you die."

I had returned at a sad and solemn time for the family.

As the day of our flight arrived, I began to wonder what had happened to Pam and the boys. I took the bus downtown to buy an alarm clock for Felix. He had trusted the roar of the jets flying over the hotel to waken him in time to drive to the airport to meet passengers. Felix gave me a proof set of Fijian coins and his sister gave me a precious piece of tapa. The traditional exchange of gifts was something for which I was never adequately prepared.

When I returned from shopping Pam and the boys were in the pool. We exchanged wild stories about our separate experiences since my midnight departure from Levuka.

They had found the elusive van for RukuRuku and had shared a bure at the resort with a Swedish girl they met. The simple resort had proven to be perfect for the children. The beach and snorkeling were superb and the travelers they met were congenial.

We talked the afternoon away until flight time. Our seats on the huge plane were widely separated, so it was our last chance to visit except for a tearful farewell at Los Angeles (LAX) when Dan's family came to claim them.

After passing through "Nothing to Declare" at Immigration, I reached into my pocket for change for a cart. On the handful of coins and a crumpled bill, there were all the symbols of Fiji...the fly whisk and lali, war club and tanoa, tabua and outrigger canoe with the strangely rigged square sail. Queen Elizabeth still looked up at me, improbably, but I no longer needed the reassurance! The fear of traveling alone was gone. In its place was a level of confidence I could never have imagined!

I glanced at the clock. If I could pick up a flight to Tucson, I could be home before dark.

The Ara Tapu, the coastal road that circles Rarotonga

Peter Jackson, captain of *Such is Life*

Chapter Twenty-Three

Such is Life

When I saw my home again, what had seemed so diminished, such a compromise from what we had before, had become an embarrassment of riches. A 1954 ranch with obsolete bathrooms and a kitchen begging to be remodeled stood palatially as measured against island homes in which I had lived. In four months of travel I had gained a different definition for quality of life. It was truly a new beginning for me.

However, profound changes can happen in an instant, unanticipated, irrevocable.

With an average of eleven inches of rain a year, the winter monsoon came as a blessing to us in the desert of Arizona. It was during a break in one of our December rains that I took a walk. The ground was wet, so I walked on the curb rather than cut through Palo Verde Park as I usually did. The film of mud flowing from the path was so thin I didn't notice it. I don't even remember the sensation of falling, but I found myself sitting in the puddle I was trying to avoid. My right arm and hand were obviously broken with the bones out of alignment.

As the doctor finished putting my arm in a cast I asked, "When will I be able to travel again?"

"You won't be able to lift anything as heavy as a suitcase for about a year and a half."

I had completed four months of research traveling eight South Pacific islands searching for budget lodgings for *The Solo Traveler.* A thousand copies were just off the press with nowhere to go.

Christmas passed, then January and February in an unproductive blur. Responses were coming from hotels across the Pacific offering *Solo* members discounts. The marketing director of the southwestern division of Air New Zealand called to see if I could go out for lunch. I explained that I was handicapped with a broken arm and couldn't drive, but suggested that she come to the house. A deep alliance was formed with an excellent airline. But, because of my limitation, my next step was uncertain.

When the cast came off, my arm seemed cemented in a thumbs-up position. For months I was unable to rotate my arm into a position that would allow its use on my keyboard. My return to the South Pacific seemed further and further away.

A letter from Father Fred spoke of an epidemic on Rarotonga. There was small mention of dengue fever in my guidebooks. A virus, transmitted by a small mosquito that bites during the daytime, causes the fever.

Father Fred wrote, "because there are quite a number who have dengue fever here, several islands refused to allow boats to come from Rarotonga for fear of getting that sickness. A PukaPuka lady who arrived here some months ago by a Fijian boat to visit the hospital to have her baby got her baby at sea with the help of the sailing crew. As she has nobody to stay with here on Rarotonga, she is in our house at the Catholic Mission for more than two months helping in the kitchen. Her island refuses to accept a boat and it may take still a few months till she can reach her island. She has a healthy, lovely baby girl. The sailors of that Fijian boat gave to the baby the name 'Queen of Fiji'. When they left they brought a nice set of clothing for the baby.

So you can see that the isolated outer islands have their special troubles as well. That island can't have any flour, sugar, coffee, soap, etc. for a long time, preferring to live without all those things than getting a fever on the island."

The virus, he said, can lay one very low with the sudden onset of fever and pain. It is referred to as "breakbone fever" because it is so painful and sometimes it is fatal.

There were letters from my young friend, Caroline, with island news and gossip, and occasional updates on island politics from other friends. Between letters I read *Pacific* and *Pacific Islands Monthly* from cover to cover. An article written by a young couple who had been at sea with their children for four years tugged at me. Their backyard was the picturesque harbor at Neiafu in the Tongan group of Vava'u. Dozens of isolated anchorages lay among the fifty closely scattered islands making Tonga a favorite home base to hundreds of cruising yachts.

Just after I read that article my son called from Florida.

"Mom, can you be out here in two weeks to go on a nine month cruise of the South Pacific?"

He reminded me of a man whom he had met the year before. Peter, an Australian, had sailed through Indonesia and across the Indian Ocean to Madagascar with his thirteen year old son, Gareth. His wife met them in South Africa, where they bought a car and spent five months touring the countryside and game parks. He said the passage across the Atlantic to Brazil was so smooth they hardly had to touch their sails.

They had stayed in various ports in South America before cruising the Antilles. His wife, who is a teacher, loves to sail, but avoids long passages. She met them again in the Virgin Islands and they traveled together through Florida.

After Gareth returned to school in Australia, Peter went to Cuba. He sailed the next two thousand miles alone, finally docking at Fort Myers when he began having engine trouble. He went home to Australia to work for a while returning with the parts he needed to rebuild his engine. While he was gone, Greg watched his boat.

"He asked me to go with him," Greg continued, "but I explained that my daughter is with me now and I just got married again. But I told him that I know someone who would go...my Mom."

I hesitated for a minute.

"Does he know that I'm 63 years old and that my right arm is only half useful?"

"I told him I thought you were about 65. It's o.k. He said it doesn't matter, he only needs someone who can stand watch while he sleeps."

It seemed simple enough. Pristine islands danced in my imagination...islands that could be reached no other way.

"Tell him I'll go. I'll be there in ten days."

Peter had moored *Such is Life* up river in a gunk hole anchorage to cut costs, so it was a few days before Greg was able to get a message to him. When he called, I was charmed by his Crocodile Dundee accent and warm acceptance.

My experience sailing was limited to Chesapeake Bay where I was in charge of the Osprey's galley. Masts and sails and rigging were the domain of the Captain and our boys. Osprey, a double masted bugeye ketch, was a heavy wooden 36' modified working boat. It was docked at a slip in front of our home, so our sailing was mostly fair weather day sailing.

While traveling, I would have only my social security to contribute to our sailing kitty, so I bought a one-way Greyhound bus ticket. It had always taken me five days to drive from Tucson to Fort Myers (two days just to cross Texas), so two days and nights on the bus seemed easy. I brought a book on basic sailing so I would at least know port from starboard.

In West Texas as the sun was setting on our first night out we lost all our oil. The coffee shop that usually closed at 10:00 stayed open all night to accommodate the stranded passengers. Whether bother or bonanza it was hard to tell because bus travelers are a notoriously frugal lot.

I joined the young man who shared my bus seat for coffee. I would guess he was near 40, polite, but with a rough edge. It was near 3:00 a.m. when the baggage was off-loaded from the abandoned bus. He suggested that we walk over to the roadside to see if our luggage was in the unguarded pile.

"My bag's not there!" he said nervously after circling the pile twice. "It has my cuffs and chains and pepper spray," he mumbled as he began frantically rummaging in the pile, then without speaking, he hurried off through the darkness in search of the driver.

We boarded a different bus that had been brought out from El Paso and, before dawn, continued our aborted trip. My seat mate, a bounty hunter, had just returned from Alaska where he and his partner had picked up a felon who had jumped bail. As we drove through the darkness, this stranger revealed a cruel world of shadowy exploits, stories from the dark underbelly of society. I was not disappointed to change buses in Houston.

Because of our delay, I arrived in Fort Myers just before midnight of my third night of travel. Peter had waited for me for nearly two weeks and was anxious to be off. Not anticipating my delayed arrival, they had arranged a rendezvous early the next morning at a dock up river. It was not fully light when the dinghy approached us through a thin fog. The only sounds were the creak of oarlocks and paddle dipping in the water.

Peter smiled up at me while Greg handed my duffles down to him. As I cautiously climbed down into the dinghy, I wondered if Greg had told him that I can't swim.

Chapter Twenty-Four

A Taste of Salt

During the days before I left home, when I called the children their reactions were varied, falling somewhere between enthusiastic encouragement and panic over Peter's plan to visit the people he had met in Cuba before continuing on to Cartegena and Panama. Cuba was a place I had never thought of visiting. Cartegena was on the State Department list of travel advisories for Americans.

I went to the library, but there were no books about Cuba. I tried bookstores with the same result. It seemed that Cuba had been erased from the geography of the Americas.

When talking to Peter on the phone, I had told him that I can't go to Cuba.

He said, "You'll be fine. You'll be sailing under the Australian flag."

Unconvinced, I called the State Department. They said that there is no way that I could get papers to go...that I would be arrested by Cuban officials for trying to enter without papers. The Department of Treasury, to which they referred me, emphasized that if I spend any money, even a penny, I would be breaking our economic embargo. I would be arrested as soon as I arrived home. I didn't want to think about it. Peter promised that he would radio ahead before we got into Cuban waters. We could decide then.

The early morning sun burnished the barely rippled surface of the water as we motored to the mouth of the river. Even at low tide, our mast barely cleared the sixty five foot fixed bridge on the Caloosahatchee River. Once in the Gulf, he set our sails to pick up the light breeze.

All day we cruised at a lazy 31/2 knots. I had time to get acquainted with the boat and unpack and stow my things.

Such is Life was much more than I expected, a sleek iron-hulled cruising yacht, forty feet overall. Peter, a marine engineer, had designed it himself and had finished the cabin to be very livable for long passages. The rich mahogany interior gleamed. Aft, on one side of the cabin were bunk beds. On the other side was a table with u-shaped benches. The upholstery-covered mattresses could accommodate three sleeping people. Above the table, a bookcase, with protective rail in front, was filled with a well-chosen library of paperbacks, quality reading to fill the doldrums days of sailing. I had once heard sailing described as weeks of boredom interspersed with hours of sheer terror. But a glance around his cabin let me know that he had brought the basic elements of home with him, with activities to occupy the voyage.

Coming down five steep steps from the cockpit, the head with rudimentary shower was on the right. Next to it, one step up from the galley floor, a large desk was built-in with radio equipment and stereo. A wide selection of tapes reflected his appreciation of music. On the other side, the galley was well provisioned. The stove, on gimbals, was centered a convenient arm's reach from cabinets and fresh food locker, with potatoes and onions hung in overhead nets. When at sea, he enjoyed cooking as creatively as one can, far from fresh supplies. Every other day, he said, he would bake fresh bread. Food, while at sea, was eaten with ritualistic pleasure. But these were things I began to learn and appreciate only as the days passed. He kept an extensive personal journal as well as ship's log.

By evening porpoises were leaping beside our bow. I was sure that was a very good omen. Peter showed me where the life preserver was and the lighted buoy.

"If I go overboard, throw them as near to me as you can. After you disconnect the autopilot turn the boat around and let the sheets go. Start the engine. Hit the button on GPS with the dot on it. It gives immediate position. But it is most important to keep me in sight. Then call the Coast Guard on 15."

He looked at me with searching, almost pleading, eyes and added, "When you bring the boat around, try not to hit me..."

The whole idea of being responsible for his rescue in a crisis challenged me to the core; yet, it all seemed reasonable enough at 3 knots.

Peter's radio was not working, but it was just a one hundred forty five mile run to Key West where he planned to have it repaired. Without the radio, we had no warning that we were running into a late winter storm with gale force winds.

Before midnight the wind had picked up and we were running at 8.2 to 8.9 knots with buffeting currents as we passed Ten Thousand Islands. There was not a light on any horizon. During my night watch, I was caught by the incredible beauty of the sea at night, even in a storm, as foaming tongues of whitecaps licked the hull of the boat; then died on the sea mounds around us. More than once I got a taste of salt as waves swept over the cabin.

During the night our delicate autopilot stopped working. My fault, I'm sure, as I turned it on and off tensely and too frequently while at the wheel trying to dodge buoys attached to lines of lobster traps and crab pots. Those lines could easily foul our gear, which would require Peter to go overboard to untangle them. We were almost upon them before they were visible in the darkness.

As the weather worsened, I went down below to get a life jacket. Peter, resting uneasily, came to attach my lifeline from its belt to the top of the cabin. Less than an hour later a wave crashed into the cockpit. The overwhelming weight of it sent me to the end of my tether. Without the lifeline I would have gone overboard in the darkness while Peter slept. I began thinking, it will be like this, or worse, if Peter goes overboard. I knew that I had to tell him that I would be totally inadequate to the task of rescue in a crisis.

Although I was wearing a sweat suit with a slicker over it, the early morning chill went to my bones, so when Peter came to relieve me, I went to the galley to make us coffee. He tied the wheel and came to sit in the cockpit with me.

"Peter, during the storm last night, when I was at the wheel I thought about our rescue drill. I would be hopeless trying to save you if you went overboard in a storm like that."

His reaction was unexpected.

"Even if you can't do everything, it's better than sailing alone! From Panama to our first landfall in French Polynesia it will be thirty or forty days, with luck. We'll be in shipping lanes, so I could never sleep more than an hour or two at a time."

"But, Peter," I interrupted, "you could find someone in Key West who is stronger and more experienced."

He quickly stopped me.

"Do you know the risk I'd be taking picking up a stranger? Do you know how many boats are stolen for drug running, with the captain killed and tossed overboard? When they scuttle the boat everyone thinks it was just lost at sea."

I remembered the machete he had hung on the wall just inside the cabin. So it's a weapon, I thought, not just a tool.

"But it's not just that," he continued. "Personalities are important when you are confined in so small a space for weeks at sea."

I felt his insistence a compliment. But, although I felt it wrong to abandon him, it was just as wrong to continue with him depending on me when I had already, during the storm, measured my ability and found it wanting.

"And it would be a tricky passage through the canal without another hand," he continued as if the matter was settled.

The closer we got to the Keys the next morning the more turbulent and gusty the winds were. It was past noon when we entered the channel to the harbor. Tacking back and forth from the breakwater to the shoals, back and forth, we came about to try it again, over and over. The sails were keeping Peter busy and I was at the wheel trying to remember if the channel markers should be to port or starboard.

The depth finder began beeping. It looked like about three meters. Too shallow. I went below to get my glasses so I could be sure. For a moment, while taking my glasses from their case, I forgot the sailor's adage, one hand for the boat.

The wave that surged through a gap in the breakwater caught us broadside, throwing me across the cabin. My head hit the desk, the ribs on my right side hit the step.

Peter shouted down, "Are you all right? Can you take the wheel?"

"I'm o.k." I lied as I crawled painfully up the steps into the cockpit. My head was swimming, my ribs aching.

A dozen other boats had sought refuge in the anchorage. At first we dragged our anchor, but once it found purchase on the harbor's bottom, we settled into the cabin. I couldn't remember when I had last slept. There were naps on the bus and three hours at Greg's house. While Peter cooked a sumptuous meal, I slept soundly waking up only long enough to eat and fell into a hard sleep again.

It seemed only half real, half a dream, when Peter shouted from the deck, "Iona, come up."

Shaking myself awake, I bounded up to the deck. Peter tossed me a fender and pointed to the boat, twice our size that was threatening collision.

"Watch your fingers, " he shouted above the wind as I held the bumper at the threatened point of impact. The smartly uniformed Captain of the other yacht and Peter worked feverishly in the bucking seas to pole the boats apart. Our anchor lines had somehow become tangled as the other boat, seeming a safe distance away, had swung around at its mooring.

When the crisis was over, Peter made coffee and suggested a game of scrabble. Words have always been my passion, but he skinned me three times before I begged off, blaming the Captain's option to use an Australian dictionary. With a wicked grin, he insisted that no handicap was in order because we were flying under that nation's flag.

All the while, I knew that this was his game and I would be hard pressed ever to win.

The storm continued for three days and nights as the water in the hold and fuel sloshed noisily back and forth while the boat tossed and rolled in waves being funneled through the harbor's entrance.

When Peter launched the dinghy over the side, he injured his arm, further complicating our situation. I watched him bob toward shore through heavy waves, reviewing in my mind instructions he had given me in the event that we began taking on water.

Reluctant to let him know how injured I felt, I took advantage of his absence to sleep again.

After dinner, Peter showed me the album of their journey. In one picture a brilliantly plumed parrot sat on Gareth's shoulder.

"You should write a book from Gareth's point of view, a book for young readers. How many young people have the opportunity to sail halfway around the world with their Dad?"

He must have grown homesick from the pictures. Putting an instructional tape on the deck, he began to practice playing the didgeridoo, the plaintive aboriginal music doing little to alleviate his quiet mood. He had brought three of the instruments with him, all colorfully decorated with unique aboriginal art.

His arm was painful and, for the moment he seemed to dread the long journey back to Darwin, uncertain whether the injury would grow worse and limit his ability to handle the boat.

"Will you ever sail around the world again?" I asked, sure of his negative answer, sure of his longing for home.

His eyes shone.

"Someday, I'd love to go around the Roaring Forties"

To even think about going around the world at those dangerous lower latitudes made me realize that he loves the challenge and rigors of stormy weather. That he loves the journey even more than the destinations.

The following day he went into town again to pick up the radio. It was long after dark when Peter came home. Greg and Chele returned with him! More aware of my injuries than I knew, he had called my son. They both agreed that it was too risky for me to go on.

Greg and Chele had gotten a room in Key West, so Peter brought them back to shore through the stormy darkness.

While they were gone, I repacked my things, leaving some of the supplies I had brought. Coffee bags for a quick and easy cup when sailing was too demanding for more. Dried fruits and nuts. Some medical supplies. But mostly, my favorite South Pacific books, notebooks and pens.

In the morning, Greg came to get me in a water taxi so Peter would not have to cross the harbor again in the dinghy. I hated leaving him that way, but I knew in the long run, I would be more hindrance than help on his journey.

The ill wind that blew had aborted my attempt to return to Polynesia, but I had a precious glimpse into the exotic subculture of cruising yachtsmen. I can see, now, beyond the glamour to the spare life at sea.

NOTE: On Saturday, March 13, 1993, during the unnamed Storm of the Century, 12 boats off coastal Florida were lost, including six fishing boats, two sailboats and a 220 foot freighter.

Before a month had passed, I was back again at my home in Tucson. I had suffered a mild concussion, the loss of a wisdom tooth and epic bruises, but x-rays had shown that no bones were broken.

The pile of mail that had come in my absence revealed a new avenue of hope for an early return to the South Pacific. Randy Keck, in his column for *International Travel News*, had written an article about *Solo Travel*, specifically about Rarotonga. He ended the article, "currently she is planning to offer and escort a small, budget conscious group to experience village life in the South Pacific. She invites inquiries."

I had forgotten my luncheon meeting with Randy a few months before when, in my enthusiasm, I had mentioned that possibility. Nearly a hundred people responded, but in the end only four people comprised this experimental sort of tour, flexible and loosely guided.

Was it really an accident that brought me home? I wondered.

A month before we left, an unexpected phone call with an invitation to Samoa opened up expanded possibilities.

Photo by Chele Kargel

Such is Life, a cruising yacht out of Darwin, Australia

Tangi Estall of Are Renga and her auntie

Chapter Twenty-Five

Return to Rarotonga

We were as disparate a group of travelers as one could imagine! Aljean, a recent Sun City widow brought her younger sister, Emmy Lou, who was seventy two. Richard, a retired banker from Florida had never traveled "budget" and made several anxious phone calls before our departure. I was the youngest in the group until Allison joined us. She was a twenty year old relative from Minneapolis, whom I had never met, the granddaughter of my cousin.

Richard's itinerary included a month in Australia and New Zealand first, scheduling his arrival on Rarotonga earlier on the same day as ours. Since he would be in Darwin, I asked him to call Peter's wife. I had heard nothing from Peter since he had left Panama and often wondered where he was or if he had returned home safely. I always felt guilty for having abandoned him.

At LAX I met Allison's plane first. A petite redhead, she was shy at first, but by the time Aljean and Emmy Lou's plane came three hours later the familial bond made conversation easy and it seemed like I had always known her.

Aljean and Emmy Lou's buoyant enthusiasm and youthful appearance made a lie of their age. Both had lived abroad on many occasions and were experienced travelers. Aljean had lived in Turkey and Honduras and Hawaii at the time of the attack on Pearl Harbor. She loved the islands as they were and hoped, on Rarotonga, to recapture the beauty of Polynesia before tourism forever changed the easy island life-style.

Just after dark we left the lights of the City of Angels behind and swung out into the velvet blackness of the Pacific night. Flights on Air New Zealand are never a disappointment with the promise of tropical islands an easy overnight flight away.

My return to Rarotonga, so long delayed, was emotionally charged. Would the island remember me, just one of fifty thousand visitors a year? It had been almost three and a half years since I was there.

I was the first one off the plane eager to make sure that the girls had brought flower eis with which to welcome my little group. I walked briskly across the tarmac. As I stepped into the arrivals lounge, the feeling of Kia Orana enveloped me as Jake sang songs of welcome. This time, not mentioning that I write, I was quickly processed through immigration and hurried to curb side to find the usual colorful chaos as men and women were greeted with eis and ei katu, garlands and coronets of flowers. Maori and English mingled with the familiar laughter. By the time my group assembled, I had found Arii who met them with smiles and kisses and eis.

Richard was already settled at Are Renga. I had asked Tangi to provide fresh baguettes and jam for each room. Richard made each of us coffee with his single-cup Melita filter and we settled on the verandah to get acquainted. He gave me a picture of himself that Peter had taken, pointing to *Such is Life* in dry-dock. They had had lunch together in Darwin.

While the others settled into their rooms to rest, Richard and I went by bus into Avarua to exchange money. I purchased a good supply of dinner vouchers at Trader Jack's and ten-trip bus passes for each tour member.

By the time we got back, everyone was up, rested and eager to go. We walked through the village to Tumunu for dinner. On the way I showed them which shop had fresh bread twice a day and the lane that led to the waterfront where a home had been converted into an ad hoc grocery and fresh vegetable market.

Richard knocked on our doors in the morning when he heard the faintest stir, to deliver to each of us a freshly brewed cup of coffee. That first morning he had already walked the plantation and met the boys who were opening coconuts to feed the pigs.

I walked to the village store to buy fresh bread. On the way back, running footsteps behind me stopped and a young man I didn't recognize called excitedly from across the road, "When did you come back?" As he approached and smiled I recognized Tero, who was just twelve when I had been there before. Then he hurried off to school.

When Allison joined us, I showed them where to wait for the bus under the flamboyant tree across the road, not yet in bloom, for late September is early spring in the South Pacific.

Orientation to "the city" was complete before lunch at Trader Jack's, located by the harbor on the foreshore. Emmy Lou had noticed a huge fish being cleaned beside the restaurant and delighted in the very fresh sashimi.

The "tour" which I had timidly offered, was a scheduled twelve days with the option of staying on independently. The purpose of the tour was to provide orientation to independent budget travel and an introduction to Polynesian culture.

I introduced Allison to my young friend, Caroline, transplanted from New Zealand four years before. They often joined us for dinner at some of the fine island restaurants, a few of them new since my previous visit. Frequently they went out in the evening with her Maori friends dancing or to the movie theater in Avarua. Allison enrolled in Greg Wilson's scuba diving course and got her PADI certification.

Richard, an avid fisherman, found a boat leaving from Ngatangiia Harbour. He came back with no fish, but an enormous grin. They had sighted a pod of four whales, three adults and a baby, frisking in the water near their fishing boat. They were the really big ones that got away!

Aljean and Emmy Lou saw every corner of the island, discovering the ancient marae and the best swimming beaches. Often Richard went with them on their wanderings, and when I didn't join them, I went to look up old friends.

One afternoon, Ina stopped to visit me on the verandah as he had so many times before. He told me that after I left one of the babies in his family had died. He was chosen to carry the small body by freighter to his family's home island for burial. Although so much about Rarotonga had changed, Ina remained the same.

After an initial greeting, one acquaintance from my previous visit handed me a copy of the underground publication *The Black Book of Shame*, so I knew that the dark clouds of political scandal still hung heavy over my beautiful island in the sun.

The tour included a day trip to one of the outer islands, Aitutaki. Since they had all decided to extend their stay on Rarotonga to 30 days, when Allison suggested that we spend more time on Aitutaki, we put it to a vote. They unanimously agreed. We went to *Island Hopper* on our next visit to town to see what could be arranged. The planned day trip was NZ$200. Using the Super Saver Fare, that is, going on Air Rarotonga's last afternoon flight and returning in the early morning, it would be only NZ$199 additional to spend a week at Tom's Beach Cottage; NZ$139 each for Aljean and Emmy Lou who would share a room. Beneath a stairwell outside the bank I counted out NZ$200 to each of them. We went back into *Island Hopper* and paid our individual reservations for a week.

Danny Mataroa was no longer dancing at the Cultural Village. Married to a beautiful Maori girl, Oropai, they were expecting their second baby. He was guide for Hugh Henry's Circle Island Tour and leader of the Tumutevarovaro Dance Team, which was playing at the Rarotongan Hotel's island night. When we went out to watch the umu being uncovered, he saw me and smiled in recognition. During the dinner break, Danny came to eat with us. He spoke of the tidal wave of change that had swept the islands during the time that I had been gone; changes that had come with appalling abruptness forever changing their culture. He was also training young drummers and dancers at the elementary school and invited us to come and watch. They were doing a program for an Elderhostel group out of Hawaii.

His feelings about encroaching change were echoed by Bart, a Kiwi who had immigrated from New Zealand. "I'm thinking of moving on to Niue," he confided.

"Where is Niue?" I asked.

"Just east of Tonga. It's a small country with a population less than two thousand. Politically it is like the Cook Islands, independent, in free association with New Zealand. It is a bit isolated."

That comment proved to be an extreme understatement!

Later that day he brought a video of Niue for me to see.

When Richard and Aljean joined me, Niue was still on my mind. Their curiosity stimulated my own. The owner of the video shop across from Are Renga offered to let us watch the borrowed video in his living room. He joined us midway.

"That's my Mom," he exclaimed with surprise as we watched a woman teeing off at the nine-hole golf course. His father was Queen's Representative of Niue.

"It's beautiful!" he said at the end of the twenty minute film. Hesitating, he added, "But that's all there is."

One quiet day at home, I saw Kura working outside. I had gotten current pictures of the rest of the Are Renga family, including his wife, Marion, and their new baby. When I asked him if I could take his picture he seemed pleased.

"We will take it by your tree," he said.

"My tree?" I asked, bewildered.

"Yes, don't you remember? You were in your room one day, writing. I was planting a tree and you came out and you held it for me."

He indicated a fine young coconut palm about twice his height. So the island did remember me!

Kura at Are Renga

Photo by Richard Filip

Aljean, Captain Nancy Griffith, and Emmy Lou aboard
Nancy's freighter *Avatapu*

Chapter Twenty-Six

Aitutaki

How could an island, whose name I have read is pronounced like a big sneeze, be so incredibly beautiful? It is frequently referred to as the most beautiful island in the Pacific.

At the time we went, Air Rarotonga flew three 18-seat Embraer Bandierante aircraft, which were made in Brazil, throughout the Southern Cook Islands.

I took a single seat. There was a large Maori man with a Tiare Maori tucked behind each ear on the double seat beside me. We cruised at about two hundred knots at ten thousand feet above a dense layer of clouds. He said that he hopes it rains because he is beginning to plant his tomatoes for market. It was very early spring. Most days were sunny, but cool and dry, still blessed by the comfortable trade winds.

The small aircraft was sweetly redolent with the heavy fragrance of multiple eis being worn by local people returning home. After a forty five minute flight we began our descent.

As we broke through the steel gray tier of clouds my seat mate pointed to the cockpit window through which I saw my first glimpse of the stunningly beautiful island. The massive lagoon has a series of large motu, uninhabited islands, around the reef's edge. Although colored brochures had introduced us to the island, nothing could have prepared me for the astonishing beauty of it!

Our *Island Hopper* "package" included transfers from the airport and return. We were met by Mr. Tom himself.

As the days passed, I learned that Taraota Tom's father was a Henry. Mr. Tom is a cousin of Geoffrey Henry, then Prime Minister of the Cook Islands. As a child, his father had been adopted out to the Tom family, so he took their last name. Though he is a Henry by birth, he has grown up outside the seat of power, frequently opposing government policies. For thirty years Mr. Tom was a policeman. After an early retirement, he held the post as Minister of Finance over all the other Aitutaki ministries, Energy, Agriculture, Marine, Education.

Throughout Polynesia, informal adoption of children is a common practice. While on the ferry to Savaii in Western Samoa I met a young woman who was going from 'Upolu to visit one of her three children. Her first was given to her husband's family, the second to her parents. This is frequently done so there will be someone to look after parents when they are old. She was delighted to be able to keep her third baby.

Mr. Tom had been raised in the sprawling beach cottage with eleven surviving of fifteen siblings. The central living room had a covered couch and chairs with bright, embroidered and appliquéd pillows. The crocheted doilies reminded me of my grandmother's house. Framed family pictures hung on the walls. Four sleeping rooms were off the main living room, two more on either side of an airy front room separated from the living room by a wall with three open, arched doorways. The communal kitchen had two stoves, two refrigerators and a double sink, with three communal baths down a short hall beyond the kitchen.

My room, #4, was Spartan but clean and pleasant with double louvered windows overlooking the garden and lagoon beyond. #3 opposite mine also had a four-poster iron bed with mosquito net. The room near the kitchen area was the one Mr. Tom's parents had; #7 and #8 were smaller rooms with no outside window.

We walked to Ralphie's Bar & Grill for dinner. A pine paneled octagon with tiled floors. It had windows all around and wouldn't have been out of place in northern Minnesota.

I wakened early and walked beyond the village, past Ralphie's to buy fresh bread.

A freighter stood off the reef. The *Avatapu* was the one about which Father Fred had written to me in April, 1991. "An American woman, Nancy, has purchased a freighter which has greatly eased Cook Island shipping. We have had no regular interisland service since the two freighters were lost."

I walked to the wharf to try to get a closer look. A large steel barge was being readied to go out to unload freight and bring it ashore. Noting my interest, one of the crew asked,

"Would you like to come out with us?"

My experience at the Keys and remembered stories of boats lost to the powerful surge and suction of the reef during changing tides made me hesitate.

"It's still as glass," they teased, indicating the flat calm of the lagoon.

The temptation was too much. I stood behind the pilothouse on the barge with one arm wrapped firmly around a steel pole. The reef passage was negotiated easily, but the barge shuddered as it nudged the starboard side of the rusty freighter.

A smiling lady, who looked more like a suburban housewife than a freighter captain, leaned over the rail of an upper deck shouting orders to the crew.

"Are you Nancy?" I asked over the din of huge metal containers being hoisted by cranes from the ship's deck to the barge. All the diesel fuel and gasoline consumed on the island comes that way.

"Yes," she answered, still smiling as I took pictures.

"I'll send you some photos."

There was no time for further conversation as she turned her attention back to the work at hand.

In the lounge at Tom's I picked up a coffee stained issue of *The Cook Island Sun*, which featured the article, *A Life at Sea*. It was further introduction to this remarkable woman. Some details extracted from the article said that she was born in New York to an Army family. Travel was a way of life. As a young woman she bought a forty two foot hull, which she rebuilt and rigged. She wrote for yachting magazines and she and her late husband, Bob, gave slide shows and lectures based on trips that took them twice around the Horn and from Antarctica to the Bering Sea.

Because of her respect for ancient Polynesian sailing skills she became involved with Awahnee Oceanic Institute. Through this involvement she crossed the Pacific from California to the Marquesas on the Spirit of Nuku Hiva, a 1974 voyage on a vessel constructed entirely without metal fastenings, fashioned from a single seventy five foot red fir log.

Her husband, a veterinarian with a shared passion for sailing died young of cardiac arrest leaving her with two children, seven and eight years old, to support.

For six years she continued to operate their small coffee plantation, but was drawn back to the sea when she was able to acquire the *Edna*, a one hundred thirty foot, seventy four year old riveted iron topsail ketch. "Five years of magic" ended when a storm pounded her onto the reef at Atiu while carrying seventy tons of cement cargo. It was an enormous loss both financially and emotionally as she was the last of her kind, a sailing, working cargo ship.

Nancy casually dismissed her four years of island service on the Avatapu as "a useful thing to do".

Allison had stayed back on Rarotonga for a couple extra days. The day before we were to leave for Aitutaki, I noticed our neighbor at Are Renga, at the house just across the lane outside my window. She was sitting on a mat embroidering a tivaevae pillow cover. I mentioned this traditional Cook Islands art form to Allison, Emmy Lou and Aljean who went with me to see it. Justifiably proud, her sister brought out several quilts which especially appealed to Allison, the artist among us.

"There will be a tivaevae exhibit tomorrow," Nga said, "would you like to come?"

Allison looked at us, "Do you mind?"

So three days later Mr. Tom and I met Allison's plane at five thirty p.m. in a light rain. She had the opportunity to hold a week-old baby on the entire flight while the mother was busy with her other children.

The tivaevae exhibits had filled all the church halls and community centers from Arorangi to Titikaveka. Colorful and intricate combinations of appliqué and embroidery, they were traditionally used for burial shrouds like masi is in Fiji. Now they are a source of pride and displayed as wall hangings and bedspreads. So difficult to make, they were given as gifts, but seldom sold. More recently they have begun to be produced commercially at Atiu Fibre Arts Studio on the outer island. During the exhibits Allison had tea in the back rooms with the women during their breaks.

Allison, with Jodi and Jean, two Canadian girls at Are Renga, did the Cross-island Trek on their own. Near the needle they were unsure of the trail. They made the wrong choice. Traveling along a white pipe on what seemed like a worn trail, they wound up on a ledge. The ridge on which they walked had sheer cliffs on both sides. Jodi slipped on loose scree and fell down a thirty foot cliff. At times she questioned whether they would survive.

One evening they went to a movie in Avarua. The usher, aware that they depended on the Raro by Nite bus to get home, stood outside to flag the bus. Then an attendant came to get them about fifteen minutes before the movie was over, while the bus waited.

Now that we were altogether again, we scheduled the day cruise to One Foot Island for the following morning.

As we learned more about it, our conversations frequently went back to Niue. We learned that its ancient Polynesian name was Nukututaha, which means island standing alone. After an unsuccessful landing attempt, Captain Cook designated it Savage Island on charts, a name, which it kept until this century. It is just three hundred forty seven miles from Samoa, two hundred ninety eight miles from Tonga, islands from which their ancestors came, referred to by Niueans historically as Fonuagalo, the forgotten lands.

Legends recount murderous conflicts and battles among the eleven clans that developed on the island. Aware that newcomers brought disease and calamity, strict quarantine was observed and even returning Niueans were not allowed to land.

In 1830, John Williams arrived with two Aitutakian missionaries. Both declined to stay because of the hostile reception, so Williams took two young Niueans with him, Uea and Niumaga, hoping to convert and return them. Sickness did follow their homecoming. One was killed; the other left with a passing whaler. Peniamina, a young man, went with him. By the time he tried to return in 1842, quarantine did not permit his landing. Four years later he again tried and was allowed after thirteen years in exile. With the Samoan missionary, Paulo, they changed Niuean life completely as clan wars ended and the people came out of the bush and settled peacefully in villages.

The driver from Viking Lagoon Cruises came to pick us up with a flatbed truck. Richard had gone deep-sea fishing, so there were only four of us.

We passed the airport, which was built on a reclaimed spit of swampy land within the reef by U.S. forces during World War II. That was long before an airport was built on Rarotonga and it is long enough, they say, with a two-way runway to handle 737's.

At the end of the road we parked at a wharf and crossed by ferry to Motu Akitua, which was occupied by the Aitutaki Lagoon Hotel. There we met an Australian couple that completed the group. Because our group was small and the glass bottom boat was out of service, we took a smaller wooden boat with a 70 horsepower motor. The lagoon was choppy and with heavy overcast and a chilly wind the day seemed a bit compromised.

Our first stop was at Muritapua Motu where everyone else went snorkeling while I explored the island. A stereo-typically beautiful South Seas dream isle, it would have been a perfect movie set.

When we arrived at our next stop, Motu Tapuaetai, the Captain told us the legend that named the island, One Foot Island.

"A man and his son had been fishing in an area of the lagoon that was tapu [that is, off limits] during that season. When warriors came to kill them, he carried his son on his shoulders and put him in a tree so there was just one set of footprints. The warriors killed the father, satisfied that the second person they had seen must have been a shadow because there was just one set of footprints."

Polynesian legends frequently speak of seasonal tapu against fishing in certain areas indicating a strong sense of care for their environment. On Niue there is a forest that is tapu to allow unhampered reproduction of coconut crabs, which are an island delicacy.

While we explored the beaches and walked across the island track, the captain and his mate, a young man named Junior, cooked fish and sausage and provided cabbage/apple salad, papaya, banana bread and vegetables for a barbecue lunch.

After lunch while everyone else went snorkeling on the reef, Allison and I stayed in the thatched shelter to rest. Junior asked Allison if she wanted him to make her a bed. He cut some limbs from a coconut palm and put her beach towel over them making a cushiony mattress. After she napped, Junior asked her if she would like a drinking nut. She said, "Yes," and they began walking around the grove to choose a nut. At each tree they paused, "Would you like that one?" he asked, "that one?" After about ten trees she explained in exasperation that she was looking for a hairy one. He smiled, quickly climbing the closest tree. He opened the outer shell, retrieved the hairy inner nut and opened it, handing her a half shell brimming with cool coconut milk.

The snorkelers returned excited about the very colorful fish at the reef that came up and nibbled at them.

We returned through choppy water at low tide. The captain stood at the wheel tensely negotiating the boat between coral outcroppings and sandbars that, at low tide, were barely submerged. At other places the lagoon was 18' deep. Marine markers indicated the channels, but he mostly navigated by colors of the water that ranged from sandy and azure in the shallows to turquoise and deep blue, indicating greater depth.

Friday night was Island Night at the Rapae Cottage Hotel. I had remembered the remarkable talent that had come from Aitutaki and the highly professional show they had given at the Sunday School building at Arorangi on Rarotonga, so I was eager to go.

Rapae Cottage Hotel was located on the lagoon about one and a quarter mile from the main village, Arutanga, where Tom's is located. The large open dining room had a high center ridgepole and beautiful thatched kikau roof. The buffet was good and plentiful, but the waiters were busy hustling drinks. When I couldn't find water or coffee on the buffet, I asked the waiter, "Is there any water?" He waved his arm toward the lagoon, laughing, and said, "There's plenty of water."

I thought he was joking, but he kept hustling drinks and ignored my request. The show was mediocre at best.

We learned that a church dance team was going to perform at Ralphie's. An impromptu show was in progress when we arrived. We stood on tiptoe to see over the crowd, were never hustled for drinks and paid no admission. It seemed like a local thing, just for the fun of it and we were made to feel totally welcome through an excellent show. The walk back along the narrow, busy road was dark.

Living on the edge of the lagoon brought unexpected surprises. One morning I woke up to see more than two-dozen outrigger canoes poling silently out toward the reef. Sky met lagoon at the distant reef line in muted shades of pale lavender. Outriggers and fishermen standing in their canoes were reflected perfectly on the lagoon's mirrorlike surface. It was a scene I had seen on postcards, which I had thought unreal.

By the time I got my camera they were already just dots on the reef. It was past three in the afternoon when the first fishermen began coming in. Proud of their catches, they held them up to be admired as the women and children ran down to the beach to meet them. I realized that they were fishing for food, not sport.

When we were on Aitutaki, there was a heated controversy over the government's plans to build a big hotel with over-the-water bungalows on the site of the government-owned Rapae Hotel. Local people were fighting it with forums and petitions fearing that the lagoon and their way of life would be seriously threatened.

One day Aljean, Emmy Lou and Richard rented a jeep and visited Marae located off the road on the southern end of Aitutaki. Allison and I walked halfway across the island to the school in which Mrs. Tom is a teacher of home economics. Her class was making a Twenty Minute Pudding. In a very large pot with a lid, they put three and a half cups of boiling water with two tablespoons of sugar. Some of the kids were busy creaming a half pound of margarine with one and a half cups of sugar. They added three eggs, one at a time, beating well, then mixed in a half tin of jam (about eight ounces). They stirred in two teaspoons of baking soda and three cups of flour, adding a half cup of coconut cream, then mixing before pouring it into the boiling syrup and simmering for twenty minutes, covered. Because most cooking is done in earth ovens rather than Western style baking ovens, they have come up with ingenious methods of cooking.

After everyone had a dish of the delicious desert, there was a serious debate on the merits and problems associated with tourism, which, throughout the islands, has become a growing threat and blessing.

Allison was asked to talk to the students and they asked her questions until school was dismissed.

--- ◄━◆◆◆━► ---

At the ice cream shop I met Ian Guinea, the fishing guide who had taken Richard out on the day of our cruise. He was a personable young man who had been guiding for ten years. His father, who was then on Mauke, had come out from England as a doctor on Rarotonga, so Ian grew up in the islands.

Ian's eighteen foot ply boat had a quiet forty five horsepower Honda motor. He prefers to take no more than two people when going outside the reef. If fishing is good, they will stay out and keep fishing until there's only enough petrol to get home, about four or five hours. From June to December, wahoo and mahi mahi are good, December to June, tuna or marlin, although any ocean fish can be caught anytime. I was surprised to learn that all the fish caught stay with the boat.

Lagoon fishing was just $60 per person, including lunch. Ian can take up to four people within the lagoon. Richard caught trevally, snapper and dogfish. Ian let him keep three trevally that we all enjoyed for dinner as Richard is, as well as fisherman, chef extraordinaire.

Metua, the young woman who had taken care of the Beach Cottage during our stay had brought mangoes from her mother's tree and drinking nuts to us. Although tipping is not considered acceptable, Aljean and Emmy Lou thought we should give her something for all she had done for us. Each of them gave her $10. I was hesitant because I realized that tipping had no place in their culture, but when she was alone, I gave her my $10 contribution. She burst into tears and pushed the money back into my hand, "I don't want your money," she cried. She wasn't angry, just pained. I searched my mind for something that might make it an acceptable gift.

"If my fruit trees were here, I could bring you apples and oranges, but my home is too far away, so I have nothing."

Reluctantly, she agreed to take the money when I put it in that context.

"I will give it to my husband and he will give it to the children's school." She explained.

Allison had met some young Europeans who were avid scuba divers and she was invited to join them. Again, she stayed back when we returned to Rarotonga.

On the morning of our departure, I looked everywhere for Metua so we could say good-bye. Mrs. Tom, whose name was Mimau, had come with him in early morning and had also disappeared, while Mr. Tom worked in his office until our flight time. I was beginning to worry that we would miss our plane when they came from behind an out building in the garden. She had brought a pail of plumeria from their home and had been busy with Metua making a floral ei for each of us.

There have been many changes on Rarotonga.

In October, 1992, Rarotonga hosted the International Maire Nui Festival, the South Pacific Cultural Competitions, as a result of winning the crown as the best dancers from all the Pacific Islands in the festival four years previous. To prepare for hosting the festival, two new roads were added along the waterfront in Avarua and the median strip has been beautifully landscaped. A complex of new buildings was constructed to house the National Auditorium, the National Museum and the National Library just a block beyond the University of the South Pacific. The old library, which was staffed by volunteers, still houses the South Pacific Collection, which includes both rare and regional books.

The Punanga Nui Outdoor Market, replacing the harbor-side truck market, was a collection of huts and stalls selling a variety of products being woven or carved on-site as well as the tie dyes and fresh fruits and vegetables that were formerly sold off trucks at the old market.

The Cook Island Christian Church at Arorangi has built a balcony to accommodate the large numbers of visitors.

Black Pearl Outlets were flourishing, even though a devastating cyclone, Martin, that struck Manihiki in November, 1997, seriously damaged pearl farms. Half the population of Manihiki has been relocated to Rarotonga until houses can be rebuilt. Some, grieving losses of loved ones, have moved on to New Zealand.

A few days after we returned to Rarotonga, when I passed Avatiu Harbour, I noticed that the *Avatapu* was in its home port. When I mentioned to Aljean, Emmy Lou and Richard that the freighter has a woman captain, an American, they decided to try to meet her.

———◆◆◆———

Aljean wrote about their meeting: *At the wharf we spoke to a woman in a very small building which seemed to be the office. She phoned the* Avatapu *to see if Nancy was there and asked if it would be o.k. if we came down. We were given directions to the ship where Nancy would be waiting for us. As we walked down the wharf to the freighter, I wondered what a lady freighter captain would look like.*

Welcoming us, she called down, "Watch your step and come aboard!" She would look at home in any American country club. She asked if we would like to see the ship. We didn't miss a thing...even had our picture taken with our hand on the wheel looking like the ship's captain.

Nancy mentioned that she has a good crew of six boys and between herself and the boys they can go through about any storm that comes up. She knows exactly what she is doing and how to do it. Continuing with our tour, we crawled around huge crates that she was delivering to the islands...boxes upon boxes of all sizes, a couple big enough for a small car, all in the process of being loaded. While the crew was busy, she kept her eyes on what was happening, sometimes calling out, "Tie that rope a bit tighter so it won't slip!" Then she would continue to explain how the engine works...what they had to do if it stopped running and how very important it is to balance the cargo in case they run into rough water. Even though she was busy, she took time to show us her ship from stem to stern. She does take passengers from island to island.

The next day they took the bus into town. As they passed the wharf, the *Avatapu* was slowly making its way out to sea. They wondered to which islands she was going.

During their visit to Nancy, she mentioned that the thing she misses most is good reading material.

Richard's determination to get to Niue became an obsession. He went to the office of Air Rarotonga to inquire about the possibilities. Because it would be an international flight, even though it was not much further than the Northern Cook Islands, Air Rarotonga was not allowed to fly that route. He then went to the office of Air New Zealand at the airport. Polynesian Airlines, near bankruptcy, had flown that route until this week. If we went on their last flight we might have difficulty getting off the island until the next unscheduled visit by a freighter. The more impossible it seemed to get there, the more determined we became to go.

Richard renewed his thirty day visitor's permit and went on to Atiu and Mitiaro. Aljean, Emmy Lou and Allison stayed a few days after I flew on to Samoa. We had become a family of sorts and I hoped that we would stay in touch.

If the purpose of the tour to Rarotonga was to teach them the joy of budget independent travel, though the numbers were small, the success rate was one hundred percent. All of them have gone back again for extended South Pacific trips, traveling far beyond the places I showed them.

During my last days on Rarotonga, I became more aware of the fallout that was still reverberating from the controversial and rowdy elections of March, 1994. The Cook Islands, a nation with half the land area of Singapore spread out over ocean the size of India had just eleven thousand seven hundred and fifty eligible voters. The turnout was an amazing eighty five point nine percent (*Pacific Islands Monthly* , March, 1994). In spite of persistent scandals over the national debt resulting primarily from the Sheraton Hotel debacle and unanswered questions, internationally, about their off shore banking, the popular, charismatic Sir Geoffrey Henry was returned as Prime Minister.

Even though island life is changing, some things never will. The sunshine, the flowers and laughter. The rich, earthy smell after a rain. Vibrant colors and a clarity of light that has inspired generations of artists. The beauty and quiet dignity of the people who are still dancing to their own incomparable drumbeat.

More changes, I know, will come. I should have written about Rarotonga when it was still a backwater, an optional stop on the way to somewhere else, when it was still innocent in the remains of its isolation. Or maybe I shouldn't have written about it at all.

Chapter Twenty-Seven

Samoa

His telephone call, just weeks before we left for Rarotonga, was a surprise.

"Eona, Pita here. I have read what you wrote about Rarotonga. Eona, you would love my country!"

His booming voice had a buoyant enthusiasm that engulfed the listener and carried me along.

"Come," he said warmly, "come and be part of our aiga."

By the time we had talked for nearly an hour, I promised him that I would come sometime in late October after returning to Rarotonga. At the time, I couldn't have guessed that this invitation from a stranger would bring me to the very heart of Samoa.

My last day on Rarotonga I met Paddy Walker for lunch at Trader Jack's. When I first arrived she was in Tonga attending a Pacific Conference on Women's Issues as she had been four years earlier when the conference had been hosted by the Queen of Thailand in Bangkok. During the intervening years when we had been out of touch she had nearly died. Medication following simple surgery on her finger had left her ill enough to require several months of treatment in New Zealand. During that time she sold her home in New Zealand and also gave up her rental on Muri Beach in Rarotonga. She was at a crossroad in her life.

Retired icon of New Zealand's fashion industry, her glamour and sophisticated bearing gave no hint of her half-Samoan ancestry. During her first seven years she had lived with her grandmother in a Samoan village. Because her grandmother was high born of chiefly parents it had been a privileged childhood.

"Why don't you return to Samoa?" I asked.

She began to answer, then hesitated and my question went unanswered.

"You must call my friend," she said as she wrote her name on a scrap of paper. "Dr. Fay Alailima. Her husband is the Honorable Vaiao Alailima. Get a copy of her book, *My Samoan Chief*."

That was my introduction into the web of interconnecting relationships that I would encounter on Samoa.

Before I returned to Are Renga to pack, I faxed my arrival time to Le Tagaloa Pita at the South Sea Star Hotel in Apia.

With traditional shell eis, Ian and Jacki, Allison and her friends, came to the airport to see me off. After good-byes, I hurried to the departures lounge where a passing stranger stopped me.

"Where are you going?" he asked.

"Samoa."

He took the ticket envelope from my hand, writing as he spoke.

"Manase. Go to Stevenson's at Manase."

He was lost in the crowd and quickly forgotten as television crews were filming the departure of Tavita Brown, the newly crowned Miss South Pacific. She and her court responded to the magic of Rarotongan drums as they joined the dance troupe that had come to celebrate her victory flight to New Zealand.

My flight, Polynesian Airlines #624 was delayed. It was well past midnight when we arrived at Faleolo International Airport. I passed through customs quickly and stopped to exchange New Zealand dollars for Samoan tala. In the glare and confusion of arrivals I found no one to meet me. I knew the airport was more than twenty miles from Apia.

As I looked for a cab, a young man approached me.

"Are you Eona?" he asked, pronouncing my name in the Polynesian way with a French accent.

"I am Serge. Tagaloa is looking for you," he said as he waved to a large Samoan man, wearing a lavalava, who strode quickly toward us.

"I am Pita," he said as he firmly grasped my hand. A shock of gray hair contradicted his boyish appearance. I was charmed by his smile.

The Frenchman picked up my bags and led the way to an ancient white truck in the parking lot. Serge apologized as he reached in the window to untie the cord that latched the passenger door. He climbed into the back seat and quickly fell asleep as we drove through the night.

The road ran along the sea through picture book villages with dimly lighted open fales. I could see people sleeping on the floor mats, others watching TVs which were placed in the center of the fale. Behind some of the traditional fales were European style hurricane houses of concrete block with jalousie windows. Traditional houses consisted of an elevated, crushed coral gravel base covered with fine mats. Evenly spaced coconut palm posts supported thatched or corrugated metal roofs. Without walls, they were open to the cooling sea breezes. It was like the setting for a romantic South Seas novel set in the last century.

As we drove, Tagaloa spoke tirelessly about fa'a Samoa, the Samoan Way.

"The Matai system will never change," he said with passionate conviction. "It is the anchor of our culture."

As we reached the city we turned inland and drove through the sleeping outskirts of Apia, the only city in Western Samoa. The South Sea Star Hotel rose out of a dense tropical garden. A narrow three-story structure, it was built mainly of corrugated metal and substantial logs. The night watchman on the first landing stirred and sleepily greeted us as we passed through an unlatched heavy screened door into the hall. On my left was a large sitting room lavishly decorated with fresh bouquets of unfamiliar flowers. Rows of chairs flanked both walls and in the center a coffee table brought a pair of couches into a more intimate seating arrangement. Floor to ceiling jalousie windows ran along the broad wall. A stunning, colorful mural reminiscent of Gauguin covered the back wall.

Without entering the sitting room, we continued down the dimly lit hall. On my right was a canteen where Serge stopped, then three closed doors marked "Bath", followed by pairs of open doors on either side. I could see that the guest rooms were unoccupied, mattresses bare, some tipped up against the wall, which was not surprising...an effort to prevent mildew by maximizing air circulation during the damp rainy season.

"This will be your room," Tagaloa said as he set my bags in the corner. He opened the windows and turned on a large fan which stood by a small desk and narrow wardrobe, all the while smiling, welcoming me effusively, sincerely, to Samoa.

We went back down the hall to a tiny office near the front entrance. He took a ledger from the desk drawer, computed my rent for the month and said, "Breakfast is at 8:00 and will be on the house."

In the canteen, Serge had begun heating water in the hot pot.

"Would you join me for a cup of coffee?" he invited, already spooning instant coffee into two mugs. The only other guest at the South Sea Star, he lived on the second floor. His Samoan wife was at their home in Paris. An anthropologist, he researched African and Pacific cultures in which chiefs claim to trace their genealogy back to deities. He told me that Tagaloa, one of four Paramount chiefs of Samoa, holds the oldest matai title in Samoa.

I was struck by the similarity between Tagaloa's name and the Rarotongan god, Tangaroa, whose whimsical well-endowed statues were everywhere in the Cook Islands; whose image appears on the reverse side of the coin which bears the likeness of Queen Elizabeth, much to her chagrin, I have read.

"Tagaloa," Serge continued, "is a member of Parliament. He was educated in the United States and Europe. Through the years, he has held most portfolios of government ministries, including Minister of Tourism. When he called you from California he was returning from leading a group of two hundred Samoans, many from his home village, on a month long tour of Hawaii and California."

Tagaloa had told me that while visiting an old college buddy in Vermont, they had shown him copies of *The Solo Traveler*. It was through that connection that he made contact with me.

I had expected to be met by the hotel's driver and was stunned by the social and political stature of the exuberant man with the unabashed grin who had picked me up at the airport in the middle of the night.

Later, after I returned home, I read in the section on Samoa in *Blue Horizons*, published by the National Geographic Society: "Of the forty seven members of Western Samoa's legislative assembly forty five are by law matai, and one member, the Honorable Le Tagaloa Pita, holds one of the country's highest matai titles. It can," according to author Gene S. Stuart, "be traced back to the creator god."

It was past three o'clock when I went to my room. Suddenly exhausted, I fell asleep on top of the bed without opening my travel bag. It seemed that I had barely closed my eyes when I was awakened by a knock at the door.

"I am Faleela," she said. "You will be having breakfast with Tagaloa?"

It was as much statement as question. It was already seven forty four, so I quickly showered.

A narrow, slippery path led through the dripping tangle of jungly garden...a miniature urban rainforest. It was a bit past eight o'clock when I opened the door at the end of the path. The dining room was deserted. There were six tables, none of them set up, with no sign of staff or kitchen.

I studied the intricately thatched roof. Ribs, close together, and beams of coconut logs were tied with sennit. Half an hour passed. I began to wonder if I was in the right place. I heard the sound of a broom on the path and went outside to inquire of the woman who was sweeping fallen leaves off the walk if that was the dining room where I was to meet Tagaloa. She said it was.

On one side of the dining room, windows overlooked the garden; on the other side doors and windows were heavily draped with a red print fabric. They seemed to curtain a fale of traditional, though not open, design. I heard a radio playing softly and quiet activity inside.

It was nearly nine o'clock when Faleela came into the dining room from the family fale. A small-boned woman about forty she wore a long straight skirt and over-blouse in unmatched prints of denim-blue colors. She asked me if I would like sausage and eggs, but I told her toast and coffee would do.

She disappeared again into the fale.

A younger woman brought a huge stack of toast and pot of coffee. She wore a Western-style nylon dress that revealed clearly that her pregnancy was advanced. It would be her fifth child, she said, the others are eleven, ten, five and three. Her husband is gone, so they live with her parents in a house nearby.

About nine thirty Tagaloa came and sat across the table. We were soon joined by Serge, then an older brother of Tagaloa who had come from his village, Salani, to do some business in the city. Platters of eggs and sausage were brought and consumed. Three times the platters were refilled, along with stacks and stacks of toast.

"You must try supo esi," Tagaloa said. Soon the girls brought bowls made of nui...a half coconut shell...filled with mashed papaya and coconut cream, steaming hot and delicious!

Three times during breakfast men came to the door and Tagaloa excused himself as they went for conferences in the room behind the curtained windows.

Although two windows were open to the garden, the slowly rotating fan scarcely moved the heavy, damp air. Tagaloa's brother mopped his brow.

"I don't know how people can live like this in the city all closed up!"

Tagaloa returned dressed in the Samoan business suit...a gray gabardine wrap around lavalava, white cotton shirt, bare feet in leather sandals with a brief case in hand.

"I'm off for Parliament," he said.

His brother left soon afterward so I had time to ask Serge questions about Samoan culture.

"It is a system that has worked for a thousand years," he began, "but is now gently, subtly going through change...a generational tug-of-war."

Land tenure and leadership are irrevocably tied together. Matai control the distribution and use of land. A village, such as Va'vau, may be made up of about two hundred related people from about a dozen families. Each family has a matai. Together, the matais form a fono or village council. Leadership is by consensus. The ruling matai is chosen more by the degree of service he has rendered rather than, necessarily, by genealogy. The more powerful matai titles are from, historically, the more powerful villages. Status is derived from affluence, not from accumulated wealth, but by how much a family or village or matai is able to give at ceremonial occasions such as weddings, funerals, birth of a child, church dedication. Fine mats, pigs, tapa, canned fish or meat, baskets of taro...these are appropriate gifts. To obtain gifts for giving, Samoans may have to ask their relatives, fa'a molemole, who are obligated to help in order to maintain exchanges and feasting.

Every guest goes home with gifts and basketfuls of food.

The matai control not only the economy, they control every aspect of village life. In this nonmonetary, agricultural society, young men contribute their total productivity by working the plantations under their matai's control. In return, they are fed and provided for by the matai for whom they work. They realize that as they mature they will, in turn, be served by the youth. The more service they render, the more status and land they gain. If they are rebellious their position diminishes accordingly and if they are totally unproductive, they can be fined or even banished.

As young people migrate overseas or enter the cash economy, the balance is delicately tipped toward the desire to retain some of their earnings. Even those that go overseas are pressured to return a major portion of their income to their matai or in response to urgent fa'a lavelave (requests for help) from their families. Severing ties with his Samoan community, with his traditional land, is like self-imposed banishment, which is the worst punishment that can be inflicted on a Samoan. Coming from a communal society, the concept of functioning as an individual is difficult to accept.

It was nearly noon when I asked Serge how to get a bus into town. He said that they would stop to pick me up in front of the hotel.

"Stand on the other side of the road, because it goes first to the University, then through a neighborhood before turning around to go back to town."

It was one of many long conversations I would have with Serge as he helped me understand the complexities of Samoan culture.

I had been told that the bus fare into downtown Apia was fifty sene. I gave my fare to the driver who carelessly tossed it on the dashboard without giving me change. The driver was a husky man wearing a cotton print lavalava and T-shirt with the sleeves torn off. His well-muscled arms, back and shoulders were heavily tattooed. I put my hand out for change. Ignoring me, he sped off.

A young man got up and moved toward the back of the bus. Catching my balance, I was grateful for the seat he had vacated, but was steaming mad over the driver's perceived rudeness. I felt furious to have been cheated, even though the ten sene difference in fare equaled less than a nickel in U.S. money, then was embarrassed over my petty reaction.

My frustration had barely cooled when we arrived at the Maketi Fou, the sprawling covered market which is the center of commercial activity on 'Upolu. Buses bearing the names of their aiga, their village, crowd nine lanes, dropping off passengers and boarding others, moving forward in turn, sometimes circling the clock tower and returning to board more passengers before leaving for their destination. If there was any schedule or order I never grasped it.

I wandered through the market where row after row of fruits and vegetables were neatly displayed for sale. There were plaited baskets of coconuts, taro, papaya and mangoes and huge stalks of bananas. Toward the back of the market dozens of vendors were selling prepared foods wrapped in banana leaves. Others were preparing Samoan pancakes, which were balls of dough dropped into boiling oil like donut holes. I chose two pancakes and ordered a cup of koko Samoa, a hot chocolate drink made of crushed cocoa beans, sugar and water, then I joined some men sitting at a picnic table.

Next to the Maketi Fou, along the harbor side, was the fish market. I continued walking along the harbor on the inland side, past the clock tower, past a fale that houses the Office of Tourism and a multi-storied government building that, I was told, had been built by the Chinese as an aid project. As I walked through Apia, the words of the poets, Rupert Brooke among them, came to mind. I thought, *this isn't it. That Samoa has somehow disappeared in this chaotic commercial city with its broken sidewalks and ancient clapboard buildings devoid of character. Desperately, I thought, if that Samoa still exists I won't find it here in the city. Alafua, the pleasant leafy residential area where my hotel is located is not part of that enchanted, legendary Samoa either. It must be somewhere else! Perhaps it is in villages such as those we passed on the way from the airport.*

On the far side of town, Aggie Grey's, a large Victorian-style upscale hotel sparkled. The high, broad breakwater, which had recently been built to protect Apia from recurrence of cyclone damage, diminished the view of the harbor, but didn't stop the breeze, which always cooled the open, tiled lobby.

Hot and discouraged, I was missing the familiarity of Rarotonga. Worst of all, I had learned that sixty sene was the correct fare to the South Sea Star. My barely concealed rage had been misdirected. I waited for the Alafua bus, recognizing the colors...green, gray and yellow, with a red roof...even before I could read the sign. Feeling contrite and embarrassed, I intended to apologize to the driver. As it pulled up to the front of one of the middle lanes, I quickly crossed the lanes between. With one foot on the boarding step, one hand on the rod by the door, the bus began to move. Rage welled up in me again as I felt his action was intentionally contemptuous.

"May I board?" I shouted as he slowed while I climbed three steep steps to hand him sixty sene. Again, a young woman rose and moved back giving me her front seat.

Having a less than sterling relationship with the bus driver, I felt isolated at the South Sea Star. Except for breakfast, which was optional with my room, there was no restaurant closer than the city three miles away. The canteen had a refrigerator and hot pot, but I missed my kitchen at Are Renga and the village stores that were so near. Most of all, I missed the contagious good humor and friendly attitude of the Raro bus drivers. I went to bed early, hungry and homesick for Raro.

The South Sea Star was basic but clean. My room, more like a dorm than hotel, was eight feet by twelve feet. Jalousie windows, floor to ceiling, overlooked a garden with two huge mango trees, papaya and breadfruit. Nine rooms on the first floor shared three baths. The third floor, which has since been enclosed with guest rooms en suite, was a mass of studs with tubs and lavatories still in packing cases. It was a breezy place with laundry lines for drying clothes and a view of the galvanized rooftops and gardens of the surrounding residences.

Before the month would pass, it was, just as Are Renga had been, my home away from home and I sorely missed my family there and every member of the South Sea Star when I left.

When I wakened, heavy snoring from the next room startled me. I met Frank, a German tourist at breakfast. He was outspokenly disappointed in the location of the South Sea Star. He had expected a beach side resort with a bar; a place he could sun and swim. Clearly, he was less interested in the unique cultural advantage of our residential location and the outstanding personalities who were our hosts. I was less than eager to take that bus again soon and the Maketi Fou was my necessary access to travel to other places on the island.

"Frank," I said, "would you like to take a chance on going to Savaii?"

I had stopped at the Visitor's Bureau in Apia and out of curiosity I had picked up a brochure about Stevenson's. It seemed to satisfy his prerequisites.

"We could share cab fare to Mulifanua Wharf where we could catch the ferry to Savaii."

I don't know if he was caught by the sense of adventure or simply a desire for beach time.

"We will leave tomorrow!" he said, adding, "I have to go into town this morning to exchange money. Would you like to come along?"

I agreed to split cab fare to avoid another encounter with the bus driver. I exchanged $100 U.S. for $244.15 WS tala.

After completing his errands he asked, "Are you in a hurry to get back? We could stop for a beer."

I had noticed that the Tusitala, a Japanese-owned hotel was near the Maketi Fou, so we walked over. The garden restaurant was pleasant. Our "waitress" was six feet tall with bulging muscles. She moved with exaggerated grace and cast winsome smiles at Frank. I was uncomfortable, but remembered the guidebook's explanation of Fa'a fafine, an accepted phenomenon in Samoa. By the guidebook's definition, *a male child who was brought up as a female due to a shortage of female children to help in domestic chores*. Some, it said, revert to traditional male roles upon reaching adulthood.

I planned to return to the South Sea Star in a couple days, so I packed a light duffle leaving the rest of my things in the room, which would be my base while in Samoa.

At breakfast the next morning we told Tagaloa and the staff that we would be gone for a few days; that Frank (who was young enough to be my son) wanted beach time and I was going to research the island of Savaii.

Samoans who have been fishing for palolo

The Honourable Le Tagaloa Pita and his wife Aiono Dr. Fanaafi Le Tagaloa. She is Professor of Samoan Studies at the National University of Samoa.

Chapter Twenty-Eight

Ferry to Savai'i

Seuoti, who was Tagaloa's assistant in managing the hotel, called a cab for ten forty five so we could catch the noon ferry. Although we were early, there was a long line at the ticket counter with hundreds of Samoans lugging boxes and bags, kids and assorted produce, all crossing the narrow straits on the Lady Samoa Car Ferry.

I gave Frank 6 WST (six Western Samoa Tala) and watched our luggage while he joined the line to purchase our tickets. Everywhere, a festive spirit of anticipation prevailed, but after boarding, a pall fell over the Samoan passengers. By the time we had climbed the narrow stair from the level into which cars and trucks were driving to the upper passenger deck, there were already passengers lying prone on benches and on the floor, heads swathed in towels or sitting with their heads cradled miserably on their arms which rested on the back of the bench in front of them. Anticipation of seasickness, even before the ferry left the dock, seemed in stark contrast to their historic role as intrepid navigators who had roamed the Pacific in seagoing canoes.

I had worn my sea bands, effective Velcro wristlets with a plastic half-marble embedded to exert slight pressure on the acupuncture point on the inside of my wrists. The hour-long crossing was smooth. We encountered a slight roll midway, but nothing to justify the misery of the traveling Samoans.

Salelologa, where the ferry lands, was a small commercial center on the Southeast coast of Savaii, the larger, but less developed of the two main islands of Western Samoa.

We had no reservations, so Frank went to find out how to get to Manase. Speaking German to a man he recognized as his fellow countryman, he learned that cab fare to Manase would be about 50 WST, but if we called ahead someone would be sent from Stevenson's to pick us up. He directed us to Retzlaff's combination store and restaurant where, he said, we could use their phone. The woman storekeeper called Stevenson's to see if they had two rooms available and to ask for transport for us.

We ordered coffee and took a table to wait for the driver. It was about three o'clock when he arrived. He introduced himself as Oke (pronounced Okay) Sene. His warm welcome gave no hint that, as manager of Stevenson's, our arrival had taken him away during two critical hours while the staff was preparing to have a TV crew from Apia televise the evening show for a promotional countrywide newscast.

As we passed through villages along the east coast I couldn't hide my excitement. This was the elusive Samoa I had been searching for! Oke Sene responded to my enthusiasm by explaining what we were seeing. We passed through seaside villages with open fales. Women and children were enjoying bathing pools. Men were poling out to the reef on paopao, light outrigger canoes, or casting nets into the shallow lagoon. Kirikiti games were being played on village greens. Then we moved inland around a lava field that had flowed to the sea, wiping out everything in its path except the grave of a young Catholic nun, where it divided and flowed on either side.

Rachel checked us in at the registration desk. Stevenson's had opened just three months before and the landscaping was not quite complete. Nineteen air-conditioned rooms were on seven acres of beach frontage. The attractive units formed a broad half-ellipse built around a garden with a huge open fale in the center, which was used for community activities as well as for resort guests. The units were constructed of corrugated metal, pre-finished wallboard interior, with mat and bamboo ceilings and louvered windows.

The furniture was all village made, mat covered for decoration. The closet was a shelf with a hanging rod. Bright red hibiscus blooms on the pillows were in colorful contrast to green and white striped canvas drapes and spreads. Windows on both front and back walls caught the breeze and provided a sea view from every room. The outer walls of the shower were made of large bamboo poles set closely together, open to the brilliant blue sky and the towering palms and stars at night.

The first time I stepped into the shower I interrupted an encounter between a long, sleek shiny-black skink and a hapless pale lizard. I startled the predator and the tiny lizard flipped over and scurried away to safety between the bamboo poles.

It was near dinner time when I finished unpacking and dressed. I found Frank sitting by the bar enjoying sashimi with a man who introduced himself as Trevor Stevenson. They invited me to join them, but I went instead to get a table near the floor show in the dining room.

At dusk, two-dozen torches lighted the way to the beach across the narrow road. The conch sounded, a single note, swelling, protracted. The men in the combo, all from surrounding villages, wore floral print lavalavas, white shirts, bare or sandaled feet. Soft songs, sad songs, love songs were filled with vowel-laden lyrics that could be understood by the heart. The single string of the uaua, a pole protruding from a pail that serves as resonator, provided bass. There were two carved hollow drums for rhythm and a rolled pandanus mat, called selo, on crossbars that sounded like a muffled drum. Two guitars completed the combo. Girls who served us kicked off their sandals and joined the combo for the dance show. Trevor's beautiful wife, Anna, danced a graceful siva while TV cameras rolled and panned the room.

As I walked home from the dining room the full moon was the centerpiece in a pouf of silver clouds, which silhouetted towering palms. Island magic.

Rita, from the W.S. Visitor's Bureau, remembered me. She was there for palolo. Her home was in the village nearby with the big cathedral. That village, she explained, is famous for the legend of the beautiful maiden who went every day to the pool to bathe. Every day an eel would come to visit her when no one else was around. She would think, *it's only an eel.* One day he spoke to her. "When I die, cut off my head and bury it." That became the first coconut tree, she said. "So when you see the eyes and mouth on a coconut, remember the eel. Remember that things are not always as them seem."

Rita glowed with pride when she told me the legend. "To this day," she continued, "women are not allowed to bathe in that pool...only men. There's another bathing pool for women."

I asked Rachel about palolo.

"Seven days after the full moon in October," she said, "the palolo rise in the sea."

"When will that be?" I inquired.

"The old people know." she answered.

I was determined to wait for that event.

I seldom saw Frank, who split his time between the beach and bars. When I went to speak to him, he was sitting at the beach bar talking to a man who introduced himself as Morton. A Dane, he was Captain of the Rarotongan Rover, a freighter in the Cook Island service leased from the same shipping company that runs the Nga Maru III. Based in Avatiu Harbor, he ran between Vanuatu, Solomons, Tonga, Samoa and Rarotonga. Four months on, four months off. Annie Brown, the girl with him was somewhere between a child and woman, beautiful, shy.

When I returned to my room I found that a dozen wasps had moved into it, so I went to Rachel to ask to be moved to another room. She cheerfully, unquestioningly, complied.

Saturday evening a dance troupe from Apia performed on the stage by the beach bar. A gate was set up and 5 WST collected as we entered. I sat at a picnic table with Annie Brown and some of her family. The show was loud and long, the dancers were mediocre as they demonstrated dances of various island nations. The Cook Island dances seemed unrepresentative of the fine talent I had seen on Raro. I was embarrassed that the show, much more appropriate to a city bar, had come to the village. Would the young boys and girls try to emulate the suggestive, untraditional moves of the dancers?

As I was pondering this between numbers a man from the village leaped onto the stage, unplugged the floor lights and "rode" a sawhorse across the stage. Throwing it down, he tore off his T-shirt and threw it off stage. His bare chest revealed that his whole torso was tattooed in an intricate design as fine as lace. The traditional dance he did put the professional dancers to shame. The show ended in disarray. The final number seemed to be an anticlimax. I wondered if this would be a matter of village pride or if it would be taken up by the village council of matais; whether he would be admonished or praised.

After the show concluded he leapt onto the stage again and kissed the cheek of each of the girls in the troupe.

After breakfast Sunday morning I hurried toward Manase to the church. A young man stopped me and asked, "Where are you going?"

When I answered, "To church," he said, "Malo," nodded and let me pass.

The church bell rang when I was halfway there. The organist who was playing as I entered was the same man who played guitar in the combo at Stevenson's. Although small in numbers, the choir he led sounded like the one at the Mormon Tabernacle. By any standard, he is an accomplished musician.

The sermon was entirely in Samoan. There was no collection, so I gave a five tala note to a man outside, asking him how I should give it to the church. He called a boy over who took it to a table in the front of the church near the altar. Twice the boy came out to ask my name as if it had to be registered. People were often confused and children amused to meet a woman named Iona, which translates into the common name Ioane, John in the Polynesian languages. It was a common name because of the impact made by John Williams throughout the islands.

When the congregation rose to leave, I followed. The choir began singing when I was halfway to the street, so I quietly slipped back into the church to listen. A girl about ten, dressed in white, came and said, "The preacher wishes to talk to you."

I followed her to the house next to the church. The pastor greeted me at the door. I slipped off my sandals and he directed me to a chair across the room. In Pacific Island homes, furniture, if there is any, is usually lined up along the walls to keep it out of the way because village Samoans usually prefer to sit on floor mats, using the furniture only when there are European guests.

He apologized for not speaking part of the service in English.

"No problem!" I said. "The music was truly beautiful."

When I asked him what he thought about tourism in Manase he said that the resort is, basically, o.k. It gives the young people jobs so they can help their families.

I said that the resort seems to not be a problem, but I didn't like what went on last night, referring to the show on the beach. I felt that the dance troupe from Apia lacked cultural integrity. Many local people attended and 5 WST at the gate may have been a hardship for larger families. Young people enviously looked through the fence feeling left out. The boom-box style electronic music was much too loud, but the thing that bothered me most was the bump and grind in what they claimed was traditional dance from Rarotonga. In four months there I had never seen such a thing.

He looked surprised at my comments and said, "That's what my sermon was about."

His wife brought us a fruit drink and sat with us. I could hear the children and teenagers busy in the kitchen. They have ten children, she said, seven girls and three boys.

"How did you meet?" I asked.

"By chance. I am from a village near Apia. She was from a village on the other side of Savai'i. It is against church law to serve in your own or your wife's village.

About customs, he said that each village, through the village council, makes laws that govern that village. Curfew in Manase from six o'clock to seven o'clock is strictly enforced. When curfew was sounded everyone had to go to his or her own home. Sa is prayer time. No one can walk through the village during Sa. After Sa everyone has the evening meal. Then they can walk around for a while. About ten o'clock everyone should go to his own fale and it is quiet time.

I wanted to ask what would happen if someone who was not Samoan would violate Sa, but I didn't ask.

As I walked home from church, Annie Brown came to the fence and called to me, "Come and see."

Walking back to the gate I entered the grounds of the beach side resort that was totally unlike Stevenson's next door. There were small open fales. On the far side, a group of women were cooking dinner in a large pot over an open fire.

"May I come back later?" I asked.

Oke Sene was sitting at the bar when I returned. I sat beside him and asked him about Sa. He said, "The curfew in Manase at six o'clock is mandatory."

"How is this village law enforced?"

"The whole family will suffer if Sa is not kept. A meeting of the village council will be held the next day to discuss this serious offence. The matai is then obligated to inform the family of the penalty."

Because we were having water problems again I bought a large bottle of Canadian Club ginger ale from the girl who was tending bar. Yesterday they had a full house and no water. After checking the pumps and filters and the whole system it was learned that someone had shut the water off at the street.

Gradually, I began piecing together the history of Stevenson's. In Samoa, only five percent of the land was "freehold" and could be bought and sold. Another fifteen percent was government owned. The rest was owned by the aigas and could not be bought or sold.

From different sources I heard rumbles of rumor about Trevor's acquisition of the land on which the resort was built. A man settled here when it was wilderness, I was told...the first man who lived here. When he was old, a woman fed him who was a half-caste and he gave her this piece of land. She married a palagi (foreigner) who was smart enough to have it titled freehold. They entrusted it to the care of an attorney in Apia.

When it came up for sale a dozen years ago, Trevor bought it, leasing part of the beach frontage from the villagers. Rumors that I heard in Apia claim that it may be contested in the Land and Title Court.

During the Colonial period Germans settled in large numbers in Samoa developing plantations and trading companies. Some of the most prominent Samoan families are of mixed ancestry.

Anna Stevenson (formerly Schmidt) is from two villages over, a beautiful, sophisticated woman who is Afakasi; that is, half-caste. Trevor was an attorney from New Zealand who had lived in Samoa for twenty years. He also owned a printing company. They lived in Apia, but often spent time at the resort.

After discussing Sa, Oke Sene told me that there had been a break-in last night during the beach performance. Someone had come through the bamboo shower wall of #9, the room I had shared with the bees when I first arrived. They had taken a lot of things, the police had been called, an investigation made. The person was arrested and the property returned.

I had noticed some uniformed men talking to Oke Sene just before I went to church, but I didn't realize that they were policemen. They wore blue gabardine lavalavas, matching blue safari-like jackets, but I had assumed that they were just people dressed for church.

Frank has gone on. When other travelers ask me how long I am planning to stay, I tell them, "Until the palolo rises."

Police Marching Band, Apia, Samoa

Chapter Twenty-Nine

Fia Fia

Christian, a young German backpacker with a ponytail, was staying in the open fales on the beach. He said that Rachel knows the Pastor on 'Upolu who has the Salani River Fales. They were very inexpensive and were in a beautiful location.

"They provide a mattress and plenty of mosquitoes," he laughed. "Rachel will write a letter for you if you want to go."

Barbara, a German girl who lives in Samoa, was showing her friends, a couple from Germany, the islands. They slept late so we often had breakfast together or sat in the big fale in the afternoon. She was a friend of Anna's and had also come for palolo.

Today Rachel said the palolo will not rise until the 26th...not tomorrow morning...but the day after. You can feel the excitement rising. Two canoes went out today from the village to check the reef.

Not wanting to risk missing the event, I asked the watchman to knock on my door at five a.m. He came down to the beach where I was sitting in the dark thinking it would be helpful if I knew what a palolo looked like!

"The moon must be there when palolo rise," he said as he pointed several degrees to the east. "When the moon is there palolo finished!" he said as he indicated its present position.

"I should be at the village for palolo," I said wistfully.

"You can go," he said.

As I walked back to my room, the young man who plays the lead guitar was sitting with the watchman. He had come to work while it was still dark even though they were singing and playing far into the night, my harmonious lullaby to sleep.

He said, "You should come to my village, not here, to take pictures."

I asked how they know when the palolo will rise.

He said, as Rachel had, "They just know. The old people know."

All day the villagers had been preparing for fia fia. Truckloads of palm branches were brought to the big fale. Men French-braided them around the fale posts. Anna and the village women were sitting on mats in the fale weaving baskets of split palm fronds. I watched them and tried it. Over and under and back, over and under and back for the top of the basket, then two sections were woven together. They were finer and stronger baskets than I had seen in either the Cook Islands or Fiji. Even with their patient instructions I couldn't get the hang of it, so I worked on nets for catching palolo. Supple green branches were bent into an oval with the ends tied together. We stitched fine netting, like cheesecloth, onto the frames. The palolo are thin, just heavier than threads they told me.

A light rain had been falling, pleasantly cool, but the men had been working all day in wet lavalavas. From eight in the morning until mid-afternoon women sat cross-legged on the mats working, laughing, talking. A world and time away, but reminiscent of an old fashioned quilting bee.

In that context, Anna's urban sophistication vanished and she was totally Samoan.

"Palolo," she said, "come out in lovely colors, almost iridescent shades of pink and green and brown, the colors of the coral. It is like a miracle to see them rising. They are swimming very fast trying to get out to sea."

"Will they rise if it is still raining?" I asked, somewhat foolishly.

"Palolo don't care if it's raining!" she laughed. "Always palolo rise when there is the first sustained rainy period with lightning, always seven days after the full moon in October on Savaii. On 'Upolu it is after the full moon in November."

This seemed very curious to me and they remained an intriguing mystery. I was thoroughly caught up in the contagious excitement.

When the rain stopped, I walked to Annie Brown's place. I was surprised to meet her mother, the same Rachel who had been trying to teach me to make a basket in the afternoon. Morton, the Danish sea captain, waved to me from the lagoon where he was swimming.

I wanted to include information about Tanu Beach Fales in *The Solo Traveler* so I brought my notebook. For a truly Samoan experience, I recommend Tanu Beach at Manase. They began renting beach fales one or two years ago on a perfect sandy beach next to Stevenson's, but in a more natural setting. Pua trees canopied the grounds providing shade to the open fales. Each fale had a name. Ioane (John) was the fale Morton had chosen, closest to the lagoon. Anetelea was in the shade on the right side of the property looking at the beach, Sir Peter Noa on a slight hill overlooking the sea. Thirty WS tala a night per person, ten tala more for a mat, chair and table. All rudimentary furniture. A blue corrugated metal building had three doors, one with a flush toilet; one changing/storage room and a bathing room which consisted of a large barrel of water, a bucket and low down, a water tap. Concrete floors. You would want to wear thongs. It was very basic.

What Tanu Beach lacked in facilities was made up for in the setting of awesome beauty. They provided papaya and coconuts but you would have to bring all your other food with you. However, dinner, Samoan style, was optional. They may have chicken, fish or pork, taro, breadfruit, pawpaws. Maybe she said chicken and fish...here the language broke down a bit. Five WS tala per person. They had no phone, but you can write to Rachel and Taito, Tanu Beach at Manase, Savai'i, Western Samoa.

As Annie was showing me around, whenever I would say, "This place is beautiful!" she would smile and say, "I know" with an extended inflection that sounded musical.

I had begun to sort everyone at Stevenson's out. There were about fifteen employees, one of them Annie Brown's uncle.

When I met Oke Sene as I came to dinner, he smiled and took the lei he was wearing and put it around my neck.

"Ula of moso oi," he said, "it is worn for palolo. They are attracted to the fragrance."

It is a feathery looking blossom or leaf. I couldn't tell, a pale golden-green.

He said, "I will go to my village to gather palolo as I always have. Adrienne will bring you to Manase village."

Adrienne, from New Zealand, was brought to co-manage the resort shortly after it opened.

"My father is half-Samoan," she said. "He was born in Apia and sent to school in New Zealand when he was twelve. I've come to Samoa to get in touch with that part of me."

The buffet table, to celebrate fia fia, was laden with delicious, unfamiliar traditional Samoan foods.

While I finished dinner, Oke Sene told me that fia fia was beginning. The Manase village choir had already assembled in front of the backdrop that had been built in the big fale during the afternoon of poles and lengths of plaited palm fronds similar to those used for roof thatch. The poles were covered with palm fronds and decorated with colorful spikes of ginger blossoms, called teuila in Samoa.

Three matai sat on one side, young men in the center, girls and women to my right. Everyone sat cross-legged on mats. Small children played on the periphery, given drumsticks, which they used to beat out the rhythm on the floor.

The women all wore long red skirts, topped by white T-shirts; the men, who were bare chested, wore ulas of moso oi or chains of leaves and an assortment of print cotton lavalavas.

One by one the women, young and old, rose to dance the siva, a sinuous, sensual, slow, impromptu dance exhibiting remarkable grace and agility. Some would dance all the way down to a near sitting position, then rise again, their movements coordinated to the rhythm of drums.

A tall young man seemed to be the choir leader. He wore only a lavalava of shimmering, iridescent material with a belt of red feather pom-poms. Lithe and graceful, he danced with masculine vigor as the young men joined him singly or in groups with guttural chants; thigh slapping, rowing threatening...their movements all seemed to hold meaning.

There were only four of us seated on the mat as spectators, two Japanese girls, Barbara and I, yet the show went on till nearly midnight. It was clear that they were dancing for themselves, for their own pleasure, for the palolo.

Rain had been almost incessant the past two days. Day-biting mosquitoes were plentiful. They were fragile looking, but wary and resilient, so I had kept punk burning in my room in the daytime, too, very effectively.

At twelve forty a.m. the generator went out again plunging the compound into total darkness. It seemed that I had barely fallen asleep when an urgent knock on Anna and Trevor's door roused me. Hurriedly dressing, I walked out into the pouring rain. Trevor told me that they were going to Anna's village, so they were leaving early, but everyone would be meeting at three a.m. in the office. I began to wonder if these people ever sleep! As Anna and Trevor left, rain came in a downpour typical of monsoons, with lightening and thunder.

A group of very loud drunken men, one a European, were in the room two doors down. Twice they pounded on my door mistaking my room for theirs. I had decided to give up on palolo because the men seemed totally unpredictable and out of control.

At four a.m. Adrienne knocked on my door and said, "It's time to go. Rachel and the Japanese girls have already gone."

We met in the bar for a cup of coffee. Adrienne, her father and their friend, Sue, from New Zealand completed our group.

Carrying lanterns and torches we walked about a mile down the beach into Manase. As we walked, Adrienne pointed out the house in which she lived. When we stopped, she put ulas of moso oi around Sue's neck and mine to insure our luck with the palolo.

In the darkness hundreds of people, fully dressed, quietly walked into the lagoon carrying nets and baskets. Because of my camera, I stayed on the shore holding the lanterns. Adrienne's Mom joined me and later, one of the drunken Samoans who proved to be a gentleman in spite of his condition. He explained that the palolo are the egg and sperm of the coral animal. He called it Pacific caviar. They appear on only one night a year in a frenzy of mating. When sunlight hits them they melt away and disappear, which accounts for the urgency of night fishing. Nothing stops the palolo or the people from gathering this delicacy.

There was no moon at all, although the rain had stopped. For an hour the village people moved in the darkness toward the reef. Lightning split the sky and we could see them in the distance.

Gradually it became light enough for us to see each other dimly. In the distance, on the reef a colorful wall of people began moving toward the beach slowly working their nets through the water scooping palolo into their baskets.

Two outriggers were the first to come in. They showed me their catch. The lantern revealed about three inches of colorful wiggly wormlike creatures in the bottom of their baskets, some trying to wriggle up the sides of the net lining the basket.

At breakfast, Trevor brought a platter of palolo. Fried in butter and onions, it topped squares of toast looking a bit like apple butter. At first the memory of their appearance in the baskets was too fresh. He teased me into tasting it and I found palolo a bit salty, but quite delicious.

Adrienne's father, Ted, was sitting alone so I went to speak to him. Since he and Paddy both had Samoan childhoods and later schooling and residency in New Zealand, I thought they might know each other.

"Paddy Walker? She's my cousin," he said.

"I'll tell her that we met. What is your last name?"

"Gray," he said, looking somewhat surprised that I would ask.

When I asked how he spells it, he said, "Grey. Aggie Grey is my mother. Adrienne is her granddaughter."

Aggie Grey. The South Pacific legend!

We spoke again of palolo.

"There is always a storm with thunder and lightning."

He speculated that, although it is the phase of the moon that triggers it, the lightning might guide them into the passages. It is in the lagoon where the passages through the coral are that the palolo can be found, where fresh water rivers run into the sea. That is how the coral reproduces and, like salmon, dies. Pink are female, brown and black male.

A young Samoan who worked for a palagi importer/exporter was waiting in the big fale for transport. Two young men from Pennsylvania joined us later. In the meanwhile I was able to ask him about the matai system.

"It is good," he said. "Everyone knows his or her place and the orderly society functions smoothly as a result."

"What about Sa?"

"Sa is kept," he said.

"What happens if someone violates Sa, if they walk through the village during prayer time?"

"They may be sent away, but only if the breach is consistently rebellious. It does not happen for a first offence. A fine would be levied perhaps a week cutting weeds in the bush garden or a fine of some food. If the offender persists, he and his whole family could be sent away. Or the fine could be, yes it could be, a hundred pigs."

"How could someone get a hundred pigs?" I asked, incredulous.

"They could. They could get a hundred pigs by going to all the members of their aiga, even those who are scattered far away, and asking for their help, explaining that they are in a lot of trouble."

By then, others had joined us. Someone in the group told of one incident, they couldn't remember the name of the village for sure. They had threatened to roast a man like a pig and even had the fire going. The pastor threw himself around the accused man saying, "You will have to roast me, too!" The threatened punishment was abandoned. Whether or not it was true, I didn't know. Perhaps it was just a bogeyman story to impress recalcitrant children. But I am coming to understand that the matais wield enormous power within the system. Yet everyone I spoke to, at whatever level of society, supported the matai system, saying in defense, that the matai are chosen and can be stripped of their power. Along with power comes tremendous responsibility for the well being of their aiga, their extended family. They stressed that everything is done by consensus.

When the palagi came, he joined the conversation. He said that suicide is a huge problem in Western Samoa. He explained that it might be young people who are caught in a system they no longer believe in and feel powerless.

When I saw him the next day, I asked Oke Sene about the pigs.

"Yes, it could happen that way. They could get a hundred pigs, but it might take ten years. They seldom assess such a hard punishment now."

Barbara and her friends offered me a ride back to Apia in her Bronco. We drove four hours around the remaining portion of the island's rim back to Salelologa.

Safotu was a beautiful village, larger than Manase, with a huge Catholic Cathedral in the center. There was a large concentration of Germans there, or part German, like Anna, whose home village that is.

We drove around another huge lava field, inland through wild country. Occasional clearings contained a traditional house amid black lava rock fences, fales on black stone bases giving the area a harsh look, unlike the fales set in coves of white sand beach. Lush jungle was being cleared, slash and burn, for new plantations. Around Assau the destruction of coconut plantations and homes testified to the awesome power of the monster cyclones, Val and Ofa. Although it had been three years, rebuilding was just beginning. The battered walls of roofless churches stood like bleached skeletons amid the ruins.

Dark clouds hovered over the mountains. High cliffs on the west coast were topped by neat, traditional villages.

We turned off the road at Taga. A small boy rushed from a booth at the roadside to collect one WST a head custom fee. In the large fale the talimalo, a council meeting of matais, was being held. Each member of the fono sat formally at a designated post according to his rank. The highest chief of the village, the ali'i, sits at the head of the fono. His talking chief or tula fale, who is the village orator, sits beside him holding the symbols of his office, the fly whisk, called fue, and the staff representing chiefly authority. At the opposite end from the ali'i sits the mayor, called pulenu'u, who is an elected official that conducts village business with the national government. They paid us no attention as we passed.

The road was narrow over lava rock tough on tires and suitable only for a four-wheel drive vehicle. Barbara's friend drove as if he was on the Autobahn.

We parked and walked over huge, flat lava rocks that led to blowholes spouting like geysers, gurgling beneath the rock platforms as waves whooshed with enormous power and sound up through a dozen holes. Like children, we tossed coconuts into the blowholes and watched them thrown high into the air by the powerful surge of water.

We arrived at the ferry landing at one fifteen after a walk on Black Sand Beach. There was already a long line of cars waiting impatiently and many trucks loaded with two by four lumber from the mills at Assau. Barbara went to the office to make sure we could get on. She returned in a hurry, uncertain whether we could board. She handed me my bag and the ticket she had purchased for me because even if the Bronco couldn't go, as a pedestrian, I could. I didn't see them again until I got off the ferry where she was waiting for me. She grabbed my bag and took me all the way back to the South Sea Star. I showed them my room, which they all agreed was an exceptional value for Samoa.

Back in Apia, I asked Serge about the things I had heard, particularly about the high suicide rate among Samoan youth. He went into greater detail with remembered examples. An older sister had scolded her younger brother in front of other villagers. He felt humiliated and drank a glass of paraquin, which is a commonly used herbicide or insecticide and is readily available on most plantations. It kills instantly. "Sometimes," he went on, "where there is no high cliff to leap from, the young person may ask around the village to borrow a gun to kill some wild pigs. Someone who hears that may go to the boy's family because there are no wild pigs around, and tell them, so stopping the potential suicide. Or they may hear and rush to the beach to stop a self-drowning. Usually it is because he has been shamed or humiliated over something he felt wasn't justified. He may fall into musu where he just curls up and goes into himself in deep depression or he may go into an angry rage where he hits things and hurts himself or, having no way to vent his emotions, to express his rage and frustration, he may kill himself.

I began to see that there is a dark side to life in Paradise.

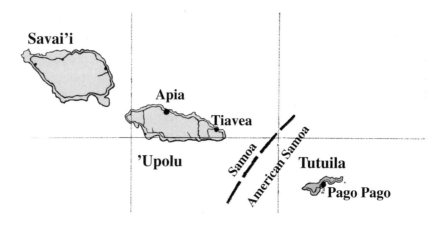

Samoa is a group of islands about 600 miles northeast of Fiji. Savai'i and 'Upolu form Samoa, formerly Western Samoa, and is an independent country. American Samoa includes the island of Tutuila.

On this map the scale is approximately 100 miles per inch. 'Upolu is about 100 miles long from east to west.

Chapter Thirty

To Nai

Mornings I awakened to the sound of bird song in the garden. Angelic voices singing hymns in the soft Samoan language often put me to sleep at night. My first evening back, Seuoti invited me to go with him to choir practice. We walked to the corner, turned left and continued around the church to a large open fale behind it. It abutted the backside of the property where South Sea Star is located. The garden my windows overlooked was behind the pastor's house.

About thirty people had assembled before we arrived, sitting in irregular rows on the mat. I joined the women while Seuoti sat with the men in the front rows. Clearly, these people enjoyed each other's company. A dozen more people drifted in before roll call was taken. A fine was levied against choir members who were absent. The ladies voices rose a cappella, clear and sweet. Deep bass of the men joined. Beautifully rendered hymns were one of the constants throughout Polynesia.

By the time I met Tagaloa's wife, Aiono, I had read most of *My Samoan Chief*. I mentioned how much I was enjoying the book. For a moment Aiono stiffened, then hesitated before saying, "It was written by my sister in law." Pita...Tagaloa...and Vai, the Honorable Vaiao Alailima, were brothers!

The humorous view Dr. Fay Calkins expressed as she first arrived in Samoa as Vai's young American bride perhaps wounded family pride. Copyrighted first in 1962, it was published by the University of Hawaii Press, a light read that explained from the outsider's point of view various aspects of Samoan culture. She also wrote a scholarly book, *Aggie Grey, a Samoan Saga*, which includes a century of Samoan history into which that legendary life was woven.

After spending my first day back home reading and writing and catching up on laundry, I took the bus into town. The market was bustling and the bank was crowded with patrons. I mailed letters to my children, then stopped at a grocery to buy WeetBix and peanut butter. Fourteen tala. I wondered how Samoans could afford groceries, at least imported items that seemed way out of reach.

I had determined that an apology was in order to the bus driver, but I didn't see him again until one of my last days in Samoa and by then he either didn't remember or didn't care.

I waited for the Alafua bus in front of an open market stall. Along with a dozen others, my bus pulled into one of the lanes. People walked between and among the moving buses with seeming disregard for safety. Buses temporarily stopped to unload market produce through trap doors in the back of the bus as well as through the front doors. Every able-bodied man stopped to help, as required. The bus was filled, then it pulled around and came into the stall twice more as passengers sat on stranger's laps. Children, without being told, always deferred to their elders, an eight-year-old to a teenager, teenager to a 20-year old, and so on. It seemed that palagi and elders were automatically given front seats.

A small girl sat beside me. Her mom was carrying a baby and two whole fishes by their tails. Two men hoisted a large woven basket of coconuts onto the bus for her, then a gunny bag filled with potatoes. More people boarded the bus along with a stalk of bananas, more palm baskets of coconuts until the aisles, the front and spaces under the seats were all full. Yet the driver kept stopping to pick up more passengers. A man about 30 got off the bus more than a dozen times to help lift produce or children off the bus and help other people board. All this was done with patience and good humor although it was unbearably hot and humid. As the bus got more crowded the small girl sat on my lap neither looking at me nor smiling the whole way, timid of the only palagi who rode the buses.

Subtle rules that govern a Samoan's conduct are apparent on the bus as passengers constantly interact, rearranging themselves wordlessly as newly boarding passengers tip the balance of status.

Seuoti preached the Sunday sermon today. I sat by his wife, Sia, who works at the University of South Pacific administration office. They invited me to come to their home for to nai, the traditional feast which is cooked in the umu, the ground oven, and served after church.

We were seated cross-legged on the floor while young men in lavalavas served us. Large banana leaves were set on the mat in front of us. We were each served a mountain of food...tender baked breadfruit, pork cooked in two ways, a whole fish each, herring in coconut cream, wieners, soup, coconut. Koko Samoa was served. Our mugs were refilled again and again by the attentive young men. We were not expected to eat all of it. The children who served us would eat what was left afterward.

Feasting was an integral part of Samoan life. Most often it was done at home or in church or community fales. The food was always prepared in umus. Restaurants were few and cater primarily to palagi with tourist prices and small portions that Samoans consider laughable.

Urban Samoan life went on around me. Sometimes, I was honored by being invited to join them. I noticed that the men in Alafua wore lavalavas ninety percent of the time, white for church, bright cotton prints for everyday. The laundry lines on the third floor were frequently filled with brightly printed rectangles of cotton cloth which were worn by both men and women.

Sunday was, necessarily, a lazy day as life in Samoa was centered on church and family. Service began at eight thirty and was finished by ten o'clock. Sia and Seuoti invited me to join them the following Sunday for Pastor's to nai. We went home to change into casual clothes. Seuoti exchanged his white shirt and tie and his white gabardine lavalava for a cotton print lavalava and shirt, half open; leather sandals for flip-flops. He carried a coconut leaf fan because it was already hot. Sia wore a lavalava, blouse and thongs, saving her white nylon dress to put on again for the three p.m. service.

In the large fale behind the church, where choir practice was held, Seuoti sat at the post designated for the talking chief. He asked me to sit at the post across from him where Sia would join me. She had gone into town with another woman to buy cocoa.

The boys have brought from Seuoti's house a leaf basket filled with baked breadfruit halves and a large kettle of soup made from pork bones, potatoes and carrots. Other women arrive with cakes and baskets of food.

There are four men seated at posts. The young pastor, Tavita (David), Seuoti and two others I had met at choir practice. Sia joined me on the mat, seated at the next post, as the boys began to serve. Ferenisi, just four years old proudly served Tavita first. He brought a pandanus eating mat, covered by a banana leaf on which was put a half breadfruit, baked, a kind of taro root and palusami, a banana leaf package containing a taro leaf wrapping coconut cream which had been baked in the umu. It was delicious, tasting somewhat like roukau in Rarotonga, but the taro leaf was whole, not chopped, and the coconut cream had congealed, almost like soft cream cheese.

Ferenisi returned with a plate that contained a chop, two kinds of pasta, a bowl of Sia's soup, a plate of fish, a plate of cake, then a steaming cup of Koko Samoa. Each item was served individually with grace and dignity. Dean, the teenage son of Sia and Seuoti, John from Seuoti's Sunday School class and two other young people served, attentive to every detail.

The pastor was the first to push his pandanus mat away. Ferenisi removed the left over food and carried it to the adjoining cookhouse. He brought an enamel bowl of warm water and clean towel, folded, on a plate because knives and forks were not used. In turn, each person's plates were removed, a bowl of water and towel brought.

The steaming kettle of koko refilled our enamel mugs. Dessert was a piece of cake the color of pumpkin.

Once a year, on White Sunday, parents serve the children.

When everything had been cleared, Sia, who was aware of my discomfort sitting cross-legged, said, "We can stretch out our legs now, but they must be covered because we are in the presence of chiefs." She pulled a mat over my legs and hers.

Conversation began as the children, who had served, retired to the cookhouse laughing and singing. The time had come for them to eat whatever was left from the plates and mats they had cleared away. Then the children washed the dishes. They learned to serve their parents and matais early and cheerfully as though it was a privilege. They knew that in Fa'a Samoa one day they would be sitting at the posts being served.

After to nai I visited Aiono and Tagaloa. I had shown him the itinerary of an Elderhostel group out of Hawaii, which had been on Rarotonga while I was there. I recommended to him that Samoa should focus its marketing on senior tours. The impact of tourism would be less damaging if the focus was on the cultural uniqueness of Samoa, which has successfully maintained much of its culture in spite of whalers and traders, colonialism and missionaries.

"Yesterday, Tagaloa, when I was talking to Joe and Tui at Tanumapua Plantation, I felt that I had reached the very heart of Samoa! I..."

He stopped me mid-sentence, his unrestrained enthusiasm bubbling over.

"That's what we will call it, Eona...the Heart of Samoa Tour!"

Barry Rose at Coconuts, Si'umu

Chapter Thirty-One

Coconuts

Coconuts is an American owned resort on the other side of 'Upolu which Air New Zealand includes in its island tours. I had decided to cross the island to visit them.

At six fifteen that morning I was waiting for the bus when Aiono stopped in the white truck that had picked me up at the airport. (Tagaloa wrote that they have replaced the truck with a new van since I was there.) She was on her way to the National University where she is a Professor of Samoan Studies. When she dropped me off at the market she said, "Take the Si'umu bus."

We rattled over mountain roads with corkscrew turns, rising higher and higher until we lost the panoramic north coast view. Over the mountain tops we were in an other-worldly cloud forest of tree ferns. Fat brown cattle grazed in chin high meadows of grass. There were bush gardens of bananas and on the descending slope, coconut plantations. I had a sensation of steep inclines as we chugged up the mountains, more so going down. When we reached the coast we turned left, passing through several coastal villages, then backtracked. The hour-long bus ride to the south coast was 2.50 WST; 50 sene more to continue on to Coconuts.

They dropped me by the roadside. A thatched shelter bore a sign, which read Coconuts Beach Club and I followed the narrow road that led toward the sea.

Coconuts, which had been built by Jennifer and Barry Rose, was a big surprise!

It is superb in design, on a gorgeous beach with a congenial staff, excellent chef and a good relationship with the villagers. It is complete with water sports equipment and rental jeeps.

If escape was Jennifer and Barry's intent, they couldn't have expressed it in a more dramatic way than through the architectural design of their tree house. Massive treetop high walkways lead to units that have views of the rainforest gardens on one side and ocean views on the other.

Over coffee in their open seaside dining room, I read their bios, which hint at unresolved intrigue. As attorneys in Beverly Hills with dual careers, they "had it all". Sometimes they talked of escaping their opulent life style in Southern California but they were ensnared by the glamour that snowballed.

Disenchantment began when Jennifer discovered, and reported, irregularities in payments diverted to a popular TV star. The response was that she should leave it alone. Her discovery had put her in the center of a legal firestorm. Honor and outrage mingled until they decided to make a break, selling everything they owned. They talked of finding a place where they could own a three-stool bar like the one they had enjoyed as a courting couple some years before. They wanted a simple place on some remote island.

But their dream's realization did not come easily. They chartered a crewed cruising yacht and sailed the Mediterranean, then the Caribbean looking for the perfect island. They continued their search in the South Pacific. It somehow came together in Samoa when they discovered the undeveloped south coast of 'Upolu.

What Michael...Mika...the chef was escaping is not so clear, but he caught their vision and is now married to a Samoan.

When I looked up from reading the remarkable story of their quest, the tide had receded to an extreme low revealing an irregular forest of coral. A fisherman in an outrigger was poling out from shore. With spears and spear guns, villagers were wading out into the knee-deep water of the lagoon, while groups of women scoured the reef and corals for edible shellfish.

As she poured my coffee, the waitress said, "This is a perfect day for gathering sea urchins."

"How do you cook them?" I asked.

She looked surprised.

"We eat them raw. Sometimes when there is nothing to eat in the house I take some breadfruit or a boiled banana and go to the lagoon and find many good things to eat."

"Like a seaside supermarket?" I joked.

She giggled. Moments later, she and another waitress had tied up their puletasi, long straight skirts, and were wading into the lagoon in search of urchins.

When Jennifer and Barry joined me, they apologized for the extremely shallow condition of the lagoon.

Mika simply laughed and said, "Somebody must have pulled the plug!"

They spoke of the transition to island life, their deep involvement with the villagers, their difficulties and the pleasures that come from living in so remote and different a place.

I asked Barry, "If you had it to do all over again would you do it the same way?"

"I'm not a visual person," he said, "but I like what's here and wouldn't do it any differently."

"I mean, would you go back to California to the life you had there?"

There was no hesitation in his answer. "Never!"

Two young boys came into the back of the restaurant with a large bottle of coconut cream they hoped to sell. While waiting for Mika they optimistically asked me, "Any money?"

"No money," I answered, disappointed to see children begging. "Do you have any?" I asked.

They smiled and turned their attention to their transaction with Mika. About 70 villagers are employed, to one degree or another, by Coconuts.

I was invited to the gift shop to see a basket of sea urchins that had been collected. The salesgirl handed one to me, a ball of thin spiny needles protruding in every direction.

"They don't bite!" she said, laughing at my timidity.

In the center of the gray spiny thing was dark, soft, pulsating flesh, a frightened living thing quivering, rearranging itself delicately in my hand.

"How do you eat them?" I asked.

"Just like this," she answered.

The bus schedules are irregular and I didn't want to miss the only bus back to Apia, that would leave between one thirty and three. A soft rain had been falling all day, growing heavier as I reached the roadside bus shelter.

Local fishermen were coming back with their catches. Each had a dozen or so lagoon fish "gilled" on the end of a stick used like a stringer. Most of the fish were six to eight inches long, colorful and varied. There were eels, octopus and fish with spines all over their skin or puffed into a ball. The fishermen all seemed proud of their catches and satisfied. I asked how they would be cooked. Boiled in water with coconut cream was the most frequent answer. They had fished all day in the rain, their lavalavas dripping as they walked.

While waiting under the scant shelter I met Fausi. He was about thirty. He had lost his father when he was eight. His Mom died earlier in the year.

"I am an orphan," he said.

He spoke with pride about Fa'a Samoa, the way Christianity permeates every fiber of life in Samoa.

His English had little accent. I asked who had taught him.

"I spent two or three years in the Bay area of California," which explained much about this urbane and sophisticated young Samoan.

"I returned in 1987 for Christmas. Mom was ill so I stayed."

"Will you go back?" I asked.

"No, because I have land here."

He grew up on his Mom's family land, his portion, fourteen acres on a peninsula.

"You have to get there by boat," he said, "because the neck of the peninsula is mangrove swamp. It is not much good for farming."

"Does it have a sandy beach?" I asked.

"Yes it sticks out into the lagoon and is all sandy with coconut palms."

"Why don't you start a resort?" I asked.

"No money."

Because he had seen Coconuts he was thinking of that kind of resort.

"Can you build a fale?" I asked.

He looked incredulous that I would ask such a foolish question. "Of course."

"How much does it cost to build a fale?"

"Only the nails," he responded. "I also have claim on my father's land, seven acres in Apia where I go and work on weekends. I also have a plantation in the mountains." (A plantation in the islands can be two or three acres or less, although he didn't say how big it is.)

But my attention turned again to his property in the lagoon. I told him about the resort at Tanu Beach on Savai'i.

He asked me to ride the bus to the end of the line with him so we could talk longer and I could see what I thought of his land. We passed through Mulivai, Lolofagauta, Salamumu...all traditional villages with lots of churches. Fausi pointed to a stunningly beautiful bay and I knew that beyond that was his land. I felt that I had touched his life with a new vision for an independent future!

The mysterious room behind the red-curtained windows in the dining room had been opened to me. I sat with Tagaloa in the center of the high-ceilinged fale, furnished Western with TV, phone and fax. It was both living room and office to Tagaloa.

He beamed as I told him of my days' adventures. I was thinking of Tagaloa's position as former Minister of Tourism as a possible source of help for Fausi.

"Perhaps you can help a young man I met," I began as I told him of Fausi and his land that would be perfect for a resort.

Before I could continue, Tagaloa's burst of rage startled me.

"That land is not his," he shouted, "it belongs to his matai and unless he is a matai he can do nothing. When people come who do not understand our culture and try to help they can cause a lot of trouble. If he tries, it will be nothing but trouble and a big headache for him."

I felt admonished and deep concern for Fausi and the problem I may have caused him.

Tagaloa suddenly changed the subject.

"If you think Si'umu is beautiful, you must see Va'vau!" he said as I rose to leave, the warmth of our relationship restored.

It is a good thing that I went venturing yesterday because it is already raining bucketsful just after daybreak. I lay in bed and remembered Manase and the stormy night palolo rose.

As we stood on the beach, Marilyn Grey, Adrienne's mom told me about a partnership in a restaurant near Apia in which Adrienne is involved.

"You must go to Plantation Homestead," she urged. "Ask for Rosemary."

Joe Annandale at Tanamapua Tropical Plantation

Chapter Thirty-Two

Tanumapua Tropical Plantation

Seuoti told me that the Plantation Homestead was open for dinner three nights a week. He suggested four thirty, so I could see the gardens. He made a dinner reservation for me at six thirty and arranged for a cab to pick me up at three thirty.

The cab driver was a member of the choir at Seuoti's church. I later learned that he was Sia's brother. As we pulled into the grounds, the driver motioned toward a man in the garden trimming plants.

"That's Mr. Annandale," he said.

As I got out of the cab, Mr. Annandale strode purposefully toward me as if I had been expected. He extended his hand.

"I'm Joe," he said and took me to a table under a shady canopy where his wife was finishing several flower arrangements. "This is Tui."

She was a beautiful woman whose dimples deepened as she smiled.

I told them how I had learned of Plantation Homestead when I met Adrienne and her family on Savai'i.

"I'm just a silent partner in that venture," she said, "more involved in the gardens."

I was astonished by the beauty of the plantation.

"How did all this come to be?" I asked.

Tui excused herself, "I must finish the arrangements."

Joe indicated a table and pulled out a chair for me beneath the umbrella.

"This was our family home," he said. "I grew up here. It was built by a German family in the early 1900's. But after World War I the Germans had to leave. The plantation came under New Zealand control. In the middle of 1944 my parents had a chance to buy the lease on this property. But let me go back a bit."

"My father's father was from Scotland. He came to manage a German plantation. He married and had three sons. He went back to Scotland and never returned. My Dad was the eldest. My Grandma, a Samoan, was house girl or washing lady to military people.

Dad left school at eleven or twelve and went to work as a stable boy taking care of the racehorses of a wealthy landowner. Dad lived in the stables with the Chinese coolies."

"In my Mom's family, my great grandpa was from Sweden, a man named August Nielson. He had gone to sea, which was a hard and dangerous life in those days. He jumped ship while they were in Samoa, on Savai'i, and married a Safun'ua girl, a tapou, the daughter of a high chief. Their eldest son was my grandfather, Olaf Frederick Nielson. Great grandpa had started a very successful trading business on Savai'i. When my grandfather was just a teenager he decided that the business should be moved to Apia, so he opened a branch there. A. Neilson is what they called it at first. It was named O.F. Nelson's later. The business was very successful. He bought a lot of property and he prospered. There were no laws then against purchase of land.

The Germans left a legacy of beautiful plantations, which the New Zealanders took over just as they began producing. O. F. Nelson married a daughter of H.J. Moors who was a close friend of Robert Louis Stevenson. He helped Stevenson get the property Vailima.

They had a family of five girls and one son who died as an infant. The eldest girl is Noue Tomasese who married one of the four Paramount chiefs. Their son is opposition leader in Parliament. He lives in the very large house built by O.F. Nelson, which you passed just before the bridge. (I remembered that house, an impressive mansion even by Western standards.) One daughter was my mother, Sina. When Mom was seven or eight my grandmother and grandfather divorced and grandfather raised the girls."

As he continued, a wealth of Samoan history unfolded in this very personal story.

"O.F. Nelson was responsible for the Mau Movement (when Samoa was struggling for its independence from New Zealand). Half European, half Samoan, he was an authority on Samoan history."

"Father was attracted to my mother. He was just a stable boy; she was the daughter of his boss, a wealthy landowner and trader." As he spoke, his eyes shone with pride and love. He continued, "Father was tall, slim, an exceptional horseman. She was also attracted to him."

"Horse racing was very popular in Samoa then. When he grew too heavy to be a jockey, he started to work as an office boy and groomed horses at night. He went to night school to learn typing and shorthand. He learned English and began getting promotions within the company. He always hoped to marry my Mom, but it seemed impossible. He studied accounting at night school and became the company accountant. Mom worked in the business, too. When he did ask permission to marry her, O.F. Nelson refused and he was devastated. By then they were in their 20's."

"After giving up all hope of marrying my mother, father had another relationship. He still worked at Nelson's. Mother never got over her first love for my father. He decided to break off his relationship and move to New Zealand. Before he left, his girlfriend committed suicide. The tragedy made everyone stop and think. It brought Mother and Father back together and O. F. reluctantly gave permission for them to marry.

"Grandfather was ill. He had been exiled and imprisoned twice for his Mau activities. Father carried on the business in his long absences. When Grandfather died, by then Mom and Dad had two daughters, Father was nominated to be his successor in the business."

"I was born in 1945. My parents had one son and four daughters. Cousin Tom grew up as a brother. Father's younger brother had gotten a girl pregnant and he went to New Zealand. Father went to the village to get the baby and his mother. His mother raised him for three years, then he was brought into our family. Tom went to sea and didn't have any interest in the business."

"My parents bought the lease on this property when I was about a year old. Father was busy with the business, which had grown to be one of the largest trading companies in the South Pacific. My mother ran the plantation. I followed my mother around and from her developed love of the land. My only ambition was to run the plantation when I grew up. Father sent the children to boarding school in New Zealand. Being the only son, he hoped that I would follow him into the business."

"They encouraged me, pushed me, into the University of New Zealand. While in Auckland, I met Tui. She was beautiful! Still is. She was the daughter of a rancher on the other side of the island. They were raising cattle. She went home to Samoa after a year. I thought when I finish the University, I'll take over the plantation. But after I graduated, father wanted me to take a Commerce course at the university of Wellington, so I took accounting."

"Tui waited for me for three years, so I knew she must love me," he grinned. "She worked as a librarian."

Serious again, he continued, "I became the internal auditor in the company. In that position I discovered a number of irregularities, which I brought to light. That caused a lot of internal strife among the five factions on the Board, which represented the five sisters, who, along with numerous cousins were involved in the business. I would never have chosen a business career. After years of stress that nearly killed me, Morris Hedstrom offered me a job that was too good in money and benefits to turn down, although it was a painful decision to leave the family business. Tui supported me. Promotions came and I was given Tonga to manage as well as Samoa."

"My parents' health was diminishing so they decided that they would have to move from the plantation house to a smaller, more manageable one. The lease on the plantation was coming up for renewal. At first they decided to build a small house where the cow paddock was, so they got a bulldozer and pushed the huge boulders aside into a pile. They now form the rock landscape around the garden. The cleared paddock is the circle drive. Then they decided to build on the freehold land three miles away in the pineapple plantation. The homestead was abandoned, but Mom tried to manage the plantation from there. That didn't work very well. They would have roll call for the workers at six in the morning, but then nothing would get done. There were about two hundred workers living in cabins around the plantation."

"In 1987 they decided to let the plantation lease run out. Tui and I talked about it. We hacked our way through the bush to where the house is. By then it was in a state of abandoned decay, having stood empty for three years. Weeds choked the yard and when I saw the house, I cried. We talked about what could be done. She shared my vision and saw the possibilities."

"It hasn't been easy. We've had two cyclones that nearly wiped us out."

I looked at the neat bed and breakfast that stood in the center of the garden with an elegant little restaurant on the first floor. Open to the garden, tables were also set on the patio for outdoor dining. Glittering tiny lights invited me inside where tables waited with crystal, linen and candlelight.

"Joe," I said, "this plantation is a national treasure!"

"They have set up a trust for it. The Canadian government may be giving us a grant to help develop the medicinal botanical garden."

He reached up and plucked some fragrant blossoms of moso oi from the tree limb above us and put them in my hand.

After a shower, Joe joined me in the Dining Room. While waiting for Tui and their daughter to join us, he told me about their work with an ethnobotanist who was gathering plants with traditional medicinal value into a nursery. He was identifying, not only known medicinal plants, but others that were being threatened with extinction, to be raised in the nurseries and reintroduced into the rainforest preserve.

When Tui joined us I asked her if it would be o.k. for me to come again when the light was better to get additional photos of the garden.

Tui told me that they also offer dinners for groups. At three thirty guests help prepare food for the umu, then tour the gardens and plantation while the food cooks. The price was $18 U.S. each, for a group of ten or more.

I mentioned that I had taken a bus to Si'umu across the mountains to the southern coast to see Coconuts Beach Resort. "You would love Jennifer and Barry Rose, the American developers."

His eyes sparkled.

"Do you remember the white sandy beach that curves to the left toward a rocky promontory?" He paused. "Tui and I had a chance to buy that. It is fifteen acres of freehold land. We were also able to lease thirteen additional acres of customary land with beach front on the other side of the rocky outcrop. We are drawing up plans for a small resort there, which we will begin building next summer."

"What will it be called?" I asked.

"Le-Ufi-Sa Village Resort. His eyes lit up again as he told me of the battle won by the Malietoas' warriors. When night came, they stopped there to rest. In need of nourishment as well as rest, they dug up the Ufi root, which flourishes there and baked it in a ground oven. It is almost pure carbohydrates. Well fed and rested, they won an overwhelming victory the next day. It is named after that event."

As he spoke, I could almost hear the drums.

The stunningly beautiful resort, which opened in 1996, was named Sinalei Reef Resort after his mother, Sina.

(Sinalei Reef Resort, P.O.Box 1510, Apia, Western Samoa;
Telephone (685) 25 191 or 26 624; Fax (685) 20 285;
E mail: Sinalei@talofa.net
Home page: http://www.talofa.net/sinalei.html

In Samoa, evening sounds are different from night sounds. Just after dark one hears the shrill of cicadas, chirp of crickets, the throaty wheezing of geckos and their clucking.

Night sounds deepen with menacing barks and growls of dogs fighting. Dogs are everywhere, small and brown, they look like they all have the same father. Toward morning, roosters herald dawn, which excites the twitter of birds in the garden.

Every morning brings a new adventure. I had met Jean through the waiter at Daphne's Restaurant. With matching gray hair it seemed that we could be twins.

"She raises vegetables," the waiter said as Jean unloaded boxes of familiar cabbages, carrots and beans...temperate zone vegetables seldom seen on these tropical islands. She stopped to speak to me and invited me to the ladies luncheon for expatriates.

I took an early bus into Apia on the day of the luncheon so I could stop at the Polynesian Airlines office to book my flight to American Samoa.

When I arrived at Aggie Grey's, they were still setting up the room for the luncheon, so I wandered around the hotel grounds.

At Aggie Grey's if you walk down seven steps from the lobby and turn right you will find the front page of an issue of the *Washington Post*, which is more than a century old. It is displayed under glass. Issue #4,003 was dated March 31, 1889. Sixteen pages for five cents. Bold headlines declared: "FOUR WAR SHIPS WERE WRECKED. TWO, THE *TRENTON* AND *VANDALIA*, WERE AMERICAN AND TWO, THE *ADLER* AND *EBER*, WERE GERMAN VESSELS. THE *NIPSIC* AND *OLGA* BEACHED. ALL TOLD, ONE HUNDRED AND FIFTY SOULS were swallowed up by the Sea at Samoa on March 15."

A map showed the shipping route from San Francisco through the Sandwich Islands (Hawaii) and sketches of four tall sail-rigged ships that were lost. It continued: *The following dispatch was received by Secretary Tracy at 10 o'clock yesterday morning; Dateline: Auckland, March 30, 1889 to Secretary of Navy, Washington, D.C. Hurricane at Apia, March 15. Every vessel in harbor on shore except English Man of War* Calliope, *which got to sea.* Trenton *and* Vandalia *total losses.* Nipsic *beached; rudder gone; may be towed. Chances against it. Will send her to Auckland if possible.* Vandalia *lost four officers and 39 men (named)* Nipsic *lost 7 men. All saved from* Trenton.

I was struck by the amazing change in communication that is now possible. This news took 15 days to reach authorities in government; an additional day before it was reported in the paper.

Sixty women attended the luncheon. Some were wives of men from the U.K., Germany, Australia and other donor nations with developmental missions in Samoa. Others were wives of men whose companies had sent them overseas. Jean and I alone were there independent of attachments. It gave us the time and opportunity to forge a new friendship.

I had barely settled into my room in mid-afternoon when Seuoti knocked at my door.

"Eona, you have a phone call. I think it is from one of your children!"

The woman at the end of the line identified herself as a journalist from Radio Australia.

"Do you have time this afternoon for an interview?" she asked.

Startled by her question, but curious, I answered, "Yes, I have nothing scheduled."

"Four o'clock then?" she asked.

"That would be fine."

I was quite elated that, finally, *The Solo Traveler* was getting international attention.

They arrived by cab. The young man who accompanied her was from a Brazilian Broadcasting station. We settled into the lounge for the interview.

Her questions immediately cut to the deeper cultural issues of Samoan life. I sometimes faltered in my answers.

"Can you tell me about fa'afa fine?" she continued.

Now that's one thing I knew something about, I thought. I told her what I had read in the *Lonely Planet Guide* ...about the cultural phenomenon in which boys are sometimes raised as girls if there are not enough girls in a family for domestic chores. I went on to explain, exactly as the guidebook had, that they sometimes revert to male roles when they reach adulthood. Ad-libbing from personal experience, I told her about our waitress at the Tusitala bar whose bulging muscles strained the satin gown she wore, and clearly, her six foot frame was unusual. I guessed that she might be an example of this phenomenon.

I took control of the interview at this point guiding her into areas about which I had personal experience. I told them about palolo fishing with the villagers at Manase.

The young Brazilian journalist was straining to the utter limits of his English, but from what he understood, he found my comments interesting and repeatedly reminded the young woman from Radio Australia to turn on her tape recorder.

Clearly, by this time I was aware that I was not giving her satisfactory information.

"I've been here just three weeks," I said defensively, "but I know someone who could help you. Tagaloa's wife is a professor of Samoan studies. You should talk to her."

She graciously disengaged herself from our abbreviated interview.

I did not catch the error until Aiono came into the lounge at six dressed in an elegant puletasi.

"Someone is coming from Radio Australia," she said.

That explained the cool detachment of the young woman from Australia who, when I gave her my card, immediately knew I was the wrong person with a similar sounding name.

It is a good thing that life had taught me not to take myself too seriously!

Coconuts

Tui Annandale at Tanamapua Tropical Plantation

Chapter Thirty-Three

American Samoa

Flights to Pago Pago (called Pongo by Samoans) left five times a day. The Polynesian Airlines office was near the Clock Tower on Beach Road. Although my airline ticket had been purchased as an extension through the Air New Zealand office in Los Angeles, they cheerfully faxed American Samoa to confirm reservations for three nights at the Rainmaker Hotel.

Seuoti again arranged for Sami, Sia's brother, to drive me to the airport. On the way Sami reminded me that taxis in Western Samoa are not metered. He cautioned me when I return not to ask the driver the fare. "Just give him eight tala. If he asks for a higher fare insist that you know the correct fare to the South Sea Star and give him just eight tala."

Although it was an international flight to American Samoa, the Polynesian Airlines commuter flights to Pago left from the small grass strip at Fagali'I Airport just east of Apia. You need your passport and go through customs. In a shed, a small portable bank opened for each flight to exchange money. You pay an Airport departure tax of twenty tala.

The thirty five minute flight to Pago was on an eighteen seat twin Otter. Weight of luggage was limited to twenty kilos each (a shade over 44 pounds). Passengers were weighed with his or her carry-on luggage.

My seat was near the open door of the cockpit. As we prepared for takeoff a book, apparently an instruction manual was between the Melanesian pilot and his European copilot who was obviously in training.

"Go for it," he instructed the hesitant trainee as we cruised uncertainly down the runway to ascent. Fifteen minutes out we flew into a dirty gray mass of clouds. Rain pelted the windshield and the sea below us disappeared in the thick mist. Clouds dissipated as we approached the stunningly beautiful island of Tutuila.

Steep, densely forested mountains rose from a very narrow coastal plain. Deeply indented bays created an extremely irregular coastline, preventing roads along the northern coast. Waterfalls coursed down mountain sides into the sea limiting the growth of coral. Without a barrier reef, breakers smashed into the rocky shoreline.

I usually research my destination so I know where the airport is relative to the hotel or town. My reservation at the Rainmaker Hotel and my arrival time had been confirmed by the Polynesian Airline office in Apia, so I assumed there would be someone at arrivals to meet me.

When I had cleared customs and looked for transport there wasn't any. A fat, grinning driver said, "Taxi?" He reminded me of a T-shirt I had seen on the Jersey shore. Below the picture of a shifty-eyed felon wearing prison stripes, the words Trust Me were printed in block letters.

I hesitated, then I turned to ask a uniformed man behind me the distance to the Rainmaker. Immediately, I knew that I had made a mistake; that something sinister, definitely not in my interest, was going on between them.

The taxi driver smirked as the uniformed man laughed and said, "About an hour. It depends on which way you go."

All my alarm bells rang! The one thing I knew was that there is only one road on the narrow coastal plain between the mountains and the sea.

As I looked up, I saw an American couple I had met at the small airport in Apia. They had told me that they were also staying at the Rainmaker. I grabbed my two small bags and ran. The driver of the van they were getting into had just put their luggage in the back and was closing the tailgate.

"Does this van go to the Rainmaker?" I asked.

"Yes, as a matter of fact, it does."

"How much is the fare?" I asked cautiously.

"Nothing," he said, "you caught the right bus. This is the Lord's van!"

The couple, it turned out, was on the advance team for the Billy Graham Crusade that was to be broadcast worldwide from Puerto Rico in March. The driver was pastor of the Samoa Baptist Academy.

As I left them, they extended an invitation. "You can catch the Mission bus. We'd love to have you join us for church." They explained that the bus comes to Pago on Sunday morning and stops at the Rainmaker if anyone is waiting there.

I was included in the series of meetings of local pastors, politicians and laymen working on the crusade. The theme that ran through all the preparations was that three things are necessary for a successful crusade..."Prayer, prayer, prayer."

The Rainmaker Hotel was the only accommodation in American Samoa of near international standards. It had one hundred eighty four large air-conditioned rooms in the main hotel and several fales. Although scenic, the harbor location was not suitable for swimming and was without a beach. More a business hotel than one for tourists, it was government-owned, impersonal and inefficient with a very indifferent staff. A conference of police chiefs from all the Pacific Islands was in progress while I was there.

Fia Fia on Friday night was just $14.95 with both buffet feast and a good show. I was seated at a table next to the buffet. The hostess soon asked me if I would mind sharing my table. He was a young man from New Zealand who lived in Hawaii and was in Samoa on business. He knew the Pacific well and was great company. A whole roast pig with an orange in his mouth smiled at me from the feast table throughout dinner.

One of the most dramatic views in the South Pacific was sunset from the second floor oval dining room at the Rainmaker. Windows spanned three sides of the curved wall providing a panoramic view of jagged mountain peaks on both sides of the harbor, which reached toward the narrow opening and sea in the distance. The sky was painted in pastel shades of pink and blue with mountains and palms darkly silhouetted.

Darkness comes quickly in the tropics. Soon ripples in the harbor reflected the green and golden lights that marked the opposite shore.

You have to accept Pago for what it is...a highly commercial port. On the walk from the Rainmaker into town, rugged slopes rise sharply from the street on your left. Houses cling randomly from the cliff sides and wherever their roots can gain purchase banana trees grow among the craggy rocks.

On your right, you pass the net repair facility for the huge fishing boats; next, the Port Authority where shipping containers like metal railroad cars are stacked four high and ten deep in places for a distance of a block or more. Busy hydraulic lifts and cranes work loading and unloading ships that are moored dockside.

The Jean P. Haydon Museum is small but worthwhile. Go through double doors behind the fale with carved posts. There is no entrance fee, but donations are requested. Several interesting exhibits include pictures showing steps in making tapa cloth, called siapo in Samoa.

Artifacts, including pre-mission weapons, models of Samoan outriggers and fine mats, the social currency of the Samoas, are displayed. One, a Royal Fine Mat, is over 400 years old.

Although the leaf samples are disintegrated, there is a collection (1974) of pictures of plants used in Indigenous Medicine explaining how each is used. In Samoan medicine all illness or injury is deemed to be trauma-caused or Aitu (spirit) caused. Some medicines are used at the site of the injury and some in ritual. I remembered Aiono showing me through her garden where many different medicinal plants are growing. One, usi, has a pungently aromatic leaf when bent or crushed, like natural Vick's Vaporub. Simmered in water, its steam is used to treat pneumonia.

Passengers wait for the ferry in a designated area just beyond the Museum.. The dock is behind a chain link fence. Tickets for Apia are purchased in a red-roofed shed by the dock, which opens shortly before departure time. ($US25 one-way). This is an international trip so a passport is necessary for non-Samoans.

Next door is the Fono where the legislature meets, a large enclosed fale. An article by David North in the April, 1995 issue of *Pacific Islands Monthly* stated, "The Fono has a leaky roof for some time, but given the efficiency of the America Samoa Government, it continues to rain in on the legislators (faipules) and their multitudinous staff members."

Two sets of shakes for the roof had been purchased, he explained, one for sixty six thousand dollars; the other for eighty eight thousand dollars but the repair was caught up in the politics and nepotism that often paralyzes government action. The roof, he said, continues to leak.

Fagatoga Square, a modern white complex of shops, lies between the Fono and the market, which, unlike the Maketi Fou in Western Samoa, is nearly deserted. At the bus terminal by the market, aiga buses can be found which go to the villages. Buses are owned either by the village or individuals. Vividly painted, most were dirty and in shabby condition. I was told not to take an aiga bus to a distant village after noon because the drivers often stop driving by two or three p.m. to stay in their villages for the night. Most villages have no accommodations.

I picked up a map and America Samoa Fact File at the Office of Tourism. On the counter was a brochure for Barry's Bed & Breakfast. *Quiet and secluded location in Leone Village surrounded by tropical rainforest.* I was eager to get away from Pago so I caught the aiga bus. The interior of the brightly painted purple bus was varnished plywood with yellow plastic-covered seats, plywood dash and header with cutout hearts and a row of green sequins rippling in the breeze from the open door as we drove.

"Do you know where Barry's Bed & Breakfast is?" I asked the driver.

I boarded when he answered, "Yes."

The road to Leone (pronounced as three syllables with all long vowels) passed through Tafuna where it turned inland through a large area of flat land with plantations. Away from the squalor of Pago the villages began looking more Samoan with large traditional fales where matai meet. Leone was a pretty village with a modern High School and neatly clipped, tall hibiscus hedges along the road.

At the turnaround point the driver, Joe, stopped. "Where is it you want to go?" he asked.

Neither he nor the other passenger knew where Barry's Bed & Breakfast was located, so I just rode with him back to Pago. It was worth the $1 each way to see, at least from the road, what village life in American Samoa was like.

On the bus, there was no cord or bell to signal stop. You just hit the wooden wall of the bus two or three times with the palm of your hand or knock on it.

When I mentioned my trip to Leone the next day at Kathy's Tours, Lua said, "I'm from Leone!" I asked about Barry's Bed & Breakfast. She said, "You'd have to take a cab from the main road. There are a hundred dogs on that road. Don't try to walk it. It's a long way. You wouldn't want to walk it," she repeated shaking her head, "just too many dogs."

The big thrill after being out of the country for a few months was to see the big orange school buses, the U.S. flag flying over the Post Office, the familiar mail trucks, the feel of familiar coins in your hand. But it really seemed like I was home when I found the ABC FAX grocery store behind the tourist office. A young couple from Taiwan operated the store. The young woman, Hui Jung Chen, recognized me the second time I came into the store. They had perfect California oranges, crisp Washington State apples and cookies, Oreos and Fig Newtons imported from the U.S. at mainland super market prices.

In this part of the tropics, the temperature averages about 80°F. year around. It was the beginning of December, the rainier season, which lasts until March and brings the island about one hundred twenty five inches of rain a year. Every day the peak of the mountain that named the hotel was wreathed with clouds. In this damp climate, building maintenance is difficult and everything quickly looks like it needs a scrub or coat of paint.

At three a.m. the wind wakened me. Palm fronds were being whipped in the ever- increasing gale with wind-driven rain beating on my window. The book *Hurricane* came to mind. Here, with the mountains at our front door, even in a storm, we would not have the problems that low lying coral atolls like the Tuamotus experience. There, the native term for hurricane, matangi hurifenua, means the wind that overturns the land.

In *The Blue of Capricorn*, Eugene Burdick wrote about the capricious unpredictability of the vast Pacific Ocean. ... *There are about one hundred and thirty typhoons a year in the Pacific. Most of them spin themselves to death over empty waters and go virtually unnoticed...the highest wave ever authenticated was 112 feet high. No sailor was surprised that it was in the Pacific.*

I fell into an uneasy sleep with the image in mind of the rusting hulks of half a dozen ships that had been driven ashore across the harbor from the hotel during Cyclone Val. Even the deep, protected harbor had failed to provide refuge during the storm. The mountains on both sides of the harbor that usually are protective barriers became a funnel for the winds.

When my flight time came, I learned that the Otter on which I had flown to American Samoa was out of service. A six-seat shuttle was flying continuously trying to fill the gap. There might be space on Friday or Saturday, but neither date had space available. Finally, they called to tell me that I could fly on Sunday afternoon.

Restless, I stopped in the lobby of the Rainmaker Hotel to watch the CNN newscast. It had been more than three months since I had seen TV, but it seemed that nothing had happened in all that time. Sarajevo...the O.J. Simpson case. The longer I was in the islands the more remote and the less relevant it all seemed.

A man from the States was also watching TV. He had been in American Samoa for six months working as an engineer laying under sea cable. Wearily, he said that they had already lost sixteen million dollars on the job because it was taking so long. Delay after delay.

Tourists were, understandably, rare, so it didn't surprise me when he asked what I was doing in Pago.

"I write a travel newsletter."

His answer was explosive and angry.

"I wish travel writers would write things as they really are!" Sardonically, he quoted, " 'For the visitor these days, there are few health risks.' Sure! Do you know what it is like being in a hotel room too sick to get up? I spent ten days in bed last July. I had a headache so severe I thought I would die. It began like a severe case of flu."

I recognized symptoms of dengue fever, a mosquito borne disease sometimes called breakbone fever because of the pain.

He also mentioned the potentially fatal risk of trespassing. Although the FBI had come looking for the gunman several times, his aiga helped him elude the police.

"If I had not known how potentially dangerous this man was, when we came into conflict I might not have been so cautious. Although access had been paid for and agreed upon, the Samoan met me with a shotgun to keep the crew off the aiga property. If I had not known about the previous shooting incident, I would have handled it more aggressively."

He repeated that guidebooks should write about places as they really are, not just about the happy, smiling friendly local people.

I was missing the courtesy of the young people in Western Samoa. School children on Tutuila wore their uniform lavalavas carelessly over gym shorts with high-top status gym shoes, a symbol of everything that has gone wrong, as we have poured money into the island, corrupting social values and replacing local customs with nothing of value.

In restaurant and grocery shop windows there were signs, "We accept food stamps." Everywhere there was trash that accompanies a careless consumer-oriented society that has lost appreciation for its land.

When I asked a staff member at the Rainmaker about finding an opportunity to visit a village she dismissed me with, "Why would you want to?"

Understandably, many of the villages aren't eager for tourists; they want to uphold their traditions and accept Western values at their own pace. Very few villages have any sort of tourist infrastructure like shops, lodging or restaurants, so what have they to gain by strangers wandering around their property?

American Samoa is at an uneasy crossroad, a blend of two cultures, not quite comfortable with either one.

I checked out early. With my two small duffles I waited at seven fifteen a.m. for the white and black Mission bus. After going into Pago where we picked up a large group of people, we passed the tip of the harbor where a dozen yachts were anchored; then with a full bus we drove back past the Rainmaker, through Tafuna which is closer to the airport, into a jungle compound called Happy Valley.

The church school teaches grades one through eight. American volunteers make up most of the staff. Tupe Magele, a beautiful Samoan girl, a senior in High School, sat with me on the church bus and graciously introduced me to the staff. Vera Vaughn, the school principal, a retired American teacher, brought me to church and afterward to an English-speaking Bible Study class. When Vera learned that I would be flying at one o'clock she offered me a ride to the airport where a group of friends were having dinner together after church.

The pilot of our six-passenger plane was a slender European woman, not over thirty. Her light brown hair was caught up in a ponytail making her appear even younger, but she was confident and skilled as a pilot.

Va'vau Beach Fale

Traveling the South Pacific

Va'vau Beach Fales

Preparing the umu at Va'vau

Chapter Thirty-Four

Va'vau Beach Fales

It was like homecoming back at the South Sea Star. Tagaloa invited me into the fale to go over his new ideas for the Heart of Samoa Tour. There would be opportunities, he said, to visit villages; for Poula and Umufono, evenings of traditional feasting, dancing and singing. Visitors would be taught to make ula, the garlands of flowers. They would spend three days on Savai'i, visit Va'vau and the beautiful beaches of the north coast of 'Upolu. Snorkeling and fishing and basket weaving. They would attend fia fia and dinner at Aggie Grey's. Then a visit to Joe and Tui Annandale's tropical gardens where they would help prepare foods for the umu. His enthusiasm was boundless. There were all the adventures I had enjoyed and more!

Laughing, he tossed a copy of the *Samoa Observer* across the table to me. Bold headlines declared PM THREATENS TO FIGHT MP. The article elaborated on an incident of the previous day when the Prime Minister (now deceased) had threatened Tagaloa with a fist fight on the floor of Parliament. Quickly, the subject went back to the tour.

Tagaloa insisted again, "You must see Va'vau!"

Aiono agreed, "It is the most beautiful place on'Upolu."

He hastily wrote a letter to the village Matais.

"Give it to Sao or Tui," he said.

Aiono added, "Take the Lepa bus."

I determined to make an early start the next day. Early morning at Maketi Fou is the most active time of day as aiga buses from all over the island arrive. Weighty stalks of bananas, baskets of papaya and coconuts, are off-loaded and carried to market stalls or set up along the sidewalk. Passengers disembark and hurry into the city to conduct business.

I searched the signs on the front of arriving buses for an hour before I spotted the Lepa bus. Waiting until arriving passengers got off, I boarded. It was not a good sign when the bus drove less than a block and parked in the shade of a large tree.

After sitting in the parked bus for a few minutes I got out and asked someone when the bus would be leaving.

"About eleven."

It was not yet eight o'clock, so I walked along the harbor to Daphne's for breakfast; then on to Aggie's. It was ten forty five when I returned to the Market. By then a large number of people were in the bus or lying under it to take advantage of the shade. As I wandered around killing time, I noticed a bus marked Va'vau and boarded.

It was a picnic scene. People were getting on and off the bus, getting drinks and bringing food back from the market. Rolls filled with barbecue pork were dropping greasy red juice on the wooden floor and seats of the bus. Legs of chicken were being passed around and all sorts of food wrapped in newspaper or banana leaves were consumed; the wrappers tossed out the open windows when they were finished.

I asked how long it would be until we arrived in Va'vau. No one seemed to understand, so I calculated, to be safe, I should search out a restroom.

I asked, "Where is there a restroom?"

I was answered by friendly but bewildered looks.

I tried bathroom, then toilet.

Someone offered me a chicken leg. I got off the bus and asked two girls, then a woman, to no avail.

Finally, sensing that I needed something, the people on the bus sent a teenaged boy to help me. When I told him what I needed, he blushed and smiled and brought me to a poolroom bar with chicken wire windows. A door marked Women was near the white double door we entered. My embarrassed young guide waited outside the door for me. I was surprised to find an immaculate white tiled bathroom.

When we returned to the bus everyone beamed their approval and satisfaction. I was one of them and they offered again to share their food.

It was a little after noon when the driver and his assistant boarded the bus. I showed him my letter from Tagaloa and asked if this bus was going there. He promised to let me off at the right place.

After donning reflective glasses the driver started the engine while his co-driver popped a cassette into a boom box, turning it to top volume. We were off. The first stop was less than a block away, Morris Hedstroms. A large middle-aged man got out and returned with two bags of rice on his shoulder. A young man got off and helped him bring the heavy bags on board. The next stop was at the Central Market. Several people got off and made purchases of huge coconut baskets full of newspaper-wrapped heaps of tobacco. Then the fish market where whole fishes two or three feet long were carried onto the bus wrapped in newspapers. Holding them by their tails, they were stuffed under seats. A carton of bottles was picked up at the Bond Store (Liquor Outlet), a tire at the Tyre Shop. After a couple more stops it seemed that we were headed out of town, music blaring.

At the edge of town we stopped at a Mobil Station, but instead of gas, picked up a carton of bottled beer that also found a spot amid coconuts, banana stalks, tires and fishes. We purchased gas at the next station, which adjoined a retail outlet for everything from candy to clothes and household goods. The bus emptied for a half hour while passengers made purchases and used the rest rooms. I had begun to realize that coming to Apia was an event and the bus is a service that brings them into town to do all their errands, so the multiple stops were necessary to accomplish this.

About ten miles out of town a car we met flashed its headlights. Both vehicles pulled over. The driver rushed to meet the woman who jumped out of the parked car and they embraced. Our driver then walked with her to the parked car and engaged in a long conversation with her companion. I relate this incident to point out again the incredible patience and consideration Samoans extend to one another. There was no comment by any of the passengers, nor curiosity or impatience displayed during the delay.

The scenic coastal road ran through small villages with imposing churches, past postcard pretty beaches with rocky headlands. The road became rougher and narrowed into a rocky lane and half as we turned into the mountains. My body ached from the unaccustomed isometric exercise as I tensed my arms and legs and buttocks to keep my place on the straight-backed board seat where I bounced and slid as the bus rattled over the stony mountain road. A deep valley plunged on our right between mountain peaks that rose on both sides of the road through Le Mafa Pass.

We turned onto a narrow plantation trail, which we followed for several miles to a small village on the opposite side of an unbridged stream where we turned around. We stopped at a compound in a plantation. A pool table with a game in progress was under a thatched roof. The driver's assistant got off the bus and after a leisurely conversation, returned.

Back on the "main" two-track road we continued over the mountains. During casual conversation, the woman who sat in front of me pointed to a trail. "That's the road 77 to Salani," she said. It was the village to which Dr. Fay Calkins had come to live decades before with her husband, Vai, long before a road had been cut through the mountains.

A few minutes later the sea lay at the end of the road. We turned east along the coast and soon the bus stopped at a narrow road that led into the bush toward the sea. The driver turned and said, "This is your stop." He hesitated, then he added, "Will you be all right?"

The woman who had pointed out the road to Salani had already told me that no bus would be returning to Apia until five the next morning.

A small board nailed to a palm tree crudely lettered, VA'VAU BEACH FALES was modest confirmation that this was my stop. A horse tied to a tree whinnied. As I walked into the bush a cow stood munching the tall grass. The road, rocky in places, cut by erosion in others, seemed impassable to vehicles. About a quarter mile later the road rose steeply.

From the crest of the hill I saw a scene that epitomizes every man's dream of the South Seas. It was all there. The deep blue of the sea beyond the foaming white line of breakers at the reef, a placid lagoon, a curve of white sand reaching far off to rocky headlands.

Coconut palms sheltered thatched roof fales by the sea. And there was not a soul in sight. Which posed the problem. To whom should I give Tagaloa's letter? I was not expected.

There was nothing else to do. I walked to the beach and then along the lagoon. Sitting in the shade of a thatched shelter, far down the beach, I saw a bearded young man leaning against his backpack. I sat down beside him on the sand. He was so like a hundred other young backpackers I had met throughout the Pacific.

"I have a letter. Do you know who I should give it to?"

"I had a letter, too, but mine didn't work," he teased.

He had been discharged from the Israeli army six months before and had been traveling since then.

"I will probably be out another year and a half," he said. "I don't think I can stop traveling..." then, growing serious, he added, "...but when does the lonesomeness end?"

It was not a casual question. He meant for me to answer it.

I told him that when I was thirty four I had come into Faith and that had wiped away the nagging soul-deep sense of loneliness forever.

He looked bewildered and asked me to explain, so there on a deserted beach half the world away from both our homes, I told this young Jewish stranger the whole story.

"I was pregnant with my sixth child and going through the inevitable search for the meaning of life...you know, the questions, 'Where do we come from? What is the purpose, if any, of our existence? What happens when we die?' Just the universal search for Truth, a quest we all make at some time in our lives. I longed for Truth...tears dripping into the dishpan as I thought about it, searching earnestly for answers to questions still too vague for me to formulate."

He still seemed interested, so I continued, " My neighbor, Martha, had four children and a semi-invalid live-in mother-in-law. Yet, she always seemed at peace above the family turmoil. She began telling me about Bible Study classes she and her husband attended. But I thought, if I had a baby sitter I'd do something FUN! But she had an intangible something I needed and one night I went to Bible Study with her. I found a taste of unconditional, loving acceptance in their midst that I had never known and was drawn to it."

By then, I felt compelled to continue. "The night my baby was born a most extraordinary thing happened that to this day I cannot explain. I only know that it changed my life forever. I was up and outside myself and as I was suspended there, somewhere between the bed and ceiling, I was surrounded by beings that were loving me so tenderly and completely that no human language could describe it. I did not see or hear them with my normal senses, I perceived them through some other sense. From that experience I knew that Truth was tangible and that I had touched it. I still did not understand the nature of this Truth. I just knew that it embodied Love. From then on, I have never been lonely or afraid of dying."

I hesitated and he asked me to tell him more.

"I wasn't a Christian then. I'd say that I was more of an agnostic. I still didn't equate this Truth I had found with God until one evening at a church meeting a circle of women were praying. I had gone to the meeting to see slides of India that a missionary was showing. While they were praying, I thought *What a lot of theological double talk, this Father and Son and Holy Ghost!* As quickly as I thought it God spoke within me, "Why should it not be so? Man was made in God's image."

In that moment I understood the reality of the Trinity. For each of us is a triune being...body, mind and spirit. I knew then that God, the great mind and Creator; Jesus who walked the earth for thirty three years (or eighty like we might) and the Holy Spirit, that part of us that is eternal and exists before we are born and after we die, are ONE. For the first time, God had become real to me."

A young woman came to speak to him. The young man told me that I should give Tagaloa's letter to her. She took it and went down a path into the bush.

"Did you know that there is no food here?" he asked.

I told him that I always travel with a little bag with my toothbrush and a change of clothes in case the unexpected happens, but that I had brought no food. I had simply not anticipated an over night stay.

He opened his backpack and took out a handful of uncooked spaghetti and a package of instant sauce, insisting that I take them.

"There's a small store in the village about three miles away." He showed me some of the treasures in his backpack including an intricately carved, museum-quality war club that he had purchased in the village.

When the girl returned, she said, "I'll show you to your home for tonight."

She took me to one of the enclosed fales and unlocked the door. The young Israeli was staying with her family in the village.

He came in to sit with me until she was ready to leave. When we were alone he said,"Please tell me the story again."

For some, life's journey is a straight path; for others a strangely convoluted trail punctuated by brief, improbable, but deeply meaningful encounters.

I was beginning to boil water to cook my spaghetti when there was a knock at my door. A Samoan man I can only describe as very handsome met me.

"I am Sao. The umu is ready for you to take pictures."

I turned off the stove and followed him down a path that led behind the fales. Under a thatched shelter heaps of coconut shells were ablaze over a four foot square pile of rocks surrounded and held in place by coconut logs.

I had been unaware that Tagaloa's letter, which was written in Samoan, had requested them to prepare an umu feast for me. A request from a Paramount Chief translates into a command that cannot be ignored. The men, who had been working in the bush all day, came home tired and hungry. My welcome was, at best, lukewarm from the reluctant cooks who were busy preparing the food and tending the fire.

One man peeled green bananas, another grated coconut, yet another peeled and quartered half ripe papaya to wrap in banana leaves. By singeing banana leaves briefly over hot rocks they become pliable and liquid-proof for wrapping food bundles, which are tied with sennit. They prepared my favorite palusami, wrapped in a banana leaf bundle placed on the hot rocks. One of the men came with a creel and fishing gear, but I pleaded with them that there was already more than enough food for a feast.

When the coconut husks had burned down to coals and ash they were brushed aside. Poles were used to level the pile of hot rocks (river rocks are always used, they said, because others can sometimes explode from the heat.) Food bundles were then placed on top and covered with more banana leaves. The food cooked for about an hour. It was long after dark when the feast was set on mats beside the umu where Sao and Tui and I were served.

They told me that they must send back with me an O So, a basket of food, for Tagaloa and Aiono to prove that they had made the umu like he requested in the letter.

Sao good-naturedly teased Tui about his great grandfather who was a German, making him an Afakasi. His name is Tui Letona Scott. Tui had been included among fifty seven people from Va'vau who had accompanied Tagaloa on the month long tour which concluded with Tagaloa's call to me from California.

The umu and the men cooking could have been a scene from centuries ago except for the iron bush knives and the wheelbarrow from ACE Hardware that carried the coconut husks.

Sao told me the history of Va'vau Beach Fales. In 1986 when Tagaloa was Minister of Tourism, he attended an EEC (European Economic Community) meeting in Switzerland.

In an effort to promote sustainable village based tourism, each small Pacific island nation was offered an EEC financed village resort sponsored in conjunction with the South Pacific Visitors' Council in Suva. The man in charge of the EEC program was Italian.

Tagaloa, who was the first full Samoan to come home with an advanced degree in Economics had done postgraduate studies in Italy and as a result, speaks fluent Italian. Vava'u was one of the locations that was suggested and it was selected because of its natural beauty and remote location. The pilot project was begun in 1991 and was officially opened in 1994. European architects designed the modern fale-style accommodations. There were six enclosed fales, self-contained with kitchen on one end, bathroom and closet on the other. Each unit has floor to ceiling jalousie windows both front and back to accommodate the sea breeze. Professionally decorated to European standards, drapes match bedspreads. There is a double bed and twin beds so each unit can comfortably accommodate three people. Fine mats cover the entire floor. A water tap is at the entrance to wash sand off your feet before entering barefoot. The units are clean and very attractive little one-room houses.

Sao and his cousin, as landowners, get sixty five percent of the income; the village, which has twelve matais in its fono, thirty five percent.

There was no moon at all, so I gave Tui my small flashlight for the three-mile walk to his village.

I believe that Va'vau is the only place in the South Pacific with no roosters. I would have to be at the roadside at five a.m. to catch the only bus into town. Sao stayed in the next fale.

"If you wake up first, wake me and I will take you to the guards who will wait for the bus with you."

It was three when I woke up. I was afraid that if I fell asleep again I would miss the bus, so I took a shower and dressed.

The moon fitfully appeared from the fragmented cloud cover as I sat on the front step of the fale watching the silver-white reef line, which defined the edge of the lagoon. I thought, What an improbable adventure this is for a timid grandmother who is always home before dark. Then the moon was lost again to the clouds, plunging the island into total darkness.

On the way to the fale where Sao slept, I ran into bushes; then the trunks of coconut palms and more bushes. While walking to the place the guards were sleeping I kept close behind Sao. One of the guards, Sao's nephew, said, "I saw you in town yesterday. You were going from one person to another asking them questions."

They waited patiently until we saw the lights of the bus reflecting off the trees as it came around the bend. He flashed the torch as a signal for the driver to stop.

It was not yet light as we turned onto Le Mafa Pass. The mountains were mere silhouettes against pale sky, but by the time we reached the north coast it was fully light. Life in the villages was stirring languidly. As we neared Apia uniformed school children were walking to school in little groups.

For the first time, I saw Apia with a sense of comfortable familiarity that overlooked the neglected clapboard buildings and broken sidewalks. Was it the soft morning light? Or had the buildings all been scrubbed and painted while I was gone? The city beside the harbor looked beautiful to me. I had begun to realize that much of the seeming neglect was a result of serious cyclone damage that they were repairing as rapidly as they could.

Instead of going home, I chose to walk along the harbor to Aggie's. I arrived at the Clock Tower in time to hear the Police Marching Band coming down Beach Road for the formal eight o'clock flag raising ceremony. My pace quickened and I stood at attention watching, admiring the smartly uniformed men in the now familiar blue gabardine lavalavas and jackets, white helmets and gloves for this formal ceremony. The martial music of the band was a strong reminder of their German colonial history.

When I got home I went to the little store by the University where I often bought hot bread that is delivered twice a day.

"I'm hoping you might have an old copy of the *Samoa Observer,*" I told the friendly young man who asked where I had been.

"I know the one you want," he said as he dug around a stack of his own used papers and pulled out the one with the headlines about Tagaloa's run-in with the Prime Minister at Parliament a few days before.

As I was having coffee in the canteen, I opened the paper. A small article on the third page caught my attention. It was about a trial currently going on. Six matai from the village of Lona east of Apia were on trial for an incident that had occurred September 25, 1993. Nuutai Mafulu had moved from New Zealand back to his village with his family. He bought a bus with his savings. When the village council of matais imposed a series of fines on him for driving the bus on Sundays, he refused to pay them. Fines were increased and the situation escalated. Outraged by his disrespect, the council met again and ordered that his home, shop, bus and jeep be burned and his animals killed. Then he was shot in front of his family. The court said, "a village council no longer has the absolute authority to impose any penalty they wish to. And if they do give out any punishment that contravenes the law, then they will be dealt with like anyone else." The judge accepted the defense council submission that there was an element of provocation.

When a matai from the village went to ring the curfew bell for evening prayers, Mafulu reportedly told him to leave the premises as the bell was on his land. The young man who did the shooting, his first cousin, was jailed. The other five who ordered that the penalty be carried out (and remember, the young man could not refuse the matais' orders under village law and custom) were each fined eight hundred tala (about US $328).

As one more do-gooding palagi who had no understanding of the demands of Samoan culture, had I given Fausi an idea that could destroy him?

My time in Samoa was coming to an end and I knew that I must go back again over the mountains to see Fausi. Could I find him? If I did find him, would he believe me? The article in the newspaper certainly gave credence to the things Tagaloa had told me about Fausi being unable to do anything unless he is a matai; that if he tried it would be nothing but a big headache and trouble for him.

With a consuming sense of urgency, I caught the Si'umu bus from the Maketi Fou at seven fifteen the next morning.

When we reached the top of the mountains we were in a misty cloud forest. We stopped for a herd of cattle crossing the road. Four men, on their way to work in their plantations, got on the bus carrying bush knives. The one who sat beside me had a rifle of ancient vintage slung over his shoulder, which he slid under the seat. We passed plantations where cyclones had stripped the tops off acres of palms. It was raining hard when we reached the south coast.

Fausi was nowhere to be found. I didn't want to leave a message, because how could I be certain that he would receive it? If he did receive it, would he respond to it and put aside my ill-advised idea?

I laid my dripping umbrella by the step and went into the covered dining patio and ordered one of Mika's superb omelettes. It would be four or five hours before the bus would leave so I had time to kill with the friendly, now familiar, staff.

When the rain let up a bit and the sun came out briefly, I asked Barry if I could get a picture of him in his magnificent tree house.

Fausi had returned so I asked him if he had a few minutes, indicating that I needed to speak to him privately. We went into the car park where he opened our conversation enthusiastically, "I heard from my sister in Hawaii. She is sending money to help build the resort."

My heart sank as I realized my worst fears for Fausi.

"Fausi, I spoke to Le Tagaloa Pita about the possibility of his helping you get started. Tagaloa's response surprised me! He was angry, Fausi, and said that unless you are a Matai you can do nothing like that."

"But we can do it!" he persisted.

"No, Fausi. This isn't San Francisco. It's Samoa and you have to do it like tradition dictates. I was wrong to give you that idea. I just didn't understand the culture."

I showed him the newspaper article about Mafulu who had been shot for disrespect to his Matai. When he finished reading the article I continued. "You must ask your matai and get his approval and cooperation or you must forget it. It would be nothing but trouble for you."

I told him about Va'vau Beach Fales. How it has been developed cooperatively among the landowners, village and matais.

There was nothing more I could do. Was he convinced? I don't know.

When I returned to Apia, I ran into Teresa, one of the Samoan girls who worked at the Visitor's Center. We had met again in Manase. She was walking with Mike Parsons, a manager of special projects for the islands sponsored by Australia. I returned to the tourist bureau with them where Mike laid out a map of Savai'i and 'Upolu and explained his mission.

He had been employed by the Western Samoa government for more than a year to develop village tourism. An area which the government designates for ecological preservation is identified and the village council approached about tourism as an alternative option to logging, for example.

There is no shortage of international development programs, but from government to individual to village level there seems to be ambivalence about tourism that seems to dam the course of development. Changes have come and more will come, but until then the matai system firmly anchors their agrarian society.

My last day in Samoa Jean offered to drive me anywhere I wanted to go. After breakfast at LeGodinet's dining room, we drove back to Tanumapua Tropical Plantation.

The soft morning light gave enhanced photo opportunities to capture the exquisite flowers.

Jean, who had owned a greenhouse and nursery in British Columbia, had worked with Tui for a few years. They enjoyed coffee in a shady spot in the garden while I took portraits of the dazzling array of tropical blooms. Torch ginger, waxy rose colored flowers as large as saucers; heliconia in foot long drops of vivid red and yellow; teuila whose spikes were taller than I am. I had stepped into a wonderland where, like Alice, I was dwarfed by exotic tropical botanicals I had never dreamed existed.

Samoa is the kind of place where even fence posts take root and grow. The garden was wild and beautiful, yet every inch controlled and balanced by an artist's eye. Paths led down a hillside into a fern valley, rising on the other side of the ravine into virgin rainforest. When I sent them pictures of individual blooms, I believe even Tui and Joe must have been surprised.

During lunch at Aggie Grey's Jean told me a story of a true incident that involved the daughter of a prominent Afakasi family. She was in Savai'i with a group of young people who were behaving in a loud way. They were reprimanded, but continued to be disrespectful. In the course of the evening the young woman's leg suffered a severe muffler burn. It was treated for months during which she went to New Zealand for medical care. She was in a wheel chair, but in spite of aggressive medical treatment, it showed no improvement.

Someone suggested that the village on Savai'i might have put a curse on her; that if she went to them to apologize it might improve. In desperation, she did. Then it healed.

The ifoga or traditional apology is part of Fa'a Samoa, the Samoan way. The person who commits the offence will bring gifts of reconciliation and may sit with his head covered for hours or days in front of his victim's fale until the apology is accepted and the relationship normalized.

I was as reluctant to let Samoa go as Jean was to see another expat friend leave. We drove beyond Palolo Deep on a road that hugged the beach just beyond Aggie's at the edge of town.

"You might be interested in this," she said as she pulled into a drive and parked beside some construction trucks. Whether in a state of demolition or repair I couldn't tell, but the sturdy magnificence, by island standards, of the old mansion was clearly apparent. We walked up the broad steps and through the open door.

A tall blonde young man rolled up the blueprints he had been studying with his architect and strode toward us.

"I am Claus," he said with a strongly European accent.

As we walked from room to room among paint buckets and ladders the workmen barely paused to acknowledge us as Claus told us what the various rooms would become.

Claus had been traveling through Samoa as a backpacker and became aware that there were few affordable, clean budget hotels. He returned from Denmark and, with a local partner, obtained a long-term lease on this spacious 100-year old mansion overlooking the lagoon, just beyond the Deep.

A total renovation was in progress. The very breezy front entrance will be a lounge; the central rooms, with high ceilings, will provide exceptionally spacious public rooms. Beyond the entrance lounge at the top of the steps will be a bar and reception room where complimentary breakfast will be provided. To the right you enter a large library/reading room with travel information and an aquarium. Behind this are two dining rooms, a communal kitchen and laundry facilities. All the things he had looked for and missed in the places he stayed will be there. Dorm rooms will be available, rooms with shared baths and self-contained doubles at various budget rates. The décor will include displays of Wendy Percival's art, he said, and the landscape will be done by Joe Annandale. It promised to be an affordable touch of class for backpackers in a beautiful, convenient location. The April, 1997 issue of *Pacific Islands Monthly* listed the Excellence in Tourism Awards for 1995. It is not surprising that the Budget Accommodation Award for backpacker hotels throughout the Pacific was given to The Samoan Outrigger.

As we left, Jean mentioned a strong undertow in the lagoon, which has caused some fatalities. Claus will have paopao available for guests use to learn canoeing, Polynesian style. As an avid diver, he will eventually add a dive operation.

In recent times, Claus Hermanson's hostel, The Samoan Outrigger, was a restaurant. In early days it was the residence of "Queen Emma" a lady of questionable reputation. Among her many lovers was the notorious pirate, Bully Hayes.

We drove north through Apia and parked to take a walk on Mulinu'u Peninsula, a place of historic significance. Tagaloa, smiling broadly and waving, passed us on his way home from Parliament.

The Peninsula defines the west end of Apia harbor as this long narrow spit of land juts out into the sea. The Fono building where Parliament meets is near the end just before the Weather Observatory. German, British, American and Samoan monuments line the shore.

When I got home to the South Sea Star I packed and lay down to rest until dinner time. Aiono and Tagaloa's two daughters were at home and Aiono's brother, a dignified Samoan doctor, was visiting from New Zealand. He had returned home to accept a village matai title. I had been invited to join them in the family fale, which is a comfortable blend of Samoan décor and Western furnishings.

As I entered, Aiono placed an ula of teuila around my neck, each petal of the scarlet ginger flower bent to form an individual "blossom". When she presented a fine mat to me I was overwhelmed. On such occasions I felt embarrassed to have been so honored and have no reciprocal gift. I was awkward in my ignorance of cultural gift exchanges, which are so much a part of island life. But what could I have given that would have been its equal?

Maria, the hotel maid, usually took a four o'clock bus home, but had stayed to see me off. She reminded me of the day I had rolled up my slacks and, barefoot, had taught her how to use the scrub brush and cleaning materials in the shower. I had bought them one day at Ace Hardware to make her work easier. We had laughed and talked together so many times since the first morning I had met her sweeping leaves from the path.

"You will miss us," she said feelingly.

Seuoti arranged passage to the airport for me on the P & F Schuster Tour bus, which picked me up at ten p.m. I joined other passengers from Aggie's and Tusitala Hotel on their way to Faleolo International Airport.

They spoke of hotel fia fias, shopping at the market and group tours around the island for lunch at Coconuts.

I longed to tell them how much they had missed. But I only smiled and agreed that Samoa was, indeed, an interesting destination.

The Honourable Le Tagaloa Pita's daughters with a neighbor, Seuoti

Chapter Thirty-Five

Time Frozen in Place

The seeds of desire to visit Niue had been firmly planted. We began planning to go, Richard, Aljean and I. I had read that there were dozens of abandoned houses there because of the severe population drain to New Zealand. We talked of getting a house there to share. It was the simplicity of the place that appealed to us. Perhaps we were each looking for something we had known so long ago before ambition and affluence, before "success" and profound changes had filled our lives with ambiguities. Rumors that Royal Tongan Airlines might begin weekly flights to Niue were encouraging.

But life has a way of asserting itself, of intruding into plans. My brother's call put life "on hold". Our mother who was eighty seven years old had fallen. She had been brought from the hospital to the Good Samaritan Home in Pine River in Northern Minnesota.

"John, I have some business I have to take care of, then I'll come."

The Solo Traveler had readers in thirty three states. I had material enough for four or five issues and could publish and mail it from Minnesota, but many details of business needed attention first. When I left Tucson I was still tense after a busy week trying to anticipate all the problems created by such an abrupt change of direction.

A blizzard delayed my flight from Minneapolis Up North. When the runway had been plowed and the wings deiced, we boarded the small Mesaba Airlines plane, stooping as we walked down the narrow aisle. A small girl, who was on her monthly trip to visit her father in Brainerd, buckled herself into the single seat across the aisle from me. As the plane skidded on its taxi toward takeoff my face must have still reflected the tension of preparing for the sudden move back home. My young seat mate looked at me with scorn and said, "You don't fly much, do you?"

For the first time in the long week I smiled and relaxed.

I have come home in the dead of winter. It is not a chapter I would have written and I cannot guess how it will end.

As I unlock the front door of my mother's house I panic. Silence magnifies echoes in rooms that are cold, familiar from my childhood, yet unfamiliar after forty years of use and change.

By the kitchen door the floorboard's creak brings a rush of memory. For a moment, firelight from the cook stove dances on the linoleum; the smell of wood smoke mingles with the fragrance of strawberry jam and hot cocoa; of fresh apple pie. But the cook stove has been gone for years, replaced by an electric one and the kitchen will never embrace us with that homey warmth again.

My room has been closed, unused, for twenty years. Like an attic, it has absorbed all those discards and keepsakes that find their way into bags and boxes. Mice have nibbled yellowed newspaper clippings and have nested in a mildewed box of old clothes. I find a small organdy dress; the khaki uniform my brother wore so proudly when he was six and we were at war.

I am not sure whether my mother will be released from the nursing home into my care. During each visit I can feel the staff measuring my intentions, my patience, my commitment and weighing it all against my lack of nursing skill, my own graying hair, my years-long absences.

At first we are strangers. We have no way to bridge the enormous gap between past and present. I've been away too long. We touch those points of memory edged with humor that we rehearse predictably each time we meet, but I don't know who she is.

She is proud of me, both cautious and desperate. She knows me as the fragile child, the spoiled teenager. Glimpses of my adult years during brief, irregular visits suggest little of my capacity or willingness to put everything aside to care for her now.

Between trips to the nursing home, I begin to sort through the dust and clutter in my room, a lonely task that is usually done post mortem. Among stacks of books and magazines and boxes of old letters...some with 3-cent stamps...I find treasures. A poem, a clipping, letters from forgotten aunts and cousins. There are affectionate letters to my mother from people unknown to me. They begin to frame my mother's life, her interests, her personality. Respect and pride replace the sense of duty that brought me home to meet her crisis.

There are shoe boxes full of letters I have written home with more than a dozen return addresses. They tell of the babies and all the funny things the children did as they were growing up. The letters became less frequent during the years I felt my marriage failing.

The day we bring my mother home in a wheelchair by medi-van it is thirty degrees below zero. Spruce boughs hang low under a fresh snowfall, which has mercifully covered all but the seed heads of weeds in her neglected gardens. The broken fence and rusted wheelbarrow take on fanciful shapes beneath the fresh snow. I hope she will not notice how warped and weathered the eaves are. It seems that she and the house are on a collision course with time.

For the first time in years I experience winter. A crystal curtain of icicles refracts the brittle afternoon sunshine outside my window. In spite of blue sky and sun, in spite of scarves and hats and mittens, frost bites my fingers and cheeks and nose, tears freeze on my lashes. But I fall into the Norwegian pattern of cheerfully enduring that makes life possible in the North.

In June Richard & Aljean go to Niue. Their letters to me, the brochures and fact files and photographs they sent to me comprised the last issue of *The Solo Traveler,* #18, which fulfills my obligation to subscribers.

"The plane coming in was full," Richard writes, "mostly New Zealand contractors who are widening the roads. It was dusk when our plane landed, dark when we got situated at Pelini's Guest House. There are three units in a former family home in the heart of Alofi. The large, well furnished kitchen is superb, with two ranges..."

"The second day there were coconuts, papaya and a huge stalk of bananas on the porch. We never knew where they came from. When I went to get a loaf of bread and saw some women doing crafts I went over and said, 'I'm Richard. I'm staying at Pelini's'"

" 'We know that,' was their response. Probably because we are the only tourists on the island during the first week."

"My travel agent arranged a round the island tour with the Postmaster who is Brenda Pelini. Leaving Alofi about nine thirty, delivery took the better part of the morning and provided a very comprehensive view of the island. The road is good, better through the villages. There are abandoned houses in the villages. Inspectors come around checking to see if the villages are clean, to see that coconut shells, which breed mosquitoes are removed. Each month a different village has a fiafia to which everyone is invited. Games are played and there are craft exhibitions and contests for husking and grating coconuts. Coconut crabs, which are kept on leashes, are raced. They have HUGE claws for opening coconuts."

"The locals are very self-sufficient. A socio-economist from the U.N. indicated that it is an ideal place to settle. There is an over abundance of food...mango, breadfruit, papaya. Vegetables available at the market, which is held once a week, include lettuce, tomatoes, cucumbers and beans. Root crops are impossible to grow because of the soil. They grow small and sideways. Bird's nest grows wild; the center of it is delicious steamed. Milk is long life, imported from New Zealand. There are a dozen bakeries that make coconut, banana and white bread."

"Very scenic views. Everything is 'owned'. Fishing grounds are jealously guarded. I heard that a man caught fishing on another man's ground was shot. Another man, someone said, was warned three times; then he was beaten to death. The penalty was two months in jail. Perhaps they told me these things as warnings, simple precautions I should take, always getting permission to fish, aware that none of the land or lagoon is public."

"I went fishing with Ernie. A tractor pulled his boat to the dock where it was put into the water by a crane. The skilled crane operator set us down very smoothly. There is a yacht club. Swinging moorings are beyond the reef to tie up to buoys of styrofoam. The reef has been dynamited to create a passage for ships to come to the wharf to unload."

Aljean wrote, "Lady Rex, the widow of John Rex Woods, the former Premier of Niue, invited us for tea. We never had the feeling of being isolated or being on a small island. After our two week visit, everyone we had met came down to the airport to say good-bye!"

There was something very final about mailing the last issue of *The Solo Traveler.* But endings are often balanced by new beginnings. The fifteen months during which I gave my mother twenty four hour care created a wealth of uncommitted time in which to write.

There were few distractions. Pequot Lakes is a village of about eight hundred people. The only things taller than the treetops are the Department of Forestry fire tower and the water tower that is, appropriately, painted like a red and white fishing bobber. Tourism, along with hunting and fishing and subsistence farming, forms the economic basis of our village life. It occurred to me that the thing I found so appealing on South Pacific islands was that, except for climate and cultural differences, life in island villages was comfortably similar to my childhood in Minnesota.

Decorating the fale posts in preparation for Fia Fia in Manase

The author in the fale of Le Tagaloa Pita at the South Sea
Star Hotel in Apia, Samoa.

Chapter Thirty-Six

Drums of Rarotonga

No two journeys are the same. Each is a product of its own time, an intertwining of people and experiences, a confluence of events and places that can never be repeated. My return to Rarotonga in April, 2000, a decade after my first visit to the South Pacific, was no exception.

The card that arrived from my friend Ben was a surprise. It simply said, "Any thought of cranking up *Solo Travel* again? If so, count me in." It was three years since I had mailed the last issue of *The Solo Traveler.*

Less than two hours later, Susan Dietz called from the *Los Angeles Times Syndicate.* She had written about *Solo Travel* in her column, *Single File*, years before.

"My column is ready to go out on the wire. I just need to confirm that your phone number is the same."

My response to her was slow.

"*Solo Travel* has been inactive for a while. I went home to take care of my mother so I couldn't travel. Now I am in the process of moving to northern Minnesota."

I thought of Ben's card, that perhaps the timing of Susan's call was more than coincidence. Susan's article is nationally syndicated. It would give me a good opportunity to begin again now that life had gone full circle and I am free to travel. I paused, "However, I would be happy to stay in Tucson to respond to any inquiries. I could offer a tour in April."

It was already October. I had commitments to care for grandchildren in Arizona in December, Ohio in January. By the first week in February I could be back in Minnesota to begin making tour arrangements. A slim margin, but I was sure that it could work.

I had just four people committed to go on the tour to attend the Cook Island National Dance Festival. Our flights were arranged for April 19, with arrival on Rarotonga scheduled for Thursday morning.

When I offered the tour I had agonized over whether to remain loyal to my friends at Are Renga, which was always my personal first choice. It was clearly a budget lodge. Or should I offer a resort accommodation of a little higher standard? I wrote to Lagoon Lodges, listed as upper moderate, for reservations. I worried during weeks when I did not receive a confirmation of the room reservations. I finally wrote again asking them to email the reply to me in Tucson where my office files and computer were still located, and I flew back to Arizona early. The email I received, just three weeks before our flight said, "Your letter was mis-sent to Tonga and we just received it. We are fully booked."

Midnight panic! There were five of us with airline reservations and no place to stay.

I waited through the rest of a sleepless night until noon (eight a.m. on Raro) and called Tangi.

She was delighted to hear from me. No problem. They had room for us. Then I called my tour members to explain that instead of Lagoon Lodges we would be staying at the budget accommodation where I had always stayed. A NZ$300 refund for each of them to help make up the difference in the room rates would nearly pay for the week they would be staying independently on Aitutaki after the tour. They were all accepting of the change. In fact, Ben and Carol responded enthusiastically, as though a vacation had suddenly turned into an adventure.

It was the first time I had booked Air New Zealand tickets through Tahiti. It was a dream flight. French waiters, gourmet food and exemplary service pampered us all the way, including champagne with breakfast!

Our stop for refueling and change of cabin crew was in a Tahitian garden frosted with silver moonlight. Polynesian music came from the lounge. A gentle breeze carried the fragrance of tropical flowers.

It was Theressa who drove the van that met us on Raro. She greeted my group with kisses and eis and an ei katu, a crown of flowers, for Ben. She had been about fourteen when I was last on Rarotonga and had grown into a gracious young woman.

"How is the family?" I asked. "James?"

"Grandfather died two years ago. He was buried by the palace in Avarua. I will show you." I felt with her a terrible sense of loss.

"Marion?" I asked, hopefully.

"She has gone to New Zealand last week."

"Kura?" I continued.

"He is over there," she said.

I saw him by the fence, watching us from inside the airport. I put my bag down and hurried to greet him.

"I am working here," he said, adding, "I will be home soon."

Striving to at least touch, our fingers were entwined in the chain links of the fence.

The Ara Tapu, the road to Are Renga had not changed, although it seemed narrower, somehow, than I remembered. Tangi was sweeping the hall with a kikau broom when we arrived and seemed embarrassed that the rooms were not completely made up. When I had been there before she had so many family members to help her.

She had the boys open a coconut for each of us while we waited. Cool and sweet and filled with island memories. When everyone was settled in their rooms she came and sat with me. We spoke easily about our families, as if I had never been away.

If I had checked my Cook Island calendar more closely I would have realized that Good Friday, Easter, Easter Monday, and Tuesday, which was ANZAC Day would all be holidays. Buses do not run on holidays. Shops, banks, restaurants, everything would be closed during most of the first five days of our twelve day tour.

When everyone was settled in their rooms to rest, I caught the bus to Avarua. After exchanging money at Westpac I went to Trader Jack's to pick up dinner vouchers and make reservations for dinner. Alarm bells rang in my mind when Sisi told me that they would be closed from Good Friday through ANZAC Day. I picked up basic groceries, survival food, so we could get by until I figured out a strategy for getting through the long holiday.

Back at Are Renga I gave everyone a ten ride bus ticket, an all day bus pass and six dinner vouchers worth NZ$30 each, which gave tour members a great deal of flexibility and independence.

After lunch we took the bus downtown for a quick orientation. It was the first night of dance competitions, so after dinner at Trader Jack's we walked across the street to Banana Court. The skill of the dancers in competition brought a rowdy response from the mostly Maori audience. But it was the drums, the incomparable, unforgettable rhythm of slit log drums that brought me back to Rarotonga.

Ben and Carol at the Right on the Beach Restaurant, Manuia Beach

Chapter Thirty-Seven

Flying Foxes and 'Uapou

Before anyone else was awake, I walked into the village to see if I could find a shop that was open. As I passed Manuia Beach Resort, the premier resort on the island during my last visit, I thought *resort dining rooms must be open even during holidays!* I walked down the sandy lane toward the beach to find the manager. Paul, new to management of the resort, was accessible and extremely friendly. I explained my dilemma; that we were a group of five people staying at the backpacking lodge just down the road and I had no idea how I would feed them until the holiday was over.

"No problem, bring your people over for meals anytime."

It was a pricey solution, but nonetheless an answer to a vexing problem.

It was just a quarter mile to Manuia Beach. The informal dining room was set right on the beach, with a thatched roof and sand floor. The breezy, open island design gave a splendid view of the lagoon and sunsets. Dinner was by torchlight around the pool. We enjoyed the friendly staff, as we became regulars there.

Tangi invited us to ride with them in the van on Sunday to the Rarotongan Hotel for lunch and the show. She and her ten year old daughter, Agnes, her son-in-law, Kura and three of his children dance in the Music Ministry from the small Catholic Church, St. Mary's, across the street from Are Renga. Tangi explained that they don't use drums on Sunday. I had little idea what to expect.

Tangi got a table for us in the covered dining room, which overlooked the pool and stage and gave us the best view of the performance. Dressed in traditional costumes for drum dances, they worship God through dance set to hymns sung in Maori. Six young men stood above the waterfall that plunged into the pool, providing rhythm through chants and hand clapping. Small children, with their mamas and grandmas in mumus, were on the left, teenagers on the right side of the pool. An evangelist explained what each of the songs was about...heaven or salvation or the love from God, which melted their hearts. People came from the bar and stood watching.

They came from the beach and tennis court and not a fork was raised during the performance. It was a ministry of love reaching out to European guests of the hotel who, perhaps, had not been in a church for decades. Yet, on this special Easter Sunday they were touched by E. Matike, the music ministry of the young people of Arorangi.

The personal interests of a small group can easily be catered to. The young microbiologist from California had expressed an interest in seeing fruit bats. Through Internet I found the staff at SPREP (South Pacific Regional Environmental Program) in Apia, Samoa. A series of references brought me to Ian Karika who promised by email to try to find fruit bats for us. With his family, he had established the Takitumu Conservation Area Project for the preservation of the rare kakerori bird.

This charming young man came roaring into our lives on a motorcycle one afternoon. Takitumu's colony of fruit bats had flown away deeper into the mountains, but he would consult Gerald McCormick of the Cook Island National Heritage. The problem with flying foxes, Ian explained, is that a colony will hang onto each other suspended in a long rope-like cluster. Hunters will shoot the one on top clinging to the branch and they all fall and can be easily captured. Because they eat fruit, the meat is considered to be a sweet delicacy. On Tonga hunting them was reserved for royalty.

Some species of Samoan flying fox have wingspans of three feet, although the kind of fruit bat on Rarotonga usually has a two foot wingspan. We all had become curious and planned to join the night hike into the mountains in search of flying foxes.

It was Ben who saw the sign "Wood-carver" beside a narrow alley that led from Arorangi toward the mountains. We followed it until it became a winding trail. I had read about Exham Wicham, historian and philosopher, as well as wood-carver. We found him in the wood shop in back of the house, a large area sheltered by a galvanized iron roof. It was filled with ancient tools, both hand tools and machines for woodworking. On a worktable a slit log drum stood on end.

"How much do you want for the drum?" I asked.

The warmth in his eyes faded.

"You don't want that noisy old thing," he responded.

He put it aside and went on to explain that it was carved for island use. After a brief silence, as if in apology, he picked up a carving of Tangaroa.

"How did my ancestors learn to carve this thing way back in 1100? Every canoe had one in front and one in back as they made their voyages. They brought with them their culture, their identity, their god. You see it is always carved in three sections. The first, the head, represents the government. It always has five cuts. And he showed us and went into great detail about the meaning of each part of the Tangaroa. The second section, the belly represents the warriors. The five fingers hold close the family, culture and heritage.

He hesitated; then he said, "This is embarrassing that my ancestors worshipped that old thing." But he went on to explain that they still dance to a living god. The third, the lower part encompasses furthering the race and carrying on the heritage. For the first time I understood that the Tangaroa statues were not just souvenirs to tease the tourists. And I understood, too, that in spite of differences in cultural expression, it was the similarities in belief that allowed the early Tahitian missionaries, like Papeiha, to make such an impact on the society so quickly.

Ben asked how tourism had changed the island. Exham told us how everyone would go down to the airport to watch the planes land back in 1974 when the airport was extended.

"I would go, too, and stand at the fence and watch. Each time, I thought I wonder if there would be cargo space for my tomatoes in that plane. One day" and he showed how he had motioned with his finger to call the pilot over to the fence, "I said to the pilot 'Would you take my tomatoes to New Zealand?' That was the beginning of shipping island produce by air. One day he brought me a check for seven thousand dollars. That was more money than I had ever seen. I bought a motorbike. Then I bought a van to take tourists around on tours. But that was too much trouble and I quit as soon as I had the van paid for. We didn't need money. We had everything here."

He waved his arm to encompass the towering palms laden with coconuts, the canopy of the mango tree outside his workshop, waxy star fruit handing in ripe golden clusters, the taro patch in the lowland, the pigs tethered beside the road.

"But for the young people now it is different. When my son got married he needed a table, so I found a fine mahogany tree. I split the trunk and showed my son how he could make a table. 'I don't want that old thing,' he said."

Exham took us out back where a half tree trunk lay abandoned in the weeds. Then he took us inside to show us the table he had made from the other half of the tree. The exquisite grain of the wood showed through the highly polished surface.

"Now he wants my table."

I wished that I had brought a notebook as the conversation went from religion to history to island economics and culture. He was a brilliant man with an agile and expansive mind. Then he spoke of the painful price of progress.

"In those days there might have been three or four people in jail. Now there are a hundred sometimes. Why?" He paused, pained, then thoughtfully added, "sometimes I wish the planes had never come."

I knew the conversation was over, but I asked again about the drum. He showed me how he had carved it in the traditional style with two bands of design and inch deep indentations at the ends.

He shrugged and somewhat reluctantly said, "Sixty dollars?" He explained that now a mahogany tree can cost a thousand dollars. I borrowed the money from Ben and walked away with the island drum.

Maria, Exham's wife, operates a backpacker's lodge. She is a smiling, good-natured woman with a kind, generous spirit. She sent us away with handfuls of star fruit.

Ben, a World War II Air Force veteran, enjoyed the long and formal ceremony downtown to celebrate ANZAC Day. We had met a woman named Poko who drives a taxi van. She helped us get through the long holiday with one adventure following another. Wednesday we began taking the bus around the island to new discoveries.

The monsoon season was officially over and we had been enjoying the dry southeast tradewinds. But one day rain came in quick and furious showers leaving the tarmac steaming when the sun came out. And the rain continued until the flood plain, which now housed nine hundred laying hens in elevated screened houses, became a murky sea. The water rose around the lodge. I wondered if the plane would fly to Aitutaki, but the storm stopped long enough to accommodate their flight. This was the independent part of their trip, the week long extension they had planned when they would venture out on their own.

My attention turned to a ten day conference on Marine EcoTourism that was being held at a church in Titikaveka. Robin, from Great Adventures in Cairns, Australia, was one of the presenters at the workshops on tour development, pricing and interpretation. I could attend the meetings each day as an observer, she said, but would not be allowed to participate or comment.

Although the workshops were productive, breaks were even more interesting. I met a one-armed Tongan who runs a rustic beach resort on an outer island in the Ha'apai group, a Frenchman from Wallis and Futuna who spoke little English, but told me that his island looks very much like Rarotonga, but without many tourists. The Minister of Tourism of Tuvalu was there, an assortment of Fijians and Steve Brown who runs EcoTour Samoa. He knew most of the people I do in Samoa.

While my group was away on Aitutaki, I went to the Police in Avarua to see if they could help me locate Mama Teiva. I had read about her in the *Features* section of the *Cook Island News*, which appears weekly on Internet. At 87, because she was going blind, her family moved her from her home on Atiu to Rarotonga. I knew that there was nowhere to have eyeglasses made on Rarotonga. I mentioned Mama Teiva to Irene and Diana, who offered to gather old eyeglasses from friends and bring them to Rarotonga.

When I explained to the police officer why I wanted to find her, he immediately made several phone inquiries. He drew a map for me that indicated her daughter's home, just beyond Telecom, not more than two blocks from Cooks Corner. Because of the policeman's call they were expecting me.

Mama Teiva was a small woman with a radiant smile. Her gray hair was caught up in a bun at the back of her head. She was sitting on a patio in front of the house. When I spoke to her, her daughter translated for us. Her gaze was somewhere in the middle distance, so I realized that perhaps blindness was already her fate. I explained that I would come back another day with some eyeglasses for her to try.

By the end of the week my group returned from Aitutaki where the weather had been perfect. They had stayed in two different lodges and had met only on the day trip to One Foot Island, but both groups praised Aitutaki for its stunning beauty and hospitality.

On Saturday Irene, Diana and I went with the glasses to Mama Teiva's. When Diana put the first pair on her, Mama Teiva shook her head in disappointment. The second pair brought the same response. But the third time, she smiled and said, in Maori, "I can see you." We were jubilant!

Ian Karika had been in and out of our days persevering in his search for fruit bats, but by the time Diana returned, the mountain trails had become impassable because of the rain.

Sunday was their last day on Raro. Diana wanted to go to the five a.m. service at CICC, so with flashlights in hand we walked into the village, waking roosters and dogs as we went. For the ten a.m. service, some went to St. Mary's while I went with others back to CICC. I whispered to Nancy that the Ariki was sitting in the front of the church with her husband in a special reserved pew along the wall near the pulpit.

It was their last opportunity to see the St. Mary's Dance Ministry. Everyone chose to go back to the Rarotongan for lunch. When Diana wanted to go to church again at five in the afternoon, they all decided to go along. The main attraction of the churches was the unforgettable Polynesian himenes, sung a cappella.

Although this was the post-tour period and I was no longer responsible, I wondered during church what we were going to do for dinner. We were the only tourists at the afternoon service. A group of people surrounded Diana and her mother who were sitting near the front; another group came to Ben, Carol, and me. They were insisting that we come along to get a bite to eat. "Just follow the crowd," we were told.

About halfway back to Are Renga, the building that had been Napa's store had been converted into a chapel, Calvary Hall. The chapel, with pews, was surrounded on three sides by rooms for socializing. There were benches along the walls and huge tables groaning under heaping platters of food. On Communion days, it was explained, they have an umukai, a feast, after the afternoon service. We were ushered past the first table to one in back. Food platters were so full and abundant there was barely room for twenty plates set, overturned, at chairs around the table. We were urged to sit. The Ariki, the Queen of the Tinomana Tribe, sat regally and somewhat sternly, at the head of the table, the young pastor at her right. My place at the table was beside the Ariki's husband. He is a jolly man with wispy white whiskers, easy to talk to, with a charming sense of humor.

"How," I asked, "does one become an Ariki?"

I remembered standing under the canopy of the frangipani trees in the light rain watching the burial of the Queen on my first visit.

He explained that Tinomana, when the missionaries first came, had three wives. The previous Ariki was the descendant of Napa, his first wife. When she died, the descendant of his second wife became the current Ariki.

"And what are you?" I asked, teasing.

"I am Tinomana Tane. I suppose I must be the Duke," he said in flawless English, laughing.

During our conversation I learned that they have nine children, four boys and five girls, three of whom live overseas. He kept urging me to take more food. I should be accustomed to eating, Polynesian style, with no utensils, but I am still shy doing so. I did eat some delicious umu roasted chicken and taro.

There was too much food to even contemplate.

"What will happen to all this food?" I asked as we had barely made a dent in it.

"It will be shared out," he answered, following the tradition common throughout Polynesia. Within minutes after we got up a dozen people from the congregation descended on the table with baskets and platters taking whole cakes and chickens and lobsters and bowls of roukou and taro and fruit. It seemed as much a food exchange as feast.

We were invited to go into the chapel for 'uapou (pronounced wapoo). My Maori dictionary defines 'uapou as a Biblical debate or discussion. But that hardly describes the happy chaos we experienced next. The debate was sung with gusto. When one side perceived themselves as having won, the victors danced tamure style down the aisle, or if they couldn't reach the aisle because of the crowd, regardless of age or size, they jumped up on the seats of the pews and danced there. Then the debate would begin again. I wished that I could package some of this unbridled joy and bring it home to our Lutheran congregation.

The plane home was fully booked, so I could get only four seats for the group and I flew out the following week.

It was a week of reunions. Ian and Jackie went to dinner with me at Portofino. I had lunch with Paddy Walker at Trader Jack's as we had six years before. She was scheduled to host the Pacific Women's Conference in November and was busy planning meetings and entertainment for the international group of royalty and prominent Pacific women who would be attending. I suggested that she come with me for lunch at the Rarotongan on Sunday so she could watch the St. Mary's Music Ministry. She agreed, after seeing them, that it might be the perfect cultural entertainment for the conference.

Bob and Tangi and I had dinner at Tumunu. Danny Mataroa and Oropai had been invited, but her father had died, so they were consumed by grief and preparations for his burial.

Kura was scheduled to leave the Thursday after my flight for Sydney where he will be working as a security officer. Marion's older sister, Manuella, lives there with her husband. He will be stopping for a week in Auckland to see Marion who, pregnant, is waiting there so the baby will be delivered in the hospital. She is living with another sister. Kura's father and his oldest daughter, Maire, are in Sydney so he will see them there.

I met Kura's mother who works as a maid at the Rarotongan. For seventeen years she had worked at Telecom, but lost her job during the recent privatization of government owned business. She said that thirty years ago she and her husband had worked in Australia picking tomatoes and plums for $9.00 an hour.

"We are beggars there, looking for jobs," she said. I shared her deep concern for Kura going to work in the city.

While waiting for my flight, I heard the sound of drums coming from the church hall across the street. I went to watch the children practice. They were a lovable barefoot, ragtag little army for God, laughing and playing, yet taking the dance practice and songs of worship seriously. Kura played the drums. His little daughter, Anna, was among the dancers. He will be taking her along to Auckland and will leave her with Marion.

I remembered the day after the others had flown home. Kura moved my things from the lodge in back of the plantation to a different apartment nearer the house. As he carried the drum he ran his fingers over its surface producing a rich and mellow sound.

"That's a fine drum," he said.

As I packed my things for the flight home, I thought of Kura, who would soon be living in Sydney far from his cultural roots.

If I brought the drum home with me it would become a dusty, silent souvenir. In Kura's hands it would come to life and be a pulsing, emotional bond to his Polynesian culture.

I packed the drum carefully in a canvas duffle that I had brought, which would make it easy for him to carry on the plane. After all, it was carved for island use.

Allison, "gone native" on the beach at Aitutaki, Cook Islands

Epilogue

Western Samoa has officially changed its name to Samoa. Our Samoan friends have announced some significant changes too.

Barry Rose of Coconuts emailed us, "I am attaching a picture of Jennifer and me that was taken in January 2001 when we were off to see the Prime Minister for the Naturalization Ceremonies. We became naturalized citizens of Samoa. So, now you can see what ten years in Samoa has done to us!"

Photo provided by Barry Rose

He added that in April he became a matai in Maninoa Village. "It was a very big event for the district and I received the matai title of Tautaimatapalapala. It is a very high title in our village and I take my duties as a matai very seriously." In closing he wrote, "You might be interested to know that one of Jennifer's favorite pictures of me (one she keeps on her night stand) is the one that you took of me standing beside a carved post in our Treehouse entrance." [See page 242.]

Pam kept in touch with Christmas cards and photos of the children.

After thirty years in Alaska, they moved to France where Dan is still involved with fish, but in quite a different way. He is now installing giant aquariums.

This 1998 photo shows Lucas, a tall handsome teenager. All the children are prospering and fluent in French. Whenever the children have free time from school they take advantage of their opportunity to travel throughout Europe.

A sad note regarding the sinking of the freighter *Avatapu* is balanced by praise given her captain for what has been described as a textbook rescue. At the time of her engine fire, according to the former merchant naval officer Margaret Hicks, "The *Avatapu* had an internationally acclaimed sailor, Captain Nancy Griffith as her Captain, a New Zealand engineer, and a top notch crew."

The twenty five passengers and crew were rescued from two life rafts and a dinghy thirty hours after the ship was hit by an engine fire two hundred miles from the Cook Islands and had to be abandoned.

Fiji Update

Nothing had been resolved by the 1987 coup in Fiji, so predictably, the smoldering ethnic hostilities erupted again.

The current crisis began on May 19, 2000, when George Speight and a group of rebels stormed Parliament and took several dozen hostages including the then-Prime Minister, Mahendra Chadhry. The Melanesian rebels demanded that the country's multiracial constitution be put aside and that Chaudhry, Fiji's first ethnic Indian Prime Minister be deposed.

Fiji's traditional power, the Great Council of Chiefs, elected Ratu Josefa Iloilo as President. In the following days, the rebels looted and burned ethnic Indian homes and businesses in civil disturbances that spread across the island nation.

Paul Alexander of the Associated Press reported the end of the nearly two-month hostage crisis on July 13, 2000. After being promised a new constitution which would curtail Indian rights, the hostage takers held a traditional ceremony seeking forgiveness by offering a bowl of kava to the last captives to be freed. Then the captors tearfully hugged the captives, who in spite of beatings the night of the coup, held no animosity toward their captors.

In November, tensions flared again in a twelve-hour gun battle in the streets of Suva.

On March 1, 2001, the Fiji Court of Appeal ruled that the interim government is illegal and should be replaced by a constitutionally elected government. However, the acting President, Ratu Josefa Iloilo and the interim Prime Minister, Laisenia Qarase maintain that restoration of democracy should be discussed by the Great Council of Chiefs.

The stated goal of the interim administration is to amend the Constitution to guarantee political supremacy and customary land rights of indigenous Fijians who make up 51% of the population of 840,000. A democratic election may be scheduled for March 2002. So the end of the story has yet to be written.

In the Cook Islands, concern mounts as the Organization for Economic Cooperation and Development (OECD) has blacklisted the Cook Islands, Nauru, and Niue for their offshore banking and money laundering that experts say might amount to an astonishing $500 billion a year, most of it through illegal cooperation of some Western banks.

As we go to press, a July 2001 deadline has been set for sanctions against countries that have not taken concrete measures to prevent illegal transfers of money from tax evasion and crime. Sanctions may prevent monetary exchange which will limit tourism in the islands.

Tourism is a major factor in the Cook Island economy with 72,994 visitors in 2000, a 31% increase over the 55,599 visitors the previous year.

While most Cook Islanders are relatively unaware of and little affected by the offshore banking, the loss of tourism dollars will affect every sector of the Cook Island economy. For our friends on Rarotonga, we hope that this dilemma is resolved soon.

Political and economic crises usually pass, so with an exchange rate of NZ$2.42 to the U.S. dollar, there has never been a better time to venture across the South Pacific toward New Zealand and a whole world of new friends and experiences. Choose a destination, do your research and just go!

Photo by Barry Rose

Over the Water Fales at Coconuts Beach Resort, Samoa

Photo by Barry Rose

A view of the Over the Water Fales from the water,
Coconuts Beach Resort, Samoa

Ben and Carol on Rarotonga

Beach fales at Va'Vau, 'Upolo, Samoa This is the picture that is shown in color on the cover of this book.

A Note on the Type and Printing

This book has been set in type using 12 point Times font for ease of reading. It has been composed using Adobe® PageMaker® on a Macintosh® computer for ease in preparation.

Composed by Penrith Publications
Cover Design by Robert E. Bell
Photography by the author, except where noted
Printed and Bound by Bang Printing, Brainerd, Minnesota

GLOSSARY

a cappella	choral singing without instrumental accompaniment
Afakasi	Samoan term for half caste; someone of half European, half Samoan ancestry
Aiga	extended family in Samoa, which requires the highest loyalty
Aitutaki	one of the outer islands of the Cook Group distinguished by its huge lagoon
Apia	the only city in Samoa, located on the island of 'Upolu; the capital
Ara Metua	the ancient, inland road that nearly circles the island of Rarotonga. According to legend, it was built a thousand years ago by a chief named Toi
Ara Tapu	the modern, coastal road that circles Rarotonga
are	in the Cook Islands, hut or house
Are Kariei	the house of entertainment in the Cook Islands
Are Renga	a plantation resort operated by a Maori family in the village of Arorangi
Ariki	ruler over a tribe in the Cook Islands
Arorangi	one of the main villages on the west coast of Rarotonga
Assau	a village on the island of Savai'i in Samoa; a lumber mill is located there
Atiu	one of the outer islands in the Cook group
Au Maru	the palace of the Tinomana tribe, located in Arorangi
Avarua	the city and capital of the Cook Islands, located on Rarotonga; population about 4,000
Avatapu	a freighter in the Cook Island service, lost by fire and sunk in 1998

Barringtonia tree	a large tree native to the Cook Islands that is the source of utsu nut which becomes a poisonous powder when crushed; used to stun fish
beche de mer	giant sea slugs that are found on the reefs of Fiji; in China used in cooking
bilo	Fijian term for a polished half coconut shell used as a cup
breadfruit	a staple in South Pacific diet; a large, globular fruit nearly as large as a soccer ball which grows on a tree with large dark green leaves; similar to potato, eaten boiled, baked or fried as chips
bure	thatch roofed house in Fiji
Cairns	a city in Australia on the north coast near the Great Barrier Reef
CICC	Cook Island Christian Church established by John Williams of the London Missionary Society; on Aitutaki in 1821, Rarotonga, 1823
cobo	traditional response to being served with yaqona in Fiji; to clap with cupped hands
coconut crabs	island delicacy; a strip of tin is often put around palm trunk to keep them from stealing coconuts
coils called punk;	smoke discourages mosquitoes when it slowly burns
Cook Islands	a group of 15 islands due south of Hawaii, as far south of the equator as Hawaii is north
copra	the dried nut of the coconut which is used to produce oil
dalo	the Fijian term for taro; both leaves and roots are eaten throughout the islands
dengue fever	a mosquito borne illness that is debilitating, though not often fatal, endemic in many of the islands
E. Matike	a popular music and dance ministry from St. Mary's Catholic Church in Arorangi

ei	a floral garland to be worn around the neck, called lei in Hawaiian, given to extend welcome and/or protection to visitors
ei katu	a crown of flowers worn by either men or women
fa'a Samoa	the Samoan Way
fa'a fafine	a Samoan custom where a boy might be raised as a girl in a family with few girls to help with chores; they sometimes revert to male roles when grown, sometimes not
fa'a lavelave	an urgent request for help from extended family members due to crisis
fa'a molemole	request for help in providing for a feast or celebration; a request is seldom denied
fale	Samoan word for traditional house which is usually oval and without walls
Fia Fia	celebration in Samoa with feasting and dancing
Fijian Archipelago	three hundred islands which comprise Fiji; about one hundred are inhabited
flying foxes	fruit bats which grow to wingspans of two to three feet and are considered a delicacy because their meat is sweet due to diet of fruit
fono	village council of Matais which wields enormous power in Samoa
himene	in Cook Island, songs of worship based on pre-mission chants
huka	Cook Island male war dance
ika mata	raw fish marinated in lime juice until it loses its translucent appearance
iofoga	in Samoa, the traditional formal apology extended by sitting outside the injured party's house with head covered, sometimes for days until normalcy is restored in relationship
isalei	an expression of yearning, remembrance
kaikai	In Cook Islands, a community feast always cooked in the umu, or ground oven

kava	the traditional drink in Melanesia made by the infusion of water into powdered kava roots called yaqona
Kia Manuia	Cook Island farewell, meaning good luck
Kia Orana	the Cook Island greeting which means may you live, or may you live well
kikau	made from palm fronds, as houses, thatch or brooms
kirikiti	a game in Samoa played on village greens every afternoon, like cricket
Kiwi	a person from New Zealand
kohl	a black cosmetic Indian women in Fiji and the Subcontinent use around their eyes
kumara or kumala	sweet potatoes, a staple food in the islands
Kulakula Village	near Sigatoka in Fiji; huge dunes rise at the coast where coral reefs are absent
Labasa	a city on the north coast of Vanua Levu in Fiji
lali	large slit log drums used as a signal in Fiji
Lautoka	a city on the north coast of Viti Levu in Fiji
lavalava	the garment in Samoa for both men and women - two yards of cloth (sulu in Fiji; pareu in Polynesia)
Lekutu	a village on the north coast of Vanua Levu in Fiji, west of Labasa
Levuka	the historic capital of Fiji located on the island of Ovalau
lolo	Fijian word for coconut cream made by squeezing grated coconut
lovo	Fijian word for ground oven
magimagi	in Fijian, cord made from the fiber of coconut, called sennitt in Polynesia
Maire Nui Festival	International South Pacific Cultural Competitions, held every four years
Maketi Fou	Samoan market
Malevu	a small fishing village on the south coast of Viti Levu in Fiji

malo	in Samoan, okay or you may pass
Manihiki	one of the northern atolls in the Cook Islands
Manuia Beach	a small boutique resort in Arorangi on Rarotonga
Maori	Polynesian people who live in the Cook Islands and New Zealand
masi	the Fijian word for tapa cloth
Matai	head of a family in Samoa, as part of fono wields much power
mata ni gone	a formal ceremony in which a Fijian child is introduced to the village of his grandmother
mataquali	the extended family of Fijians who live in the bush
Matavera	a village in Rarotonga
Maui	an ancient Polynesian god
Mauke	one of the southern Cook Islands
Maungaroa	a high mountain peak on Rarotonga
mbula	Fijian greeting
meke	Fijian dance
Melanesian	people who live in the Fijian Islands and those to the west of Fiji
Mitiaro	one of the southern Cook Islands
moso oi	worn as an ula for luck in palolo gathering in Samoa
motu	small offshore islands usually at the edge of the lagoon, frequently uninhabited
Muri Beach	an exceptionally fine beach with three motu offshore
Nabouwalu	a very small village on the southwest coast of Vanua Levu where ferries dock
Nadi	a city on the west coast of Viti Levu, Fiji, near the international airport
Nassarawaqa village	a small village on the north side of Vanua Levu, Fiji
Nga Maru	a freighter in the Cook Island service

Ngatangiia Harbor	on Rarotonga, the historical site where the voyaging canoes left Raro for New Zealand about 700 years ago
ochre	red powder used by Indians at pujah to put a tikka on their forehead
Ovalau	one of the Fijian islands that was, historically, a seat of power
PagoPago	the capital of American Samoa, pronounced by locals as Pongo
palangi	Samoan term for foreigners
palolo	egg and sperm of coral animal which is released seven days after the full moon in October on Savaii; seven days after the full moon in November on 'Upolu
palusami	leaf of the taro cooked with coconut cream
pandanus	a small tree whose leaf is used for weaving fine mats throughout the islands
papa'a	Cook Island term for foreigners
papao	Samoan word for a lightweight outrigger canoe called vaka in Polynesia
Papeete	the capital of French Polynesia on Tahiti
Papeiha	missionary from Raiatea in French Polynesia who was brought to the Cook Islands by John Williams. He is buried in the church yard in Arorangi
pareu	two yards of cloth used as garment in Polynesia for both men and women, called sulu in Fiji; lavalava in Samoa
pate	slit log drum of the Maoris
Penrhyn	one of the northern atolls in the Cook Islands
Perth	A city on the west coast of Australia
Petersburg	A fishing port on the intercoastal waterway in south Alaska
pujah	Hindu religious ceremony
Punanga Nui	the outdoor market in Avarua, Rarotonga
punjabi	female's garment from north India, with slim pants and a long tunic

puri	Indian flat bread which puffs delicately when cooked in hot oil; made for holidays
punk	mosquito coils
Raiatea	the island that is historically the spiritual center of French Polynesia
Rakahanga	one of the northern atolls of Cook Islands
Rarotonga	the largest of the fifteen Cook Islands
rito	the finely woven white hats ladies in the Cook Islands wear to church
roti	Indian flat bread baked on a grid
roukou	in the Cook Islands, taro leaves in coconut cream, like palusami, but chopped
Ruku Ruku	a rustic resort on Ovalau
Sa	mandatory prayer time every evening in villages in Samoa
Savaii	the largest and most traditional island in Samoa
sandalwood	in Fiji, shaved finely to put on hair for cosmetic appeal
sari	traditional female garment for Indians
sea urchins	a sea creature eaten raw and considered a delicacy in Samoa
sele levu	means big knife in Fijian, the all purpose tool of the Fijian villager
sene	cent in Samoan money
sennit	Polynesian term for string made from fiber of coconut tree
sevusevu	mandatory gift or offering given to the chief of a Fijian village before entering to seek his protection, usually yaqona, or given as a gift on returning to ones own village
siapo	Samoan word for tapa cloth
Sigatoka	a small city on the Coral Coast of Fiji's Viti Levu
siva	sinuous, sensual dance by Samoan women of all ages

sulu	Fijian name for garment worn by both men and women; a lavalava
supo esi	mashed papaya and coconut cream, served hot in nui (half coconut shell) in Samoa
Suva	the largest city in Fiji, on Viti Levu
tabua	whales tooth, a very special gift given in formal ceremonies in Fiji
tala	Samoan dollar
tamure	the rapid dance typical of Tahitian and Cook Island girls
Tangaroa	god of the Polynesians which appears in carvings and on coins in Cook Islands
tanoa	large carved bowl on three legs that is used for mixing yaqona in ceremony in Fiji
tapa	cloth made from the inner bark of paper mulberry and worn in ceremony in Fiji or used to wrap body for burial
taro	root crop that is one of staples throughout the islands, leaves are used for roukou/palusami; it is grown in patches in wet land
tapu	Polynesian word for taboo
ta'unga	a high priest in Polynesia
Taveuni	the Garden Island of Fiji
Te Reinga	one of the high mountains on Rarotonga
Terora College	similar to our High School, on Rarotonga
teuila	Samoan word for ginger blossoms
Tiare Maori	small white, very fragrant gardenia prized throughout Polynesia for eis
tikka	the red dot put on Indian's forehead in Hindu worship ceremonies
Tinomana	the High Chief of Arorangi when the missionaries came in 1823
Titikaveka	a village on Rarotonga
Toi	a famous legendary chief who lived a thousand years ago on Rarotonga
Tonai	Samoan feast after church on Sundays
trevoro	in Fiji, a ghost

'Uapou	a Biblical debate, sung and danced...more like a joyous riot
umu	Polynesian ground oven
ula	in Samoa a garland of flowers worn around the neck, like a lei in Hawaii
utsu	nut of the barringtonia tree, which was crushed and sprinkled on water to stun fish
'Upolu	the more developed island of Samoa where Apia is located
Vaka Viti	the Fijian Way
Vanua Levu	the second largest island in Fiji with very little tourist infrastructure
Vanuatu	a Melanesian island west of Fiji
vasu	male hereditary position of almost unlimited power
vinaka	thank you in Fijian
Viti Levu	the more developed island in Fiji where both Nadi and Suva are located
yaqona	the drink in Fiji made from crushed kava roots
trochus	a highly prized shell in the Cook Islands
Tubakula	an affordable resort on the Coral Coast of Viti Levu, Fiji,
turanga	powerful Fijian chief

INDEX

Traveling the South Pacific
can be ordered by calling or writing:

Book Passage
51 Tamal Vista Blvd.
Corte Madera, CA 94925
1-800-999-7909

If you like this book, watch for some of the present and future releases from Penrith Publications:

A Bedtime Companion compiled and edited by Robert E. Bell. This is an anthology of quips, quotes, humorous anecdotes, and cartoons which the editor has collected over a fifty year period. Planned release date is November, 2001.

Traveling in Alaska, Without Reservations by Evangeline Brunes. This a description of the writer's adventures traveling in Alaska during the winter months, and telling the readers how they can do the same thing on a limited budget, safely and pleasantly, meeting the real people of this, our northernmost state. Planned release date is October 2002.

Beyond Petra, Without Reservations by Evangeline Brunes. An authentic journey into Arab history and culture. The author tells how any one could do the same on a limited budget. Planned release date is October 2003.

Buying Green Bananas by Evangeline Brunes and Robert Bell. When a person reaches a certain age, he or she often is reluctant to buy any green bananas because there may not be enough time left for them to ripen. In this book, the authors tell of their experiences "buying green bananas", starting a new business after reaching the age when most people expect them to go sit in a rocking chair somewhere and die gracefully. Planned release date is October 2004, provided the bananas ripen properly.

Penrith Publications, LLC
7340 Penrith Drive, Mechanicsville, VA, 23116, USA
(866) 746-8150 Fax: (804) 746-8190
email: penrithpub@aol.com

Notes

Notes

Notes

Notes

Notes

Notes